Understanding marketing and financial information

Produced for the course team by Andrew Lindridge and Haider Ali (Marketing) and Graham Francis and Michael Lucas (Finance)

Contents

Chapter 1 What is marketing?
What is marketing?

Marketing is traditionally viewed as a process by which organisations anticipate and satisfy customer needs at a profit. Most marketing ideas and concepts have been created with the commercial or for-profit sector in mind. However, in this book, we argue that all managers can improve the performance of their work unit by *choosing and applying relevant ideas* from marketing. In our view, marketing thinking is not only useful for businesses that sell things but in service and not-for-profit contexts too. In this sense we might see marketing as a process in which an organisation improves its relationships with its stakeholders – those who have an interest in the organisation, whether staff, recipients of services or funders. This may include improving communications, improving products and services, improving resource flows, or all of these.

The idea that marketing could be applied to non-profit organisations, such as public sector (state) organisations or voluntary organisations and charities, was introduced in the 1960s by Kotler and Levy (1969). Instead of viewing marketing as an activity whose sole aim was to generate profit, they argued that not-for-profit organisations could use marketing to help to deliver a process that met a societal need.

Sargeant (2005) argues that marketing can bring the following benefits to not-for-profit organisations:

- Marketing can increase customer/client satisfaction through understanding their experience of using the organisation's product/service.

- Marketing can be actively used as part of a not-for-profit organisation's fund-raising activities.

- A not-for-profit organisation that undertakes marketing may be encouraged to review and understand its key strengths and weaknesses and respond to them accordingly.

Many people associate marketing mostly with 'selling' or 'advertising' but marketing comprises far more than this. It covers the identification of customers (or the stakeholders with whom better relationships are sought through marketing), grouping them into 'segments', researching their needs, expectations and behaviour, and designing product or service offerings that will meet their needs and expectations. This involves selling and advertising, of course, but it also includes the design of the product or service itself, the price that is charged for it, and the place and means through which it is offered. All this will be discussed in more detail in later chapters.

It is easy to see how marketing can improve relationships with external stakeholders, particularly customers. For example, a city council may wish to provide the schools, playgrounds, museums and health clinics that the city's people want. In the for-profit sector, businesses want present and potential customers to buy the food in the supermarkets, the clothing in retail stores, the programmes broadcast on TV. We apply marketing also to the machinery sold to farmers to help grow food, the sewing machines sold to clothing manufacturers, and the TV cameras sold to TV companies. We expect large businesses to have marketing departments but this does not mean that only the people who work in a marketing department have a role in marketing. It is argued that the companies that are most successful at building relationships with their customers are those in which everyone is focused on the customer, that is, customer-oriented. Public and not-for-profit organisations will often not have a marketing department, but we find people doing marketing in a number of parts of these organisations. These organisations and, indeed, many for-profit ones are not selling products – tangible items such as a camera which you can own – but services such as education, insurance, refuse collection, health care and so on.

It should be clear by now that marketing is not only important for people working directly with customers, in marketing departments or who have marketing in their job title. It is also useful to apply marketing to activities and employees who support core processes of providing and running schools, preparing and delivering food or running museums. Information technology (IT) people who design information systems and HR people who provide specialist services to all employees also indirectly support an organisation's relationships with its stakeholders. An aspect of this is sometimes called internal marketing. Here, too, marketing serves to improve relationships, but now with an organisation's internal stakeholders. Again, this improvement may include improving communications, improving products and services, or improving resource flows.

Because many marketing ideas are more readily understood in the for-profit sector this book will have more pages on this than on other sectors. After an introduction to the marketing idea we will therefore often discuss this idea in terms of the following contexts (sometimes all, sometimes only some of them):

1   the marketing idea in the *for-profit* sector: products and services for *external* customers and consumers – often a longer section than those that follow

2   the marketing idea in the *not-for-profit* sector: products and services for *external* customers and consumers

3   the marketing idea for *external stakeholders* other than customers and consumers

4   the marketing idea for *internal* customers and consumers: an example would be an IT department providing a service to other departments in the organisation.

Marketing in different contexts

Most marketing ideas have been developed in the for-profit sector so our definition of marketing will begin here. The UK Chartered Institute of Marketing describes marketing as a management process that *identifies, anticipates and satisfies customer needs at a profit.* In this definition:

> *Identifies* refers to a recognition that the for-profit organisation's potential or existing customers have a need that is not *currently* being satisfied and

which can be satisfied. This relates to the idea of improving the relationship with customers.

Anticipates refers to an estimate of how much the organisation's potential or existing customers will buy.

Satisfies refers to whether the product or service they buy satisfies customers' original needs. Again, this relates to our idea of improving the relationship with customers.

At a profit refers to making money by charging customers more than it costs the organisation to satisfy their needs.

This definition leaves out a key detail which is that marketing considers people's wants as well as needs. People have a physical need for water without which they quickly die. There is no actual physical *need* for the water to be flavoured, fizzy, or transported many miles, even from one continent to another. But one of marketing's greatest successes – or failures depending on one's outlook – is to build up people's desires for a wide range of 'water with additions' and 'water from a named source'. This is a *want*.

In its original setting in the for-profit sector, then, marketing can be seen as giving people what they want, when they want it, where they want it and at a price they are willing to pay for it. To achieve this, an organisation must be able to satisfy its customers' needs. A customer need represents something that motivates a customer to seek out a product or a service to satisfy that need. Marketing provides a means to satisfy this need, that is, achieve customer satisfaction. Customer satisfaction refers to the customer's subsequent feeling of whether the product or service satisfied their need.

The term 'customer' usually means the person or organisation buying from your organisation. This may be the same as the 'consumer', the person or organisation actually using what has been bought. For example, someone buying food for their own consumption is both the customer and the consumer of the product. On other occasions the customer and consumer may not be the same person. For example, when a parent buys breakfast cereal for a child, the parent is the customer and the child is the consumer.

Let's look at a not-for-profit context now, say, a city's public authority (the council) wanting to improve leisure facilities for people living in the city. Marketing in this context is about anticipating the leisure needs and wants of the city's inhabitants and satisfying them, for example, by providing swimming pools or theatre space. 'Profit' might be more difficult to assess but profits need not be financial: the elected members of the city council might gain in popularity and perhaps be re-elected as a result of successfully anticipating and satisfying the needs and wants of the citizens.

The context of *external* stakeholders, other than customers and consumers, can be illustrated by a not-for-profit organisation, such as a charity providing relief in emergencies caused by natural disasters. The 'consumers' of the organisation's services might be the people affected by the disaster. However, the marketing challenge for these organisations lies more in securing funds and resources. Many voluntary organisations have highly professional marketing departments whose main activity is fundraising. In this context marketing might be best understood in terms of anticipating and satisfying the needs and expectations of key external stakeholders such as donors (those who provide funds). For example, the organisation might offer them up-to-date and in-depth information on how their donations are being used. The benefit to the organisation – the 'profit' – will be securing a greater flow of funds into the organisation from the donors.

The context of *internal* stakeholders who are closely connected with the product or service provided to external stakeholders, can be illustrated by the human resources department of a company offering financial services to individual customers. Although the human resources department is not directly responsible for customer contact many of its internal stakeholders are, such as the organisation's financial advisors who deliver services to customers. So when designing training for the financial advisors, the human resources department must anticipate and satisfy their needs and expectations, for example in terms of offering training on improving customer contact. The 'profit' for the human resources department in this case might be an improved relationship with the financial advisors' department.

Finally we can also consider marketing in the context of *internal* stakeholders who are *not closely connected* with the product or service provided to external stakeholders. An example is a department of a university that decides on the internal processes and procedures to be observed when a new course is to be offered. A faculty wanting to offer a new course would have to anticipate and satisfy the needs and expectations of the department setting the procedures, for example, by completing forms in good time and with all the required information in order to be able to offer the new course. Being able to offer the new course to students would be the 'profit' in this case. In situations like this we may have a conflict in which the internal stakeholder may want something different from the external customers and consumers, in this case, students.

Differences between sectors

While marketing can be relevant and important both to the not-for-profit sector and for-profit organisations, there are a number of important differences between how the for-profit and not-for-profit sector conduct their marketing activities. Lovelock and Weinberg (1993) have identified a number of these differences, which follow.

> *Funding* A profit-orientated organisation generates its profits from selling a product or service to its customers. This means that they generate all (or most) of their income from one group of external stakeholders, their customers. This is often not the case in the not-for-profit sector where the people who demand and use the service (the customers and consumers) are frequently not those who are paying for it. For example, a hospital has customers or clients (patients) but does not often receive money directly from them. The hospital instead may receive money from taxpayers via the state or from private insurance schemes. Therefore, the money needed to run the hospital may not necessarily come from its customers but from non-users.

Objectives The indirect relationship between users and funders of not-for-profit organisations means that non-financial objectives are generally more important than in for-profit organisations. Where a for-profit organisation may measure its marketing success in terms of achieving financial objectives, this is generally not true or possible for not-for-profit organisations. Such organisations tend to offer services that cannot, or not easily, be measured in financial terms, such as education, hospital treatment, social care and so on. Not-for-profit organisations may measure their success through setting non-financial objectives. For example, an AIDS prevention charity may set an objective of educating 10,000 people about AIDS prevention.

What is offered Where a profit-orientated organisation usually delivers some form of a product or service, this is not always the case for not-for-profit organisations. Although many not-for-profit organisations offer some kind of service, some have as their sole aim a change in social behaviour, for example, to persuade people to stop smoking.

Public scrutiny Ethics (moral values and rules) and corporate social responsibility (a commitment to behave ethically and to address social and environmental concerns) are relevant to both for-profit and not-for-profit organisations. However, although very few for-profit organisations are open to public scrutiny, not-for-profit organisations generally are. Typically, not-for-profit organisations are funded by state governments or by public donations. This means that there is a greater public interest in, and scrutiny of, how these organisations spend their money and what services they deliver.

Marketing as process and marketing as philosophy

The Chartered Institute of Marketing definition is what Crosier (1988) calls a 'process' definition of marketing. This means it looks at the processes of delivering marketing. It views the marketing process as a combination of planning, researching your existing and potential customer's needs, and coordinating your organisation's marketing strategy. All the examples in the different contexts given above essentially relate to the process of marketing something to a customer or other stakeholder.

In contrast to process definitions of marketing are those that define it as a concept or philosophy. These regard marketing as an organisation-wide belief which drives everyone in the organisation to satisfy customer (or stakeholder) needs in everything the organisation does. Every department and every employee has the task of adding to customer satisfaction through every aspect of their job. Examples are the receptionist who ensures he or she is always friendly and approachable when greeting people in the reception area, and the finance director who wants to make it easy for people to purchase the organisation's product or service. This is called a market-oriented approach.

These two types of definition of marketing are not incompatible. Indeed, it can be argued that a market-oriented approach is important in order to make marketing processes work effectively. However, throughout this book we tend to focus mostly on the process oriented view of marketing.

From our various examples of marketing in different profit and not-for-profit contexts, you may now have a better idea of how marketing relates to your job. Nonetheless, you may harbour some misgivings about seeing your job in terms of marketing. In fact, many people dislike the idea that what they do has anything to do with marketing. This is because the word 'marketing' is often understood in a fairly negative way and marketing as a process or as a philosophy is not without its critics. In particular marketing has been criticised in two ways:

It places too much emphasis on profits and the for-profit context. While marketing is relevant in not-for-profit contexts, it is true that marketing is mostly considered in the for-profit context. Many of the concepts developed in marketing therefore need adaptation to make them useful in other contexts.

It encourages excessive material consumption. Particularly in the for-profit context, marketing is generally associated with trying to get people to buy and consume more. For example, a car company might encourage people to want to buy a high-status car which costs more and provides bigger profits for the car company. Equally, many marketing efforts are criticised for focusing on immediate gratification of relatively minor wants rather than focusing on larger, long-term needs. This emphasis by marketing ignores the wider social and environmental implications of a materialistic lifestyle.

Customers, consumers and clients

An understanding of marketing requires a clear understanding of the terms customer, consumer and client. The customer is the person buying from an organisation. The customer can also be another organisation, for example, when a bookstore buys from a book publisher. The customer will *also* be the consumer *if* the person or organisation uses what has been bought. This is not the case with the bookstore: there the bookstore is the customer of the publishing company and a person buying a book from the bookstore is likely to be the consumer.

Here are two simple examples that highlight the distinction:

- You choose, buy and eat an ice cream. Here you are the customer and consumer.
- Your child chooses and eats an ice cream but you pay for it. Here your child is the consumer and you are the customer.

The second example is of interest because marketing activity is likely to be focused on the consumer rather than the customer. Consumers and customers may not share the same view, and marketers often use the influence that consumers (in this case, children) have over customers (in this case, parents). For example, marketers advertise tempting toys or food items during breaks in children's television programmes or by placing sweets within reach of small children in supermarkets. They are thus attempting to use children's 'pester power' to persuade parents to buy the goods in question. As a result they are often criticised for addressing the wants of children without much consideration of the expectations of their parents, the customers.

When we look at purchases made by organisations, in most cases, customers and consumers are not the same. Many purchasing decisions in organisations are made by purchasing departments. As a manager you may be allowed to take decisions to buy items costing up to a certain amount of money. An exception might be for products used in many parts of the organisation and which are supplied by another department, for example, ink for printers and printer paper. For these and more expensive items, many managers are required to use the equipment and materials which someone else in the organisation has chosen – and these buyers may or may not respond to managers' needs or wants. We will look in more detail at the buying behaviour of individuals and organisations later in the book.

Customers and clients

Now we turn to the difference between customers and clients. The term 'client' is generally associated with the provision of professional services (such as accountancy and legal services). In these contexts, the specific service being provided is normally discussed and agreed between client and provider. While the client has more influence over the specification of the product or service being provided, the service provider – the marketer in this context – is often in a position to advise the client as to what his or her needs and wants actually are, and then charge fees for delivering services that meet these needs. You should immediately recognise that the power balance between the marketer and the person being provided with a product or service can be quite different according to whether the person is a customer or a client.

In recent years it has become customary to use the terms customer or client for the recipients of public and not-for-profit services. Before then, these recipients were called passengers, patients, students and so on. These more traditional terms had the advantage of indicating to service providers the needs and expectations of these service recipients. It is argued that calling everybody a customer reduces every service to a commercial transaction – and many people would be unhappy to think that their relationship with their doctor or teacher is nothing more than a commercial transaction. This is partly an issue of terminology and becomes less problematic if we recognise that many aspects of marketing are useful and appropriate in not-for-profit contexts.

In the not-for-profit context we might consider the example of a doctor in the UK National Health Service (NHS) wanting a patient's blood sample tested. Here, the patient is the doctor's client and the doctor then becomes the customer of the blood testing laboratory. The laboratory must deliver a prompt service to satisfy the expectations of the doctor as a customer and the patient as a client.

When we look at *internal* stakeholders, an interesting feature is that 'consumers' often have no decision over what they consume. For example, in an organisation's wage and salary payment system there is usually no choice of products or suppliers if an employee wants to be paid. There are exceptions, however. For example, all IT systems within an organisation may be provided by the IT department but the internal customer or consumer may be able to influence the design.

In addition, while we can see clearly who is paying for a family's ice creams, holiday or car, in *internal* marketing contexts it is often not as clear who is paying and how much is being paid for the services or goods supplied. If you are a budget holder, you will know what items are charged to your budget. But if you are not the budget holder you may have little or no idea of what internal services actually cost.

Exchange, fairness and satisfaction

A core concept in marketing is *mutually satisfactory exchange* between the organisation and its customers or stakeholders. In a for-profit organisation this would normally involve a customer paying an agreed sum of money in exchange for a product or service supplied by the organisation. In a not-for-profit context and in 'internal marketing' between people or departments within an organisation, the concept of exchange still applies but is slightly different. This is because the organisation (or individual or department) concerned may not see financial profit as evidence of a successful exchange. Instead, it may exchange a service against some form of positive outcome considered to be of equivalent value, for example, political support, a return service, or good working relationships. For example, if a voluntary organisation organises a party for children from disadvantaged backgrounds, the exchange value might lie in the children enjoying themselves and having a positive, self-esteem-building experience.

For an exchange to be thought of as mutually satisfactory it usually needs to be regarded as fair, that is, two things of equivalent value (financial or otherwise) will be exchanged. However, what is considered to be fair will differ between different people: external stakeholders may have a different perspective from that of a manager in an organisation. Fairness is not easy to define, but as a general rule we consider decisions to be fair if they are free from unjustified bias or dishonesty.

Dissatisfaction will arise if the exchange is regarded as unfair in some way, perhaps because one exchange partner feels that they are getting less than they are giving, or less than other customers or stakeholders are getting from similar exchanges. In a free market-place, exchange partners who think they are not getting a fair deal can walk away and seek more satisfactory exchanges elsewhere. In reality, however, not all exchange partners and stakeholders have equal power and it is often not possible for one party to walk away and seek a better exchange.

There can be a number of reasons for this:

- They cannot expect to get a better deal elsewhere, for example, because all suppliers offer a similar standard of service or because they are dealing with a monopoly supplier, as is often the case in public services.

- They are locked into an agreement they cannot easily change; for example, in times of high unemployment it is often not possible for employees to walk away from their current employers even if they feel unfairly treated.

- They do not know whether or not they are getting a good deal because they lack sufficient product knowledge of the product or service. This is often the case because the supplier generally has more knowledge about the product or service than the consumer.

This lack of equality means that organisations can often decide how they want to engage with their stakeholders and perhaps give more attention to those stakeholders with more power and financial resources. Therefore, in any exchange the amount of power held by the exchange partners will influence the level of fairness of the exchange.

For a customer or stakeholder, fairness may be linked to the level of satisfaction that arises from an exchange. Satisfaction can arise only after the exchange has happened and perhaps after a product or service has been used. The product or service will be evaluated by comparing what we expected to experience with what we actually experience after the exchange has happened. Customer satisfaction and what contributes to it will be discussed in more detail later in the book. For now it is sufficient to say that, generally, if a product or service meets or exceeds expectations the customer or stakeholder will normally think that they had a fair exchange. If the product or service failed to meet expectations, however, then fairness will often be judged by how the resulting dissatisfaction is resolved. The following is an example of an exchange which proved to be unsatisfactory and which raises difficult questions about fairness.

John wants to buy a birthday present for his grandmother, a keen cook, but his job is poorly paid and he needs to be careful about how much money he spends. He decides to purchase a cookery book by a well-known chef. On her birthday, however, he discovers that a cousin has already given his grandmother a copy of the book. John's grandmother says she would like some new cooking utensils instead. John returns the book to the bookstore with the original receipt to ask for a refund. However, the store manager tells him that it is company policy not to give cash refunds, only to exchange one book against another. John, however, does not want to buy anything else from the bookstore now because he needs the money for the cooking utensils he wants to buy for his grandmother.

This example presents an interesting issue around fairness. On the one hand, the manager is following organisational policy. As an employee the manager does not have the power to override company policy. If the manager were to give a refund he or she might face disciplinary action by the employer for breach of the policy. On the other hand, refusing the customer a refund feels intuitively quite harsh, and perhaps unfair, to a customer who bought something unsuitable through no particular fault of his own and cannot easily afford to buy a replacement gift without a refund. While it is not in the power of the manager to override company policy, the manager is now also exerting power over the customer by applying the company policy strictly. In this case, fairness seems hard to achieve when neither of the two people directly involved in the exchange has the power to act freely. It is a typical example where it is difficult for the manager to provide customer satisfaction. A change in organisational policy would be needed to ensure this.

Marketing and ethics

Considerations of fairness, power and satisfactory exchanges bring us to the question of ethics in marketing. Marketing ethics refers to the question of whether particular marketing activities can be considered morally right or wrong. Ethics imply choice. We have seen that power relations affect how decisions are made but this does not mean that a manager or an organisation must or should willingly accept unfair exchanges or apply this power to the detriment of others. Consider the following cases in terms of their acceptability.

- A manager gives an extra discount to a customer who is a personal friend.

- An organisation charges a higher price to less wealthy customers on the basis that they buy less from the organisation.

- A local health authority refuses to provide a drug to cancer patients on grounds of cost, while neighbouring authorities provide the drug.

While some of this may be quite common behaviour, fairness is an issue because different people are being treated differently purely on the basis of their power in relation to an organisation or its managers. Fairness or justice is one of the key questions raised by ethics. Marsden (2005) suggests that a consideration of marketing ethics should involve in turn:

1 recognising and describing moral issues that arise from marketing activities

2 using various ethical theories and frameworks to analyse critically these moral issues

3 establishing a set of codes, rules and standards for assessing what is right or wrong regarding the marketing activity being undertaken.

What does this mean in practice? The first step, concerned with recognising and describing a moral issue arising from a marketing activity, can be applied to the example of the customer, John, seeking a refund. One moral issue centres on his lack of wealth and his need for the refund to buy another present. If no financial refund is offered the customer will suffer. Another moral issue might centre on whether the customer is entitled to a refund even if it is company policy only to exchange goods and there was nothing wrong with the book. Another issue might centre on the possibility of the manager losing his or her job as a result of giving a refund and breaking company policy.

The next step identified by Marsden is to use ethical theories to understand the moral issues arising from a marketing activity. An ethical theory is a systematic way of approaching ethical questions from a particular philosophical perspective. Western moral philosophy has developed a number of different ethical approaches. Three ethical theories that are commonly used in considerations of marketing ethics are utilitarianism, deontology and virtue ethics. Each may lead to a different conclusion when applied to the same ethical dilemma.

Utilitarianism is concerned with the consequences: the quality of a marketing decision or action is assessed by looking at the consequences. In deciding whether something is unethical, you assess the likely costs and benefits of the decision or action for each stakeholder and make a decision based on what produces the greatest benefit for all concerned. This is a principle often used in public policy decisions, where policymakers have to take the course of action that is likely to produce the greatest overall benefit for the greatest number of stakeholders (for example, all the inhabitants of a region). In the example of the refund, we could argue that the greatest level of utility for all concerned would be produced if the company changed its refund policy and gave full refunds for items that proved unsuitable after purchase. This would be the best outcome for the customer. It could also be a desirable outcome for the manager who would not have to refuse a refund to a customer whose need he or she might sympathise with. A change in policy might be to the detriment of the bookstore because it might lose some revenue. However, this might be true only in the short term. The longer-term benefits of increased customer satisfaction and better company reputation could lead to more business overall, to the company's benefit.

The second theory, deontology, is concerned not so much with the consequences of action but whether the underlying principles of a decision are right. According to this view ethically-good decisions are made by adhering to key ethical principles, such as honesty, truthfulness, respecting the rights of others, justice and so forth. Applying this theory to the refund, we might make a decision on the basis of the neediness of the consumer and the principle of justice and fairness. The manager might decide that it would be unjust for the customer to be given only a credit note if the store does not actually offer anything John wants to buy with that credit note. On the other hand, it might also be argued that the refund policy of the store was clearly stated, there was no fault with the book, and therefore the customer had no right to a refund if he made the wrong decision to buy the book in the first place.

The third theory, virtue ethics, views marketing ethics from the perspective of the moral integrity of the individual involved in making the decision. A morally-good decision is one that is based on the virtuous character of the person making the decision. Moral virtues include honesty, courage, friendship, mercy, loyalty and patience. In our example, if the manager decided to make a refund this might be based on the virtue of mercy (in taking the customer's plight into account) and courage (in defying the store policy). On the other hand, deciding to stick with the store refund policy, the manager might invoke the virtue of loyalty to the bookstore owners and their policies.

It should be clear that making ethical judgements is rarely clear cut. Depending on the viewpoint taken, different ethical principles may well lead to different decisions. Often it is appropriate to look at an ethical question using different ethical theories before making a decision. Managers in public-sector organisations often will have to make difficult decisions about which stakeholder needs they should satisfy if limited budgets mean not all stakeholder needs and expectations can be met fully. In many public sector and internal marketing contexts, the customer or stakeholder has relatively little say over the kind of service they are to receive. Thus, questions of an unequal distribution of power are more acute in the not-for-profit and internal marketing sector, where one or both parties to an exchange are often locked into existing arrangements and cannot walk away if they are dissatisfied with what they are receiving.

References

Crosier, K. (1988) 'What exactly is marketing?' in Thomas, M. J. and White, N. E. (eds) *The Marketing Digest*, London, Heinemann, pp. 16–27.

Kotler, P. and Levy, S. J. (1969), 'Broadening the concept of marketing', *Journal of Marketing*, vol. 33, no. 1, pp. 10–15.

Lovelock, C. H. and Weinberg, C. B. (1993) *Marketing Challenges: Cases and Exercises* (3rd edn), London, McGraw-Hill.

Marsden, D. (2005) 'Marketing Ethics' in Littler, D. (ed.), *Blackwell Encyclopedic Dictionary of Marketing*, Oxford, Blackwell, pp. 206–7.

Sargeant, A. (2005) *Marketing Management for Non-profit Organizations*, Oxford, Oxford University Press.

Chapter 2 Customer satisfaction
Customer satisfaction

Customers have expectations of the products and services they buy and use, and it is the task of organisations that provide these products and services to make sure that they meet, or even exceed, those expectations. If they do this, customers are likely to be satisfied. If they do not do this, and the expectations are not met, the customers will be dissatisfied.

There are three elements which contribute to a customer's expectations, and we show them in Figure 2.1.

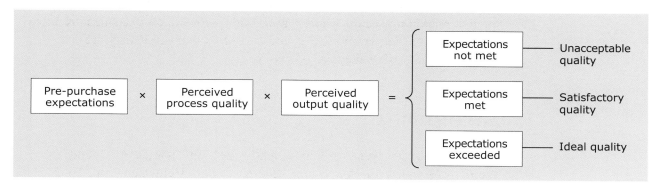

Figure 2.1 The roots of customer satisfaction

(Source: based on Berry *et al.*, 1985, p. 47)

This model shows how a customer's expectations and perceptions of the various aspects of a product or service will affect their final assessment. The model suggests that a customer forms expectations before a purchase. These arise from word-of-mouth recommendation, past experience, external communications and the customer's own needs. The customer will then assess these expectations in the light of their experience of the purchase. They will assess both the process and the output. In other words, they will consider the way the product has been delivered to them (what is known as the intangible service part of the product) and the quality of the product or service itself (the tangible part). The relative importance of each of these elements will depend on the product and on what the customer perceives to be most important. The outcome will be one of three states:

Expectations met The customer will be satisfied

Expectations not met The customer will be dissatisfied

Expectations exceeded The customer will be very satisfied, but will probably increase their expectations to take into account the new level of quality they have received. In future, the customer will probably want the product or service to meet this new level of quality just to be satisfied.

Parasuraman *et al.* (1991) showed that customers have two levels of expectation: adequate and desired. The first is what they find acceptable, and the second is what they hope to receive. The distance between the adequate and the desired levels is known as the 'zone of tolerance', and this can expand and contract according to circumstances. The two levels may vary from customer to customer, and from one situation to another for the same customer, depending on what else has happened to them that day, whether they are in a hurry, and so on. You can probably remember situations in which you have accepted services or products which, in other circumstances, you would have refused or been disappointed by. The zone of tolerance is shown in Figure 2.2.

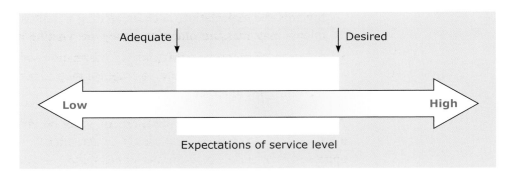

Figure 2.2 The zone of tolerance

(Source: Parasuraman *et al.*, 1991, p. 42)

If one accepts that this is how customers subconsciously evaluate products and that there is some tolerance in their evaluation, the meaning of responsiveness to customers becomes clearer. Ideally, organisations, and more particularly their employees, will always try to operate within a customer's zone of tolerance. To do this, managers need to understand what customers want from them and their organisation and whether or not their customers' expectations are being met. If managers realise that a customer is dissatisfied, they need to adjust their behaviour in order to change the customer's view. This is being responsive to the customer's needs. Of course, it is not always possible to respond immediately; other people may need to be involved, or the resources may not be available. However, even if the response cannot be immediate, it is important that feedback is given to the organisation, so that next time the customer can be satisfied.

A closer look at customer expectation

As we have seen, customers form expectations about a product or service and their experience of buying it. These expectations can be confirmed – the experience of buying a product or service meets or exceeds expectations – or they can be disconfirmed (Oliver, 1980). In this case the experience a customer has will challenge the expectations they had before the exchange. For example, a hospital patient about to undergo surgery has a positive expectation of a successful operation. However, the person has a poor experience in hospital: it is under-staffed and the surgical procedure is more complex than the surgeon anticipated. The patient develops complications that require a longer stay in hospital and a longer recovery time. In this case, the patient's initial positive expectations are disconfirmed by what appears to be a negative experience, despite the inevitable uncertainty over surgical procedures. The patient now has a new, negative expectation for any subsequent hospital visit. If the patient had had a positive experience, it would provide a positive expectation about a subsequent visit and offer reassurance to the patient.

Expectations represent a combination of:

- previous experience – either by the customer themselves with that product, or a competitors' products, or someone else's previous experience

- situational clues – the customer encounters a situation which contributes towards the expectation, such as visiting a dentist and seeing smiling clients may reassure others that they are visiting a good dental practice

- external information – this can be information gained from advertisements, friends and colleagues, magazines and other sources including the internet.

Although managers and organisations may not be able to completely control a customer's satisfaction processes they can attempt to influence them. One approach is to influence customer expectations, for example, by explaining carefully to customers what levels of service or product performance they can expect, the time frame in which they can expect them, etc. The other approach is to improve your customer's experiences of engaging with your product or service, for example, by improving actual service levels or product performance or giving more information or instruction on how to use the product or service.

Customer satisfaction and quality

Most people agree that quality is a desirable thing. Organisations invariably emphasise the quality of their products and services. It is difficult to find anyone who is *against* quality (excluding unscrupulous traders and organisations that knowingly provide sub-standard goods and services). But what is meant by 'quality'? The word is frequently used to mean quite different things. Indeed, there are many different definitions of quality which, when summarised, can refer to 'perceived' quality (the experience of quality by the customer or client), the measurable characteristics of a product or service, the customer or client's perspective on fitness for use, fitness for purpose, conformance of the product or service to a specification, and value for money. Quality can mean excellence (based on perceptions), or lack of defects (based on conformance), or value for money (Jackson, 1998). Quality is also considered to be relative to what something *should* be. Quality can refer to decisions, documents, information, outputs or processes in addition to products and services.

Slack *et al.* (1998) argue that all these definitions really mean one thing: that quality is consistent conformance to customers' expectations. *Conformance* emphasises the need to meet a clear specification. *Consistent* highlights that conformance to a set of measurable characteristics must be constant. *Customers' expectations* recognises that a product or service must meet the expectations of the customers, which by implication incorporates a consideration of what they expect to pay. What should be clear is that, however quality is defined, satisfying customers is central to it.

Customers' requirements

Buying a product or service can be seen as a problem-solving or desire-satisfying process, in which customers seek to match product or service attributes with their needs or wants. In this process, they look at the available products to see which is most likely to offer the benefits they seek. Bank (1992) points to five elements that customers take into account when considering quality. They can be thought of as five questions:

- Specification 'What can I expect when I buy or use the product?' The specification should enable potential customers to determine whether the product is likely to meet their needs.

- Conformance 'Will it do what I expect?' Any shortfall in conformance to the specification is bound to lead to dissatisfaction.

- Reliability 'Will it continue to do what I expect?' Clearly, customers will value a car that always starts first time.

- Delivery 'When can I have it?' It is important to distinguish between two aspects of delivery: availability and dependability. Availability is about when a product will be ready for a customer. Dependability is concerned with the adherence to a delivery time once that is agreed.

- Cost 'How much do I have to pay?' A purchase is an exchange, in which a customer obtains goods or services by offering something of value in return. Customers will be satisfied if the price they pay, whether in money or in some other form, equates to the value they place on the goods or service.

People's judgement of quality is largely a matter of how well their experiences live up to their expectations. Their expectation of a meal at a railway station snack bar is likely to be very different from their expectation of eating in an award-winning gourmet restaurant. People are likely to want different eating experiences on different occasions. Judgement of quality may depend on how well an experience lived up to the expectations of an occasion.

We can use the five elements of specification, conformance, reliability, delivery and cost to judge the quality of the experience, but, using the example of eating at restaurants, in each restaurant different elements will be emphasised. If you eat at a Japanese restaurant you may be more concerned with specifications (what can I expect when I eat there?), whereas when you eat at your local Italian restaurant you may be more concerned with conformance (is it what I expected?). If you are eating at a food outlet in a large chain you may be more concerned with reliability (is it the same as last time?). However, in reality, expectations are likely to comprise a mixture of these elements, in different combinations in each case.

Different customers are likely to have different expectations, even of the same product or service. Also, different customers may perceive the same product or service quite differently. Some customers may see a meal as a means of enjoyment with family and friends, while others may be using it as a business opportunity to entertain their customers. In short, the quality of a product or service is whatever customers perceive it to be. This makes it essential that providers understand quality from their customers' points of view.

In some situations, customers may not be able to judge the technical aspects of a product or service specification. For example, you may be unable to judge the quality of the medical aspect of an examination and diagnosis you receive at a visit to your doctor. You may therefore judge the experience by the doctor's manner, the receptionist's attitude, or even whether you had to wait longer than you expected.

Shortfalls in quality are likely to arise when there is a gap between what customers expect and what they consider they are getting. When such gaps exist it is almost bound to lead to customer dissatisfaction.

Customer expectation of service quality

As a manager it is important to understand how customers' perceptions of service quality are formed. Parasuraman *et al.* (1985, 1991) identified a variety of aspects that determine a customer's perception of service quality. These are:

- tangibles – offer some physical evidence that the service has been delivered
- reliability – it is important to honour the promises your service says it will deliver and get the service right the first time
- responsiveness – ensure the organisation is ready and willing to respond to customers' needs
- communication – using simple, easy-to-understand language; keep your customers informed about the service being delivered to them
- credibility – ensure your organisation is honest and trustworthy in how it deals with its customers
- security – customers value confidentiality, and financial and physical security in their service exchange with an organisation
- competence – ensure that all your employees have the right skills and knowledge to deliver the service
- courtesy – customers value friendliness, politeness and respect
- understanding/knowing the customer – employees must know and understand what their customers want from their service encounter
- access – make your service as accessible and approachable as possible.

What can you do?

Of course, managers may not always be able to put customers first and respond to their needs if there are major organisational constraints. But identifying constraints is not an excuse for inaction. There generally will still be things managers can do, and one important task in managing customer satisfaction is to identify what these things are.

One of the most important things is to allow staff – and managers – to take calculated risks and learn by doing. As McKenna puts it:

> Because there are no signposts or established paths to [successful] management, organisations can really do no more than grope their way toward it. Every day they grapple with the unknown – what is yet-to-be – much like an artist facing a blank canvas. They take a calculated risk and act on what they do know, even when that little is far outweighed by all that they don't know about the appropriateness or consequences of their actions.

(Source: McKenna, 1997, p. 160)

It is not easy for managers and organisations to implement this, because it gives employees the right to make decisions, to use their initiative and to make mistakes. However, it is important if employees are to make sure that customers, whether external or internal, are satisfied.

Organisations that are serious about meeting customers' expectations will invest time and money in staff training and good information systems which will provide accurate and timely information for staff to use. Finally, managers and organisations need to remain open to new ideas. If staff feel they can make suggestions that will be listened to, they will be encouraged to think a little more broadly about their own jobs, what their customers want and how to achieve it.

The right to make mistakes, to training, to good information systems and to openness are vital if employees are to put their customers first. While you may not be able to affect the whole of your organisation, making a start in your own team could improve your customers' satisfaction.

References

Bank, J. (1992) *The Essence of Total Quality Management*, Hemel Hempstead, Prentice Hall.

Berry, L. L., Zeithaml, V. A. and Parasuraman, A. (1985) 'Quality counts in services too', *Business Horizons,* May–June, pp. 44–52.

Jackson, T. (1998) 'New-style quality is just a fiddle', *Financial Times*, 29 December, pp. 12–13.

McKenna, R. (1997) *Real Time: Preparing for the Age of the Never Satisfied Customer*, Boston, Mass., Harvard Business School Press.

Oliver, R. L. (1980) 'A cognitive model of the antecedents and consequences of satisfaction decisions', *Journal of Marketing Research*, vol. 17, pp. 460–9.

Parasuraman, A., Zeithaml, V. A. and Berry, L. L. (1985) 'A conceptual model of service quality and implications for its future research', *Journal of Marketing*, vol. 49, no. 4, September, pp. 41–51.

Parasuraman, A., Berry, L. and Zeithaml, V. A. (1991) 'Understanding customer expectations of service', *Sloan Management Review*, spring, pp. 39–48.

Slack, N., Chambers, S., Harland, C., Harrison, A. and Johnston, R. (1998) *Operations Management* (2nd edn), London, Pitman.

Chapter 3 Market segmentation, targeting and positioning
Market segmentation

Most organisations, regardless of whether they are for-profit or not-for-profit, want to maximise customer satisfaction. However, customer needs may vary in numerous ways, for example, how often they use a product, what they use a product for and how they use the product. An organisation is unlikely to be able to satisfy all the wants and needs of all of its customers at the same time. Instead, organisations need to find a way of identifying which of its customers are the most important to them and strive to satisfy them first. This does not mean that the organisation will neglect its other customers, but simply that it has identified that different customers have different needs and this will require different ways of satisfying these needs. This process is called market segmentation.

Market segmentation refers to the process of dividing customers, or potential customers into different groups and segments, with each segment having the same or similar requirements (McDonald and Dunbar, 1998). While this may sound like a very profit-orientated approach, consider this definition of market segmentation applied to people who make gifts to charitable organisations:

> ...the process of dividing a varied and wide group of [donors] or potential [donors] into smaller groups within which broadly similar patterns of needs exist.

> (Source: Wilson, Gilligan and Pearson, 1992, p. 91)

Both these definitions refer to segmenting customers in a similar way but for different types of organisation. There are five important aspects of these definitions.

1 Customers/stakeholders can be grouped together in various ways to help organisations to meet their needs. This focus can save the organisation money and time and increase its effectiveness.

2 Managers can use the information about their customers to design products and services which meet their customers' needs better. When there is competition in a market, 'better' will mean 'better than the products or services offered by competitors'. When there is no competition, 'better' may mean 'better than currently, thus leading to greater customer satisfaction'.

3 The definitions assume that the notions of product, place and price can be used to further enhance customer satisfaction. Where the customer has choice, this should increase their willingness to choose a particular product. Where the customer has to accept what organisations provide, then the definition emphasises that managers may well be able to improve satisfaction.

4 These definitions imply that customers' wants and needs can be explained and even predicted from information about what they have in common.

5   The second definition shows that market segmentation can be applied to for-profit and not-for-profit organisations as well as internal markets (and internal stakeholders).

Importantly, segmentation assumes that the needs of each segment will differ. For example, some customers may bulk-buy products and others may buy small amounts regularly; others might celebrate different religious festivals, such as Christmas (Christians), Diwali (Hindus and Sikhs) or Hanukkah (Jews) and buy products specifically for these purposes. Internally, a training department of a large organisation, for example, may segment its internal customers depending on whether they require standard training, or something specifically designed for them. Differences between segments are relevant only if they refer to their needs and uses for a product. If there is no difference in customer needs then they can be considered as one group regardless of other differences, such as age or location.

Market segmentation has a number of advantages for an organisation. It forces the organisation to identify who its existing and potential customers are and what their needs are. This encourages the organisation to develop its marketing strategy to better suit the needs of each segment. In turn, developing a better marketing strategy makes the organisation more competitive in the market-place – and a more appropriate marketing strategy and focus on customers can lead to increased customer satisfaction.

These actions encourage an organisation to develop better marketing relationships with its customers by encouraging greater communication.

However, market segmentation also has a number of disadvantages. An organisation's focus on many different market segments may result in a more-individualised marketing strategy for each segment. This may increase costs and can reduce the profitability of the segment. Alternatively, poorly-handled or poorly-resourced efforts to engage with many different segments may result in miscommunication and customers feeling disengaged from the organisation and cynical about its marketing strategy.

Segmentation is not just a tool that is used at a strategic level and where there are many different customers, of course. The principles can be applied at all levels of an organisation and to situations where the actual numbers of people are relatively small.

Market segmentation methods

How an organisation goes about grouping its customers or potential customers into market segments will depend on the type of organisation it is and on the nature of its customers. There are different approaches to market segmentation. These can be applied to for-profit and not-for-profit organisations and internal markets or stakeholders.

Demographic variables

Many markets in which the customers or stakeholders are individual people can be segmented using differences in age, gender, socio-economic status, family size, income, religion, ethnicity, education or nationality. These all represent *demographic* differences in a population. This is a popular method of segmentation because it is easy to apply to a group of customers. For example, an organisation relying on donations for its income, that is, a charity, could segment its donor market in this way because donor behaviour is influenced by demographic variables. In different stages of their lives, people will normally have different levels of income and interests, affecting their ability and willingness to donate. Five segments relevant to this sector are set out below.

> *Elders 70+* Most have a low income but are free of debt. They like to support many different charities but because of their limited funds, make only small gifts. They often like children's groups, animal welfare and health causes related to their own experiences.

> *Seniors 60–70* Seniors tend to respond well to appropriate direct mail from charities, particularly those concerned with children, animals and local causes. They have a strong 'waste not want not' attitude, hold traditional views and hope for a better future for their children and grandchildren.

> *Thrivers 50–60* These are normally more active than the previous 60+ group; they often are healthier and more active. They are not old, they own their own homes and are many are recent beneficiaries of legacies from their parents. They tend to give to overseas charities, to health charities and to groups who preserve heritage and the environment.

> *Settlers 35–50* Settlers who are building their careers and families; they often have good incomes but spend most of their money on mortgage repayments to pay for the house they live in and on their children. Charity support is likely to be based on their own interest or a specialist interest rather than on generalised philanthropy. They are most likely to support organisations concerned with human rights or children.

> *Starters 20–35* These people are experiencing and enjoying their independence. Their expenditure often exceeds their income and they tend to be self-focused rather than philanthropic. They are often concerned about inequality in the world and about the environment legacy of past generations.

(Source: based on Sargeant and Jay, 2004)

Psychographic segmentation

Psychographic segmentation uses individuals' lifestyles as a means of grouping people together. For example, an individual's hobbies, aspirations, attitudes, political beliefs, magazines read and so on can all be used to group individuals. This approach ignores such factors as ethnicity and age, and instead focuses on lifestyle. It is a popular approach because lifestyle shapes behaviours and, in turn, wants and needs that organisations can then satisfy.

A good example of psychographic segmentation is provided by Wells (1975) who identified eight lifestyle groups among male consumers from which consumption behaviour can be predicted. For each of these segments he calculated what percentage of the male population belonged to each group.

Although these segments and their relative size were identified in the 1970s they are still relevant today because the behaviours (and relative size) have not changed significantly.

Group 1: the quiet family man – 8% of all males

The quiet, family man is self-sufficient, shy and wants to be left alone. His life centres on his family. Of low economic status and older than the average age of all males in the population, he watches television. He avoids buying consumer goods and does not seek pleasure by buying clothes and eating out in restaurants.

Group 2: the traditionalist – 16% of all males

The traditionalist is typically the oldest group, with a low level of education and of low socio-economic status. This male feels secure, has high self-esteem and is concerned with the welfare of others. When shopping he is conservative, tending to buy well-known products from well-known manufacturers.

Group 3: the discontented man – 13% of all males

Older than the average, with a low level of education and of low socio-economic status, this male feels that life's opportunities have passed him by. When he shops for products he tends to be risk conscious.

Group 4: the ethical highbrow – 14% of all males

Contented with family life, friends and work, this man is sensitive, concerned about the ethical implications of his consumer choices and is responsive to other people's needs. He cares about quality so when he buys products he is likely to spend more.

Group 5: the pleasure-orientated man – 9% of all males

This man views himself as a leader and rejects whatever appears to be feminine. Self-centred, his buying behaviour focuses on reinforcing his sense of masculinity. Purchases are rather impulsive.

Group 6: the achiever – 11% of all males

This man is typically young, highly-educated and hard-working. He is motivated by success, prestige and power. He favours diversity in all aspects of his life. He is status-conscious and his buying behaviour is motivated by this. More than males in other groups, he likes good food and places emphasis on his enjoyment of music.

Group 7: the 'he' man – 19% of all males

Motivated by an exciting and action-packed life, this man believes he is capable and dominant. His lifestyle often reflects that of an unmarried man even though he may be married. Well-educated, his shopping habits focus on reinforcing his 'man of action' image.

Group 8: the sophisticated man – 10% of all males

Typically the best-educated of the men in the eight groups, this man is younger than the average of all males in the population and of high socio-economic status. He is an intellectual who is concerned about social issues. He admires men with traits similar to his own. However, he wants to be dominant and the leader in a group. He typically buys unique and fashionable products.

The above categories would be useful for an organisation selling products or services to individual consumers. For example, an expensive hi-fi manufacturer may decide that Group 5 (the pleasure-orientated man), Group 6 (the achiever), Group 7 (the 'he' man) and Group 8 (the sophisticated man) are all image conscious and, therefore, more likely to purchase their product. However, this method of psychographic segmentation can also be useful within an organisation. For example, a human resource department might be able to determine male employees' training needs based on these categories. Employees belonging to Group 3 (the discontented man) may be unmotivated and unproductive at work and training may increase their self-esteem and, therefore, productivity.

Behavioural segmentation

Behavioural segmentation is based on customers' attitudes to, or knowledge, response or use of a product. Although this approach to segmentation can take many different forms (such as segmenting on the basis of how much your customers know about your product), typically three types are used:

Brand loyalty status This segments the market on the basis of how loyal customers are to a product. People who buy only a particular brand could be categorised as very loyal, while people who buy whatever is cheapest are not. A supermarket might want to give money-off vouchers to customers who are not regular shoppers in order to encourage loyalty.

User status An effective way to segment the market is to identify who uses your product and how often. For example, a hospital may find that 70% of contact nursing time is spent on patients over the age of 65; nurses could be offered additional support in dealing with this age group.

Benefit segmentation People buy/use different products because they are seeking benefits, but the benefits sought may be different. Thus, the market can be segmented on this basis.

Benefit segmentation can be applied to healthcare. The following example is drawn from a study in the USA by Lynn *et al*. (2007) who argued that previous government healthcare studies tended to segment the market on the basis of the services used. Instead they argue that the healthcare market should be segmented on the basis of the users' needs and, more importantly, on the benefits users are seeking. Lynn *et al*. (2007) identified eight different segments, set out in Table 3.1 with examples of representative individuals.

Table 3.1 Behavioural segmentation of a population's healthcare needs

Population segments	Population example	Benefits sought by segment	Provision required	Health care goals
Healthy	Dan, a 37-year-old carpenter, usually books appointments with his doctor for an annual check-up and medical tests and for minor conditions such as a sore throat.	Longevity by preventing accident, illness and progression of early stages of disease	Doctors' surgeries; health clinics; public information on occupational health and general health	Staying healthy
Maternal health and infant health	Sara, 30, had regular contact with her doctor for contraception and general health monitoring. Two years ago she was referred to a gynaecologist for fertility treatment. She was then monitored through a normal pregnancy and delivery. Her newborn's checkups and immunisations follow national guidelines.	Healthy babies, low maternal risk, control of fertility	Prenatal services, delivery and perinatal care; fertility control and help with fertility problems	Staying healthy
Acutely ill, likely return to health	Luciano, an 18-year-old student, fractured his leg playing football. After being taken by ambulance to his local hospital for emergency treatment, he received physiotherapy to rehabilitate his leg and maintain his body strength. He returned to football eight weeks later.	Return to healthy state with minimum suffering and disruption	Emergency services, hospitals, doctors' surgeries, medicines; short-term rehabilitation services	Getting well

Table 3.1 Continued

Population segments	Population example	Benefits sought by segment	Provision required	Health care goals
Chronic conditions with generally 'normal' functions	Monique, a 49-year-old teacher, has hypertension and diabetes. She attended classes to learn to manage these long-term conditions but both are occasionally out of control resulting in a visit to her doctor. The doctor also sends her reminders for regular checkups and monitors her for possible complications.	Longevity by limiting disease progression; doctors need to be aware of condition and physical limitations and act accordingly; caregiver support	Support and self-help education, doctors' surgeries, hospitals and emergency treatment	Living with illness or disability
Significant but relatively stable disability, including mental disability	Tom, a 56-year-old telemarketer, is a former soldier who is paralysed from a gunshot wound. He lives with his brother in an adapted apartment and pays for personal care. He has a motorised wheelchair and transport for shopping and outings. He has been suicidal at times and often has urinary tract infections. He has a care plan and medical 'home team' coordinates care services.	Autonomy, rehabilitation, limiting progression of disability; help with adaptations and equipment to aid domestic and work life; caregiver support	Home-based services, rehabilitation and institutional services; assistance with adaptations and equipment to aid domestic and work life	Living with illness or disability

Population segments	Population example	Benefits sought by segment	Provision required	Health care goals
Dying with short decline	Brenda, 68, has terminal cancer. She is exhausted and losing weight. After several unsuccessful treatments, she has accepted hospice services that will allow her to stay at home till her death. The hospice clinicians manage her pain and other symptoms, and she is able to complete her life as satisfactorily as she can.	Comfort, dignity; caregiver support; preparing client psychologically for death	At-home services; hospice and personal care services	Coping with illness at the end of life
Dying with long decline, limited reserve and serious exacerbations	Simon, a 75-year-old former executive, has severe mobility problems due to smoking. He is supplied with oxygen at home and has a complex regimen of drugs and treatments. He and his family have learned to manage his condition but also a nurse is on 24-hour call for guidance and urgent home visits. He has a care plan that specifies limited intervention to prolong his life.	Avoiding exacerbations, maintaining function, and specific advance planning, for example, level of intervention to prolong life.	Self-care support, at-home services, 24-hour access to medical guidance and home-based care	Coping with illness at the end of life

Table 3.1 Continued

Population segments	Population example	Benefits sought by segment	Provision required	Health care goals
Dying with long decline from dementia and/or frailty	Marie, an 88-year-old grandmother, has dementia. She cannot walk or communicate. Her daughter provides most of her care. Marie attends a daycare centre three days a week for baths, diversion, and caregiver relief. The local health service helps with monitoring needs and coordinating services. Marie's daughter has authority to make decisions and has decided her mother should not be admitted to hospital or resuscitated if the need arises.	Support for caregivers, maintaining health and mobility and specific advance planning, for example, level of intervention to prolong life	Home-based services; mobility and care devices; caregiver training for family members; support and nursing facilities	Coping with illness at the end of life

(Source: adapted from Lynn *et al.*, 2007)

Segmenting organisational markets

Organisational or business-to-business markets differ from consumer markets because there are often relatively few customers in the market. Some of these customers may be the few very large ones who dominate the market, buy large quantities often and have high purchasing-power. Not-for-profit organisations are also often interested in segmenting organisational markets. For example, an organisation giving advice on environmental issues to small and medium sized businesses might segment its customers according to size, industry segment, level of environmental impact, or whether or not they have used the advice agency's services before. A not-for-profit organisation looking for donors might segment business organisations according to whether they are likely to make donations to charities, to support campaigns and so on. How organisational markets can be segmented depends on the nature of the market and the organisation that is segmenting it. Bonomo and Shapiro (1983), cited by Sargeant (2009), provide the useful classification scheme set out below.

Organisational market segmentation criteria

Demographic

- industry type or sector
- company size
- location.

Operating variables

- technology used
- user status (i.e. heavy, medium, light users)
- customer capabilities based on their level of need or expectation.

Purchasing approaches

- buying criteria – what the organisational customers focus on, for example, price or service levels
- buying policies – for example, whether they buy through public bidding
- current relationships – whether they are already customers or not.

Situational factors

- urgency, that is, how urgently the product or service is required
- size of order.

Personal characteristics

- loyalty shown to suppliers
- attitudes to risk, that is, the risk an organisational customer is willing to take when buying products or services
- buyer-seller similarity.

We have seen how commercial, not-for-profit and business-to-business organisations can segment their markets. Although each operates differently, they all segment their market on the same basis, that is, grouping customers, clients or consumers on the basis of a shared, common need.

Segmentation as a tool for managers

Segmentation – the division of a market into distinct groups of customers – is often considered at a strategic level, for example, at a senior and top management level of an organisation. But segmentation can be a useful tool for managers working at lower levels in other parts of an organisation. The decisions they have to take with respect to segmentation may not necessarily be in terms of choosing which segments to target. Rather it may well be that once the organisation has chosen the segments, managers throughout the organisation have to decide how best to serve the needs of chosen customer segments and support the organisation's marketing efforts with respect to those segments. This may be achieved through:

- liaising with the sales team to ensure that the needs of your organisation's customers are known and are being met
- assessing how your existing marketing strategy is appealing to your targeted segments (this may be achieved through analysis of sales figures by segment, location and so on)
- identifying market and channel trends
- identifying and communicating to senior management new market/ product trends and how these are affecting the segments
- ensuring that staff have the appropriate training to meet the needs of each segment, such as in a hospital with elderly patients
- identifying and communicating wider external market trends and industry dynamics in the segment to contribute to future strategies and projections.

If your customers are primarily internal it may still be helpful to segment them according to what they need and expect from you. You may have little choice about which ones you target but you may still be able to prioritise. More importantly, by considering the needs of each segment you may be able to deliver a better service to them, possibly at less overall cost or effort.

There are some additional issues to consider. Segmentation is often presented as if it is entirely planned. This is not always the case! An organisation may have segments that it *wants* to target but this does not mean that those segments want to do business with the organisation. Furthermore, other segments that an organisation never intended to target can show a preference for what the organisation can offer. The challenge for many managers thus becomes one of trying to answer the following questions:

- What are the common characteristics of the people who are buying or receiving our products or services?
- What is it about these characteristics that make these people prefer our organisation's products or services?
- Could this information be used to attract more such customers or to improve our offering to them in order to increase satisfaction?
- Should this information be communicated to more senior managers? This is likely if a manager finds that the segments showing an interest are different from those whom senior managers express interest in targeting.

Segmentation strategy can emerge over time, therefore, and managers who have direct contact with customers can have an active role in shaping that strategy. Those managers who have no direct contact with customers often benefit from an awareness both of the external customer or stakeholder segments the organisation is serving and from segmenting and prioritising the demands of their internal stakeholders.

As a manager you may well have customers who have very specific needs and their importance means that you have to offer them a far more specific service than would be the case for other customer groups. You may feel that you are dealing with a number of segments or a single group. If you provide a service internally, you may feel that each of your customers may want something slightly different and you have to work hard constantly to fulfil the precise needs of every one of them. If this is the case, then it is worth considering what those customers have in common, rather than how they are different. In this way you might be able to standardise the products or services you offer in some way to make your own role easier and to be more effective.

On the other hand, you might be in the opposite position – of offering exactly the same product or service to all your customers without any clear idea of whether they would prefer something different from you or your department. In this case you might need to move to a differentiated approach.

Targeting

Once an organisation has identified and divided its market into distinct groups of customers and potential customers it will need to decide which of these segments it needs to devote more time and resources to. Normally the segments selected are those most likely to achieve the organisation's marketing aims, or wider objectives. In the for-profit sector targeting is the process of identifying which of the numerous segments offers the greatest opportunity to achieve marketing objectives, such as increased profitability or market share.

Targeting is also useful for not-for-profit sectors but here the organisation's objectives may be different. For example, the target segments for a government road safety campaign designed to change behaviour will be those shown to have a higher accident rate, such as young males. However, targeting for the not-for-profit sector does not mean that other segments are ignored. For example, in the UK, local public authorities have a duty to collect waste from everyone; however, those segments that have a greater need for regular waste collection may be targeted. These segments might include hospitals, where waste may need to be collected more often, for example, daily rather than weekly.

The decision about which segments an organisation should target depends partly on whether the product or service is a new or an existing one. For a new product or service, targeting should be conducted after the initial identification of the organisation's market segments and those most likely to meet the organisation's marketing or wider objectives. In the case of existing products or services it is possible that people who do not like what the organisation has to offer have stopped buying or using its products or services, or ceased to provide the organisation with resources such as financial donations. In this instance, the manager needs to consider whether these segments are worth targeting. If they are, then the reasons why customers have stopped buying a product or using a service need to be addressed. Alternatively, if the segment is no longer of value to the organisation then the segment should no longer be targeted.

The criteria for targeting may include:

Segment size and growth potential A segment should be of a reasonable size and offer sufficient reward for the organisation to select it. For a for-profit organisation this may be a group of customers most likely to purchase the product or service. In the not-for-profit sector, it may be a segment that fulfils political requirements. For example, children under ten years who abuse dangerous drugs may be a better target than a reasonably sized and growing segment such as adults using soft drugs.

Measurability A segment needs to be measurable in terms of size, 'profitability', scale of provision required, purchasing power and needs. For example, an organisation receiving donations from the public to provide shelter for homeless people will want to measure the results of its targeting. Measurement might include how many people were offered accommodation and how effectively donations were spent.

'Profitability' of the segment Profitability may be non-financial such as a reduction in the number of people smoking. A segment might be large and growing but it might be difficult for an organisation to make a profit by providing products or services for this group. For example, in the USA low-income families are a large market segment. However banks may not wish to target these families because they do not provide a profit; servicing this segment often costs the banks money. In fact, in certain US states banks are obliged by law to offer products to this group of customers, regardless of their profit potential. A not-for-profit example might be potential donors of money who have very low incomes. Here, it might it be more 'profitable' to target wealthy potential donors.

Current and potential competition The fewer competitors the more likely the organisation is to find the segment attractive. However, there may be few competitors because the segment has not yet been targeted by competitors or because there is little to be gained from targeting that particular segment. This criterion can be applied to many sectors.

Capabilities of the organisation In many sectors it is important to match the resources and capabilities of the organisation with the needs of the segment. For example, if the organisation identifies a segment of customers in another country for whom a product is likely to be attractive, it will need to be certain that it has the financial and human resources and capabilities to launch the product in that new country. In some cases, stakeholders will demand that a product or service is provided. For example, a hospital with a shortage of medical staff is not able to stop treating accident and emergency patients.

Accessibility An organisation needs to have access to the segment targeted.

These criteria must be considered in combination. An organisation will need to think about the choices it has in relation to the segments it has identified. It needs to decide which segments and the number of segments to target because there will usually be limitations on the resources available. These limitations may be money, time or knowledge about the segments.

When the market segments attractive to the organisation have been identified, managers need to decide how the organisation is going to target these segments. A number of approaches are available to organisations.

- *Undifferentiated targeting* The organisation treats all customers in the same way and ignores any differences between segments. This may be a valid approach because the expense of addressing differences between customers may be too high compared with the possible benefits. Publicly-funded hospitals tend to take this approach on the basis that everyone is equally entitled to medical care.

- *Differentiated targeting* This approach assumes that different segments need to be treated differently. This may cost time, effort and money, but the benefit to the organisation could be that customers are more satisfied as a result and are more loyal to the organisation. For some organisations there may be legal reasons for dealing with different markets in different ways. For example, mental health services may need to allocate more services and provision to different segments on the basis of age, ethnicity and so on.

- *Focused targeting* When the organisation has the freedom to choose and when resources are limited or the product or service is a specialist one, the organisation may focus on only a few segments. The advantage of this approach is that the organisation can develop a good reputation in a specific area of the market. The main disadvantage is that it may be difficult to find other customer groups if a problem arises with the existing segments or if the needs of a segment change. For example, if fewer children are born in an industrialised country, marketers of children's products may find that they can sell less quantity of the same product, but this may be compensated by the fact that parents now need to provide for fewer children and can thus spend more per child. A greater variety of children's products and higher qualities may therefore be demanded.

- *Customised targeting* In the for-profit sector, this approach was traditionally reserved for customers who required a highly specialised product or service and were prepared to pay for it, for example, a made-to-measure suit. Similarly, legal services often need to be customised to meet individual clients' needs. However, with the development of sophisticated database technology and, more recently, the ability of customers to communicate directly with organisations via the internet, many other types of organisation are able to tailor their products and services more closely to their customers' individual needs. For example, some charitable organisations use information about their donors to develop segments based on size of donation and reasons for donating. Organisations can then approach individual donors to ask for further donations, based on the reason for the original gift. Consider an organisation that carries out a wide range of activities in developing countries to provide health care, clean water, sanitation, education and self-help initiatives. If a donor previously gave money for education, the organisation will contact the donor to ask for a second donation for education. This may well produce a further gift.

Positioning

Positioning describes the process by which an organisation aims to create a favourable image in the mind of its customers and to differentiate its product or service offerings from those of its competitors. An example is Singapore Airlines' use of the slogan 'A great way to fly' accompanied by pictures of cabin crew, excellent in-flight food and modern aircraft. How an organisation positions its products and services compared with those of competitors depends crucially on how the company and its products and services are *currently* viewed by customers. For example, Aldi is a German supermarket that prides itself on selling good quality food, from manufacturers who are unfamiliar to customers, at a low price. If Aldi tried to re-position itself as an 'upmarket' or luxury supermarket selling top brands, it would fail. The market does not see Aldi stores and what they offer as 'upmarket'.

However, there are situations in which positioning is not a useful concept. For example, if you manage the wages system in the organisation for which you work, the company is likely to consider it unnecessary or even inappropriate for you to use resources to try to build an image of a 'great' wages office amongst the employees you serve. However, it will be important for you to position the wages office favourably in the mind of the finance director.

There are a number of different ways in which marketers can differentiate their offering from those of their competitors, such as product or services features, appealing to the needs of a specific market segment and brand image. To understand the range of different positioning options open to marketers, consider the laundry products market. Some powders, liquids and tablets are sold on the basis of price – they are cheap. Others are sold on the basis of performance – they wash whiter or help to maintain the colour of items being washed. Yet others are positioned on their ability to wash at low temperatures or without ingredients known to be harmful to the environment. All of these are benefits that customers want. However, because different market segments attach different priorities to each benefit, manufacturers are able to take advantage of this by offering different products for each segment.

This does not mean that, just because a segment attaches importance to one benefit such as luxury, all the other benefits are redundant; they are simply lower on the list of priorities. To be effective, differences between an organisation's own product or service and that of competitors need to be:

- important enough to customers to choose the product or service in question
- related to a distinctive and valued feature of the product or service

- of benefit to the customer
- communicated to and visible to the customer
- related to product or service features that are not easily copied by competitors.

Positioning as a concept is important because it takes account of the fact that, usually, customers have a choice. Looking at the alternatives from the customer's point of view, we need to appreciate that the customer will see the alternatives as occupying different 'positions' in terms of what they can do, how much they cost and what image they present. For example, a visit to a dentist incurs costs not just for treatment, but also in time and expenses in travelling to the dentist. The person receiving treatment will encounter a reception space, a receptionist, a furnished waiting room and so on, and then the dental surgery, all of which will create an impression.

Using positioning maps

Positioning maps can be used to show how customers view an organisation's offerings, in comparison with those of competitors. This allows marketers to assess whether the position that their products and services occupy is the preferred one, based on their marketing objectives, or whether repositioning is required. The map can also provide marketers with insights into the marketing strategy. This is the planned combination of elements used to market a product or service and which are under an organisation's control. These elements, called the 7Ps, cover:

- the *products* or services offered
- their *price*
- the *place* where they can be bought or used
- how they are *promoted*
- the recruitment and use of appropriate staff and *people* in their delivery
- the systems used to in deliver a service (*process*)
- *physical evidence* that allows the consumer to make judgments about the product or service and the organisation providing it.

To achieve the 'right' mix, the elements are adjusted until a combination is found that best serves the needs of customers and profitability or benefit to the organisation. A positioning map can help marketers to identify how the elements and their mix (the 'marketing mix' of 7 Ps) need to be changed in order to change the position of a product or service in the market-place.

The example below shows how positioning maps work. It uses an imaginary American university, Bloomsville, which wants to understand how its potential students perceive the university compared with competing universities.

First, marketers need to identify the key attributes of a product or service — that is, the attributes that customers regard as important in meeting their needs. Relatively quick methods for doing this including running a focus group — a type of qualitative research in which a group of customers are brought together to discuss a product or service — and interviewing experienced staff who deal with customers and understand their preferences.

The focus in this first stage of mapping centres on how the organisation's offerings are currently perceived by customers. The marketer should be able to form a list of key attributes.

For example, Bloomsville has conducted three focus groups consisting of, respectively, potential students, existing students and graduates. In each group, participants were asked to describe what they thought about Bloomsville, the university's competitors and, importantly, what they thought they would experience or did experience at Bloomsville. The following factors emerged:

- convenience (being able to study at times that fit with work schedules)
- cost
- course duration
- academic reputation
- recognition and prestige (amongst employers)
- standard of teaching
- applicability of teaching material to business practice
- courses/modules that can be used to build towards future qualifications
- quality of university life.

Of these, the factors mentioned most were 'academic reputation' and 'quality of university life'. Bloomsville decided to use these two factors to position itself in the academic market. So, in a second information-gathering exercise, Bloomsville asked potential, existing and past students to rank Bloomsville and its competitors on these two dominant factors.

Then, Bloomsville drew up its positioning map using the two factors identified – 'academic reputation' and 'quality of university life' – and the rankings. The map consisted of intersecting axes, ranging from low to high, labelled 'academic reputation' and 'quality of life', as show in Figure 3.1 Preparing the positioning map.

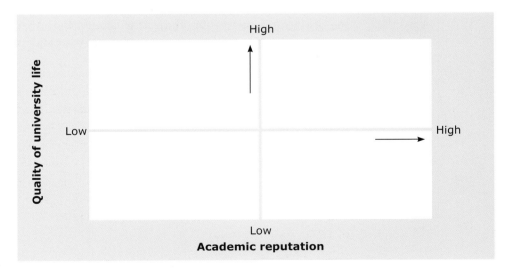

Figure 3.1 Preparing the positioning map

(Source: Sargeant, 2009)

Then Bloomsville took the rankings of competitors on the two factors and placed the competitors on the positioning map, along with Bloomsville itself. This result is shown in Figure 3.2 Initial positioning map for Bloomsville.

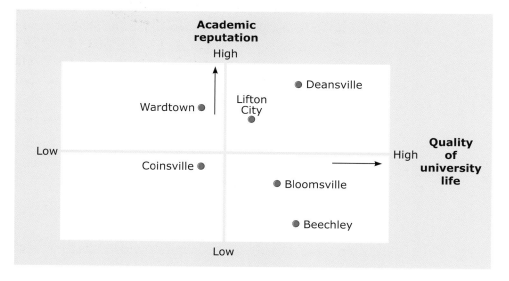

Figure 3.2 Initial positioning map for Bloomsville

(Source: Sargeant, 2009)

The resulting map revealed that Bloomsville's potential and existing students and graduates viewed the university as offering higher-than-average quality of university life than most of its competitors but having a lower-than-average academic reputation than most competitors. One competitor, Deansville, was ranked high on both factors – the position in which Bloomsville aspired to be.

It was now clear to Bloomsville how it was seen by potential students, so it could now adjust its marketing strategy. These adjustments would aim to reposition Bloomsville in the minds of potential students as a university with a strong academic position and offering a good quality of life. If successful, the university's new positioning map should look like the one in Figure 3.3 Amended positioning map for Bloomsville, showing it as a university offering a high academic reputation and high quality of university life.

Positioning maps are used by organisations to create a new image of themselves or to maintain their existing image in the market. However, the desired image must be based on the actual quality of the product or service in as far as this influences the image customers have. For example, Bloomsville's repositioning will be successful only if it acts to improve its academic education, otherwise its repositioning efforts will ultimately fail. In some cases, products or services have already been improved, but the 'old' image or reputation remains. Here, repositioning can take place on the basis of improvements made.

Even if an organisation has no competitors it can still use positioning to create a positive image in its customers' minds. For example, a local hospital may want to emphasise the quality of its service. It is also important to remember that non-direct competition may still exist; for example, patients have the opportunity to be treated at a private hospital instead of a publicly-funded one provided they are willing to pay.

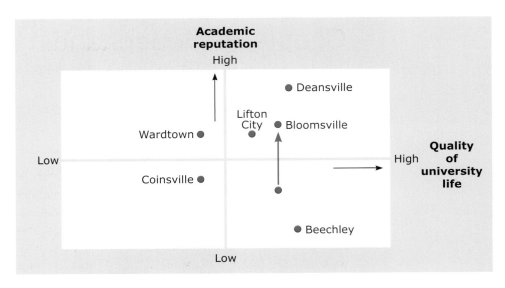

Figure 3.3 Amended positioning map for Bloomsville

(Source: Sargeant, 2009)

It is helpful for most managers to understand how their organisation positions itself in the eyes of important stakeholders. However, positioning can also be used in the context of your professional and career development. When you undertake your job you may want your most important stakeholders to see you in a particular light, for example, that you are the best person to do a particular job. Thinking about your important stakeholder segments and your positioning in their eyes may allow you to decide how you want to be perceived and what you need to do to achieve that perception. In other words, you are positioning yourself.

References

Bonomo, T. V. and Shapiro, B. P. (1983) *Segmenting The Industrial Market*, Lexington, Lexington Books, cited in Sargeant, A. (2009) *Marketing Management for Nonprofit Organisations*, Oxford, Oxford University Press.

Lynn, J., Straube, B. M., Bell, K. M., Jencks, S. F. and Kambic, R. T. (2007) 'Using population segmentation to provide better health care for all', *Millbank Quarterly*, vol. 85, no. 2, pp. 185–208.

McDonald, M. and Dunbar, I. K. (1998) *Market Segmentation* (2nd edn), London, Palgrave Macmillan.

Sargeant, A. (2009) *Marketing Management for Non-profit Organisations*, Oxford, Oxford University Press.

Sargeant, A. and Jay, E. (2004) *Building Donor Loyalty: A Fundraiser's Guide to Increasing Lifetime Value*, San Francisco, Wiley, p. 79.

Wells, W. D. (1975) 'Psychographics: a critical review', *Journal of Marketing Research*, vol. 12, no. 2, pp. 196–213.

Wilson, R. M. S., Gilligan, C. and Pearson, D. (1992) *Strategic Marketing Management: Planning, Implementation and Control*, London, Butterworth-Heinemann, p. 91.

Chapter 4 Understanding and influencing customer behaviour
Understanding and influencing customer behaviour

How can organisations influence customers to achieve the outcome they want? For-profit and many not-for-profit organisations are primarily concerned with getting customers to buy the products or use the services they provide. This assumes that customers have a choice. For example, people are likely to be able to choose the food they eat, the clothes they wear and the furniture for their homes. These are examples of products usually provided by the for-profit sector, but people may have choices over services that are often provided by the public sector, such as schools, hospitals or leisure facilities. While you may not have direct contact with your organisation's customers, your role as a manager will be linked in some way to satisfying their needs. Understanding how your organisation's customers behave, what they expect and how their needs can be satisfied is therefore an important aspect of any manager's job, whether you have direct contact with customers or not.

There are situations where external or internal customers have no real choice about who they purchase from. This may be the case in some public sector organisations or internal markets. For example, someone who wants their rubbish collected is usually limited to using a collection service, if there is one, or taking the rubbish to a local collection point. Similarly, when we consider internal products and services provided by one part of an organisation for another, managers of those departments receiving the product or service often have relatively little choice about who to go to, to obtain what they want. There is normally only one department that pays the employees' salaries, or provides IT or human resource services. Individuals are generally not able to make independent 'buying' decisions in these cases. While the models of buyer decision-making may not be as directly applicable in these specific cases, a general understanding of buying decision-making is nonetheless useful for managers working in most contexts, not least because 'no choice' situations may change. For example, in many countries, people can now choose who supplies utilities such as telecommunications, gas and electricity whereas, in the past, there was only a single supplier of each of these.

In marketing terms, the key to organisational success is keeping customers satisfied so that they continue to use the organisation's products or services and, ideally, tell others about them. Understanding what makes customers happy involves understanding the process by which they make a decision to purchase a product or use a service. From this perspective, almost every department in an organisation makes a contribution to support the customer in this decision-making process. For example, a person who cleans the floors in a hospital is not only helping to create an impression of cleanliness for clients; the cleaner also makes a vital contribution to hygiene and, therefore, to keeping patients healthy. The hospital's record of hygiene and the first impression of cleanliness may enhance its reputation.

While customer decision-making is an interesting subject in itself, some aspects of it will be more useful for your own work context than others. This may be the case if the organisation you work for has no desire to encourage customers to purchase a product or service, but instead wants to bring about a change in behaviour. In this sense getting the customer to do what the organisation wants is a behaviour change. Anti-smoking campaigns are a good example of this. In these instances the decision-making process as described for purchasing decisions has less obvious relevance. Instead we need to understand how we can change our clients' negative behaviours into positive ones.

Of course, understanding customers' decisions or clients' behaviours and how to influence them is not enough. In order to attract these customers and clients and keep them satisfied, organisations need to adapt to their customers' expectations and behaviour and create a suitable marketing mix that will satisfy customer needs.

When customers can choose

Managers can most easily find a way to influence their customers if they understand their decision-making process. Customers' purchasing decisions can be influenced by a wide range of considerations. By the purchasing decision-making process, we mean the process through which a customer reaches a decision to 'buy' a product or service. This may be a short and fast process, or it may be more complex and lengthy, depending on the individual customer and the type of purchase. Figure 4.1 shows the decision-making process for a 'high-involvement' purchase. A high-involvement purchase is one where customers commit a considerable amount of time and effort to reaching a decision. Examples include buying a car or a pregnant woman deciding whether to give birth in hospital or at home with the services of a midwife.

Figure 4.1 The decision-making process

The process begins with the recognition of a problem (a need or want) and ends with coming to terms with the purchasing decision that is eventually made. The process can be illustrated with the example of a mother and father deciding which school for 11–16 year-olds their daughter should attend. While this example refers to a not-for-profit situation, the same process applies to for-profit situations, such as buying a plane ticket.

The parents live in a large city which has a choice of secondary schools. Some of these schools are faith-based and accept only or mainly pupils of a particular religious background (such as Catholics), some are single-sex schools accepting only boys or girls, some select their students depending on their academic ability, and some have no selection criteria for entry but give priority to children living in a particular area of the city.

Problem recognition

For the parents, the need to choose a school has arisen because their daughter is 11 years old and it is time for her to change from primary to secondary education. It is a legal requirement for children to continue schooling after the age of 11, so 'problem recognition' has been forced on to the parents by the law.

In this case problem recognition arose as a result of an external force – the law – but problem recognition can arise in many ways. A need may be *internally* generated (such as hunger) or *externally* influenced by situational factors (such as seeing an advertisement for an appetising food). Problem recognition can be very simple or quite complex. An example for a very simple form of need recognition would be to think, 'I have no food to eat tonight, so I need to go to the shop and buy some.' An example for a more complex form of need recognition might be someone hearing of an earthquake which has left many people homeless, realising that these people need help, and therefore deciding to donate to a charity that helps people in disaster zones. In this case. The news item triggered a need to do something to help the victims of a disaster.

Usually there is little that an organisation can do about the internal processes involved in problem recognition except to recognise them. Any influence on these processes is likely to be indirect and difficult to control. However, organisations can sometimes influence external stimuli – inputs that arouse action – that might lead to problem recognition. This is often done through advertising, for example, food items advertised during an evening television programme may stimulate the viewers' appetites so that they then go out and buy that product.

Information search

The parents have received various prospectuses from a number of schools that their daughter could attend. They requested these after finding out about possible secondary schools from a list provided by their child's current school, through an internet search and by asking friends about their own children's experience of secondary schools in the city.

In this second step, customers seek information to find out how a problem can be solved. A significant and expensive item, such as a car, will probably involve collecting a considerable amount of information. However, deciding to buy a sandwich or putting some coins into a collection box next to a cash till to help a voluntary organisation that monitors animal welfare may require little information gathering. In these cases, a quick 'memory scan' of things a person has eaten before in similar circumstances, or recognising the organisation to which you are making a donation, will provide sufficient information. From the perspective of an organisation trying to influence the customer, this is the point at which it needs to ensure that information is available to a customer.

Information evaluation

The parents have read the brochures and have started to rank the schools in terms of their own and their daughter's preferences. These preferences are based on a selection of criteria the parents have formed with their child which meet their respective needs. These include:

- academic reputation
- examination performance
- cultural diversity
- tolerance of difference between pupils in terms of their background
- proximity to home
- preference for a state-funded school.

It was perceived by the parents that the religious schools were not as tolerant of difference as they would like, so they were ranked lower. In contrast, ethnically-diverse schools were ranked higher along with those that have a strong academic reputation and examination performance.

Once customers have enough information they will try to find some way to evaluate what they have learnt in order to be able to distinguish one product from another. Evaluation often requires some form of selection criteria to be applied to the information. In our example, evaluation is being done in a rational, logical and systematic way, but this is not the case in all situations.

Customers often draw on impressions or emotions and give reasons such as: 'I liked the look of that one'. In most cases, information search and evaluation are done together: people review and evaluate pieces of information as they get them.

Decision

The parents and child have now chosen two schools they like. The parents favour the single-sex girls' school which they believe will encourage their daughter to focus on her academic studies and prepare her for university. The school is culturally diverse and prides itself on its academic performance. In contrast, the daughter has chosen a mixed-sex school whose academic performance is not as good as the single-sex school. However, it offers a wide variety of after-school clubs that aim to increase student confidence and life skills. These are what attract the daughter. A decision has to be made. After considerable discussion, the single-sex school is chosen. However, the daughter has been assured that she will be allowed to join various clubs offering activities such as horse-riding that will help to develop her confidence.

The ease or difficulty of making a decision will depend on the outcomes of the previous stage. If only one product or supplier emerges, the decision may be relatively easy. If there is a choice to be made between two or more products or services, then other criteria for selection may need to be generated. Again, an organisation can influence the decision. For example, a for-profit organisation could offer superior after-sales service, a loan to buy a product, or a technical support service. A not-for-profit organisation, such as a hospital, could use a website to publicise endorsements from previous patients about the quality of the hospital service.

Post-purchase dissonance

The daughter is worried. Has she made the right choice? Many of her friends are going to the mixed-sex school that she had originally wanted to attend, and she will now have to make new friends at the girls' school. Her worries, however, are lessened when her new school writes to her inviting her to spend a day at the school. The aim of this induction is to reassure new students about their decision to study at the school and to familiarise them with their new surroundings.

The period of doubt and uncertainty that arises after a purchase has been made is known as post-purchase dissonance, when customers try to rationalise the choice they have made. Eating a snack that satisfies our hunger does not need too much thought about whether we made the right decision. If we did not find it satisfying, we may decide not to buy that particular item again. Choosing a school is different and we may take some time to overcome our doubts. An organisation can reduce post-purchase dissonance by ensuring that the product or service lives up to the customer's expectations and by reassuring customers about their decision. In our example above, the school has offered this reassurance with an induction day. Organisations increasingly use advertising to provide this reassurance. For example, advertising may not be intended to convince people to buy but instead to convince people that they have made the right choice. This is often used by charitable organisations to show existing and potential financial donors the results of projects they helped to fund. If an organisation does not deliver what it has promised, however, opportunities for repeat purchases or donations are threatened.

Benefits and limitations of the model

The model of the customer decision-making process has a number of benefits for managers in situations of high customer choice. It provides managers with a framework for undertaking marketing activities. For example, raising awareness of a product or service will be appropriate at the information search and evaluation stages, and activities that might encourage customers to make a decision in favour of the product or service that an organisation is offering will be appropriate at the decision stage.

However, the model generalises complex human behaviour and presents it in a simplified form. It also represents a complete process – one that customers may not go through. There are three main reasons for this.

- In many situations and locations people may be under time pressure to make a decision and may not be able to evaluate different options.
- People may feel that they do not have the knowledge or ability to evaluate different options and may buy on the basis of convenience. This is often the case with technical products, such as video cameras.
- People may not recognise that they have a need before thinking about a purchase and may buy on impulse. For example, they may see a product offered at a very low price, assume that they have the chance to buy a 'bargain' and make a purchase.

Influences on customer behaviour

A decision to make a purchase may not be made by the customer alone. Decisions are often made in consultation with others, for example, by a family or a work group who all have an influence. Individuals are also influenced by a wide variety of factors around them in making purchasing decisions. These include personal, situational, psychological and social factors. These factors influence the customer decision-making process and customer behaviour in a wider sense. Understanding these is important, so that organisations can influence their customers' decision-making process or change people's behaviour in a wider sense (for example, a campaign designed to encourage people to have their children vaccinated against serious diseases). Figure 4.2 shows the influences and the stages of decision-making that customers may go through.

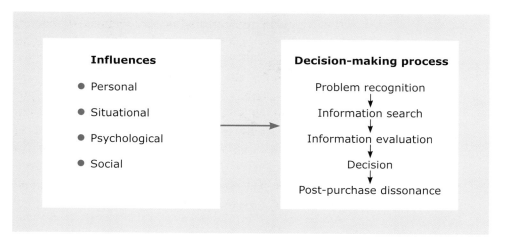

Figure 4.2 Influences on the customer decision-making process

We will explore these influences through the example of a family choosing a holiday destination. The same influences apply to not-for-profit situations.

Personal factors

Personal factors relate to those influences that relate to the individual. Among such factors are demographic factors and the level of involvement required in the decision-making process. Common demographic factors that influence what people buy include characteristics such as age, gender, ethnicity and so on.

> For example, when choosing a holiday destination, a father might prefer the destination that would allow him to spend time with his own parents and extended family who live in another country. The children, however, might prefer a customised, outdoor adventure holiday.

Situational factors

Situational factors refer to the external environment that surrounds and influences us and the decisions we make, consciously or unconsciously. Influences might come from the economic or political environment, changes in technology or wider societal changes such as a greater interest in environmental and ethical issues.

> In the example of a family choosing a holiday, the parents may be concerned that one of their preferred destinations may not be safe because of political unrest. The children have been learning at school about the impact of different forms of travel on the environment and try to persuade the parents to choose a destination that does not involve long distance air travel. (This fits well with their preference for a holiday in a nearby mountain area, offering internationally-renowned facilities!)

Psychological factors

Psychological factors refer to the mental or emotional influences that affect the customer decision-making process. This wide range of influences can include the mental processes by which people attend to and respond to information, the ability to empathise with others, the need to belong to a certain group and one's level of family orientation. People select, organise and interpret information to form concepts that help them to create a meaningful picture of the world. These concepts shape their behaviour. Customers' willingness to donate money to a charitable organisation will be influenced by their concept of 'charity' – the provision of help to the needy. Individuals who take the view that 'charity begins at home' may give only to charities that operate locally or in their home country. Other people may take a much wider, perhaps global view of charity.

Many purchasing decisions are not made using a rational process. Rather, people use their emotional responses to situations and products or services to help them make decisions. Even for decisions involving significant risk, such as buying a house, people are more likely to make emotional than highly rational decisions. Making decisions based on emotions can be sensible. Emotions are useful and highly-evolved shortcuts to decision-making. Without such shortcuts it would be impossible to exist in a world in which every decision – big and small – needed to be carefully considered. Psychological factors mean that marketers should make as much, if not more, effort to understand customer emotions as they do to understand rational decision-making.

> In the holiday example, the father has strong emotional ties to his own parents, brothers and sisters and their children and feels comfortable with them. While his wife and their children understand this and enjoy visiting the family too, they are reluctant to spend every annual holiday in the same way.

Social factors

Social factors refer to how reference groups, such as families, friends, peers and colleagues, influence customer decision-making by acting as a source of information. For example, the family is an important reference group which provides a set of values and beliefs that influence its members' thought processes, including their motivation to purchase certain products or services. The wants and needs of a customer's spouse and children will have a direct impact on the customer.

In the holiday example, the children want the kind of holiday that their friends would approve of. There is considerable pressure on them at school to have exciting, adventurous holidays. The children's father, however, feels considerable social pressure on him to spend time with his own parents and extended family.

All these factors will influence different people in different situations to a different extent. Sometimes, psychological factors will be important. At other times, colleagues or the family will be the most important influence. In some decisions, all the factors will play a significant role. Organisations and their managers need to understand and identify the most important influences on their customers' decision-making, so that they can adapt their marketing actions. In some cases, it is possible to influence the customer decision-making process through advertising that aims to change customers' perception of the product or service offered.

The organisational buying process

Organisational buying behaviour refers to the purchase behaviour of organisations. Organisations who manufacture products need to purchase raw materials; resellers, such as supermarkets, need to purchase items to sell to the public; local and national government departments buy services such as waste collection and disposal; and hospitals buy drugs, surgical tools and beds. Most organisations buy office equipment and consumables such as paper and printer ink. Unlike individual, private customers, whose decision-making tends to involve only a few people, decision-making by organisational buyers is more complex and their purchases are often of high financial value.

Three main features of organisational buying behaviour are:

Rational reasons for purchase Although organisational buyers often make decisions on an emotional basis (e.g. if they like a salesperson), there is a greater expectation that decisions can be explained rationally.

The need to justify There is a need to justify buying decisions so that it can be shown that the organisation's money has been spent prudently. This can lead to conflict between a manager making a purchasing decision and other stakeholders who demand extensive justification for even relatively small purchases. This is the reason a manager may make a complaint such as: 'This printer cost only £50, but documenting the decision and getting approvals took 10 hours of our time.'

Limited choice Organisations often limit managers' choices when making purchasing decisions. The organisation might impose quite strict specifications concerning the IT equipment that can be purchased, for example, and on the supplier. Managers often spend considerable time finding ways to avoid such strict limitations.

How does an organisation make purchasing decisions? Robinson *et al.*'s model of the organisational buying process (1967) is still one of the most useful models. This model distinguishes between three types of organisational buying decisions, set out below. Each type of decision requires a different amount of effort on the part of the purchasing organisation.

Re-buy Here the same product or service is bought again from the same supplier. This type of organisational buying behaviour requires almost no effort and time to come to a decision.

Modified re-buy Here a slightly modified version of an existing product or service is purchased, for example, office stationery with new letterheads or a more comprehensive cleaning service. This requires some effort in the decision-making process, because the modifications will need to be negotiated with existing suppliers or new suppliers need to be found.

New task Here the organisation buys a product or service it has not bought before, for example, a new piece of machinery for a production process. This requires the most extensive decision-making process because the organisation has no previous experience with the product or service or the suppliers.

'New task' buying is the most complex type of organisational buying decision and has eight 'buy phases'. These are:

1   recognising or anticipating a need that needs satisfying

2   identifying features of the product/service needed and determining the quantity required

3   specifying the purchase requirement clearly

4   seeking potential suppliers

5   assessing potential suppliers for their ability to satisfy the original need

6   choosing one or more suppliers

7   agreeing contracts and specifying the terms of business

8   seeking feedback on and evaluating the buying process to ensure that the organisation's original need was met.

Although this model has been criticised for being too simple, it does provide a fairly realistic idea of how organisations make their purchasing decisions for 'new tasks'. The number of people involved in the decision-making will depend on the cost and the complexity of the purchase being made. To attempt to simplify the purchasing process, buyers may use a method of purchasing known as 'systems buying'. This involves buying all the components needed to perform a particular activity together. This has obvious benefits for suppliers who can sell not just single products, but a complete range of goods. Computer manufacturers are an example: they may carry out initial consultancy work to specify what hardware a customer needs, provide and install it, and provide training for the customer's staff.

The organisational decision-making process is influenced by other factors:

- the environment in which the organisation operates
- the organisation itself (its values, beliefs and how it operates)
- interpersonal influences on the 'buying centre'
- individuals' ability to influence the buying decision.

Perhaps the most interesting of all of these is the third one, interpersonal influences on the buying centre. Relatively few important or complex organisational purchases are made by just one person. Generally they are made by what is called a buying centre, composed of all the individuals and groups who participate in the purchasing decision-making process. These individuals and groups share some common goals and the risks arising from the decisions. Webster and Wind (1972) identified seven roles that may be played in the buying process:

- initiators, who request that something is purchased
- users, who will actually use the product or service
- influencers who include, in particular, technical personnel
- deciders who make the decision
- approvers who formally authorise the decision
- buyers, normally the department with formal authority to make purchases
- gatekeepers, who are those with the power to allow or stop suppliers reaching other members of the buying centre.

Not all these roles will be found in every organisation. Further, there may be more than one individual in each role, for example, there may be a number of users and several influencers. The formal roles or job titles of individuals may not necessarily reflect their role in the organisational decision-making process. However, the key principle is that a range of different people will be involved. For example, when organisations send their staff on training courses the initiators may be individual members of staff, their line managers, or perhaps the training department. Individual managers or employees are the users of the courses; the training department may be the influencer, line managers may be the deciders and the human resource department may be the authoriser for staff attending a course. Line managers may also be gatekeepers in that they may decide whether or not to suggest training to a member of staff.

The challenge for managers is to identify the different groups of people who are party to a decision, the role that they play and their needs and wants. They also need to evaluate the relative importance of each person or group to ensure that the needs of the most important ones are given priority. Finally, in order to assess how to appeal to the different stakeholders managers need to consider which elements of the 'marketing mix' can be used, that is: the products or services offered, their price, the place where they can be bought or used, how they are promoted, the recruitment and use of appropriate staff and people in the delivery of a product or service, the systems used to deliver a service (process), and physical evidence that allows judgements about the product or service and the organisation providing it.

Organisational buyers differ from individual, private buyers in important ways. According to Wilson (1999), organisational buying involves:

Additional needs Organisations have additional needs, for example, the making of profits and legal obligations to their customers.

Procedures that need to be followed Organisational buying involves formal policies and procedures, such as order forms and purchase contracts. Buying also tends to involve more people.

A chain of demand In organisational markets, demand is derived, i.e. demand for industrial goods and services only arises as a result of demand in consumer markets. For example, without consumer demand for cars, there would be no demand from automobile manufacturers for car parts.

Professional buyers Organisational buying is usually done by professionals who have access to more information than individual, private customers and consumers do, allowing them to make more-informed decisions.

However, while organisational buyer behaviour can be considered to be more rational than its consumer-buying counterpart, individual customers and consumers are becoming increasingly rational in their buying decisions. This results from developments in information technology which improve suppliers' ability to communicate with them. Further, Wilson (1999) argues that consumers do not only buy for themselves but, like organisational buyers, they often buy on behalf of others. It is also the case that organisations are frequently exposed to the same personal and external influences as individual buyers when making buying decisions.

Changing people's behaviour

Many organisations aim to influence their customers to make decisions – to buy a particular product or service, give time or money to a charitable organisation or ask for a particular service from another department in the same organisation. However, some organisations seek something different. Their efforts are not aimed at increasing the organisation's profit or its share of the market or use of a service. Instead they aim to encourage people to behave differently, for example, to eat more healthily, stop smoking or recycle their waste. This is known as social marketing.

Attempts to change an individual's behaviour are complex and complicated by a variety of external and internal influences on individuals. Consider the example of an organisation that is trying to encourage people to eat a healthy diet. No matter how much an individual is exposed to information on healthy eating, if a person's family and friends continue to eat unhealthy food the individual is likely to continue to do so as well. A different approach is needed that addresses these wider influences and tries to change them from negative to positive.

One approach to creating a behaviour change in a group is the behavioural ecological model. This recognises the limitations of attempting to change individual behaviour. The easiest way to show how this model works is through an example, set out in Table 4.1. The example includes a number of strategies aimed at different groups (who all influence each other) to try to reduce obesity in children, an increasing problem for many societies. The table shows who is targeted (level) and how (strategy).

Table 4.1 An example of the behavioural ecology model

Level	Strategy
Individual	Develop education programmes focusing on health: this may lead parents to purchase healthier foods so that they are readily available to children in the home
	Design programmes to help parents overcome constraints on a healthy lifestyle, such as lack of time to prepare healthy meals or lack of opportunities for the family to be physically active
	Encourage positive attitudes towards physical activity
	Improve parents' knowledge of nutrition
	Stimulate parents to encourage their children to take physical exercise
	Encourage parents to interpret advertising messages for their children
Local	Encourage schools to include more physical education and to improve children's knowledge about how to be physically active
	Advocate access to school facilities at weekends and during holidays
	Develop initiatives such as cooking classes in school or 'walking bus' programmes that involve two or more adults taking a group of children to school on foot
	Eliminate arrangements whereby suppliers of unhealthy foods sponsor schools
	Introduce stricter standards for food supplied to children in schools
Community	Advocate the development of more recreational facilities for children
	Increase the availability of healthy foods
	Increase funding for education and social marketing
	Reduce visibility and restrict supply of less healthy food items, such as products with a high content of fat/sugar
	Require health warnings on high-fat foods and high-sugar drinks
	Restrict food advertising during children's TV programmes
Social structure	Change attitudes to childhood inactivity to make it socially unacceptable
	Encourage the media to develop a greater focus on healthy role models and behaviours
	Encourage or legislate for greater restraint on the marketing of less healthy food products to children
	Encourage fast-food chains to produce more diverse menus and lower-fat menus

(Source: based on Dresler-Hawke and Veer, 2006)

This example of a social marketing strategy for a government department or a large not-for-profit health foundation involve the work of many managers at relatively senior level. But some aspects of the example will be applicable in other, more local and more limited situations. Many management tasks in a variety of contexts are to do with encouraging staff or other stakeholders to change their behaviour, for example, to adopt new working practices. So, while influencing the social structure of a society is beyond the scope of most managers, the behavioural ecology model shows how behaviours can be influenced. These ideas can be used in many more circumscribed situations.

Who constrains and encourages customer behaviour?

Customers' or clients' behaviour will be partly influenced by other people or organisations. This influence, which can constrain or encourage customer behaviour, can range from someone offering advice, to an organisation providing misinformation about another organisation's products or services.

Managers often need to identify what these constraining and encouraging influences are, where they have an impact in the decision-making (or behaviour change) process and how they might be reduced or encouraged (as appropriate). By understanding these influences, organisations can often achieve desirable outcomes for themselves. For example, if government organisations provide school children with information about 'environmentally-friendly' behaviour the children will often encourage their parents to adopt such behaviour too. It is, of course, possible to use such influences in less benign or unethical ways. For example, shops have been accused of unethical behaviour in placing sweets near cash tills where children are most likely to see and demand them. Attempts to reduce fat and sugar intake in a population may be undermined by fast-food restaurants giving money-off vouchers.

When considering influences on buying decisions it is helpful to distinguish a number of different, influential, roles that people or organisations may play. These include:

> *Initiator* These people, organisations and stakeholders recognise there is a problem or unmet need that needs satisfying or changing. They will begin the decision-making or behaviour change process to resolve this problem or meet the need.

> *Decision-maker* Decision-makers are those who make the decision to purchase the product or service or begin the desired behaviour change. An organisation making a large donation to a charitable organisation may ask a committee to make the decision. Alternatively, attempting to change the eating habits of a community may involve identifying the community leaders who can advise the community to make the decision to change its behaviour.

> *Purchaser* In buying decisions, the purchaser is the person who purchases the product or service and pays for it. In behaviour change, the

equivalent of the purchaser is the person or group or society making the desired behaviour change. For example, when attempting to change anti-social behaviour among a group of late-night bar visitors we would consider this group to be the 'purchaser' of the desired change in behaviour.

End-user In buying decisions the end-user will be the person, organisation or stakeholder who uses the purchased product or service. This can be someone who has not been involved, or little involved, in the decision-making process. When considering behaviour change, the people, groups or society benefitting from the behaviour change are the end-users.

Identifying the variety of people, organisations and stakeholders who play different roles in buying decisions or behaviour change does not recognise the nature of their influence, however. When considering the nature of the influence, it can be helpful to classify these people, organisations and stakeholders into two categories: influencers and gatekeepers.

An influencer is any person or group who exerts some influence on the buyer decision-making process or the behaviour change. They exist in all of the above categories and their influence can either be negative or positive. For example, in a hospital, an end-user (a patient) can be a positive influence on getting a new drug accepted by a doctor. A positive comment, such as 'That new painkiller worked better than anything I've been prescribed before' would offer a positive, reinforcing, message for the doctor.

Gatekeepers are people, organisations and stakeholders who have the power to deliberately allow information to get through to those involved in the customer decision-making or behaviour change – or to block it from doing so. For example, a secretary may filter telephone calls to a purchasing manager of an organisation and thus make it either easier or more difficult for, say, a sales representative to reach that purchasing manager. It is often known who these gatekeepers are and they can sometimes fulfil a valuable function in protecting decision-makers from unsolicited information or sales pitches. From a marketing perspective, however, gatekeepers can be a hindrance and marketers often try to circumvent them. Getting information to the target group is of paramount importance to a marketer. If a gatekeeper blocks this information, marketers need to find alternative ways of reaching the target audience that 'get round' the gatekeeper. This may involve approaching the target audience in person or by letter, email, or advertising, in situations where the target group is present but the gatekeeper is not.

This can be done by networking. For example, the managing director of a charitable organisation might be able to approach the managing director of commercial organisation at the golf club they both belong to, to secure a donation. If you want to approach the manager in a different department at work but find you are blocked by the department's gatekeeper, you might arrange to attend the same staff social event as the manager. Similar situations arise in consumer marketing. A husband wants to buy a new TV but his wife acts as a gatekeeper, deliberately providing her husband with negative messages and information about the cost and the financial impact on their holiday plans. The sales person (as an influencer) may respond with messages and information to encourage the purchase of the television with information about attractive credit terms and the store's returns policy should the couple change their minds about their purchase.

References

Dresler-Hawke, E. and Veer, E. (2006) 'Making healthy eating messages more effective: combining integrated marketing communication with the behaviour ecological model', *International Journal of Consumer Studies*, vol. 30, no. 4, pp. 318–326.

Robinson, P. T., Faris, C. W. and Wind, Y. (1967) *Industrial Buying and Creative Marketing*, Boston, Allyn and Bacon.

Webster, F. E. and Wind, Y. (1972), *Organisational Buying Behaviour*, Englewood Cliffs, NJ, Prentice-Hall.

Wilson, D. T. (1999) *Organisational Marketing*, London, International Thomson Business Press.

Chapter 5 Delivering value in exchanges – products and services
Value, quality and marketing relationships

Customers do not just buy a product or service because some marketing manager has cleverly categorised them into a segment. Nor do customers necessarily buy because the organisation has decided that they are important enough to be communicated with. Customers buy from organisations because they believe they are going to experience something special in their exchange. This can be called 'value', which occurs when the benefits of using the product/service exceed the cost. In this chapter we are going to review delivering value in exchanges from two perspectives.

First, we are going to explore how services differ from products and how this presents a number of problems surrounding quality. We shall examine how these problems occur and how they can be resolved.

Second, we are going to explore why organisations increasingly want to develop a relationship with some groups and not others. Often, the difference in value between one provider and another does not lie so much in the product or service itself but in the long-term relationship they have with customers. In this sense, marketing becomes a question of establishing and maintaining good relationships with customers. If we see marketing as improving relationships with stakeholders, then we need to analyse how the relationship might be developed further.

In many cases marketing relationships are fairly basic and there is no great wish on either side to make it deeper or more meaningful. For example, in many marketing relationships with consumers, say, in the purchase and consumption of low-value items such as ice cream, even though you hope that the customer will buy your product again, it is unlikely that you will want to make extensive contact with every customer. You may wish to print a customer information telephone number or website address on the ice cream packaging. But that is all. Similarly, while a city will want to have a website page on waste collection, and send a message to each home perhaps once a year, it is unlikely that it will want to make regular contact with every customer.

With a high-value product such as a car, however, it is more likely to be cost-effective to build regular post-purchase contact. This will include increased contact with people who choose and use a car, but it will be more important to build a good relationship with the corporate buyer of ten or more cars per year.

Building good long-term relationships is likely to be most important for both providers and customers when repeat purchases are likely and/or when there is an element of trust involved. Many people like to keep buying certain high-value items (such as the car in the example above) from the same supplier. It is even more important for many people to go to someone they know and trust for essential and confidential services, such as health care and financial or legal advice. Most people do not like to change their lawyer every time they need legal advice but prefer to keep going to a known and trusted family lawyer.

Building good marketing relationships is often not easy but takes time and effort. When there are multiple stakeholders then developing relationships may well be even more complex. As an example, consider organisations whose aim is to reduce antisocial and criminal behaviour by young people. Once the organisation has identified those young people who are unlikely to behave badly, it would seem appropriate to *reduce* the organisation's relationship with them to a low level. Similarly, once the organisation has identified that another organisation is already in contact with a particular antisocial person or group of people, it seems cost-effective again to *reduce* our organisation's relationship. This releases resources to *increase* the relationship with active stakeholders – the police, schools and colleges, the city, sources of funds – and those antisocial or at-risk persons or groups that are not yet targeted by other organisations.

Understanding how services differ from products

Most developed countries are commonly referred to as service-based economies. In using this term, it is recognised that these countries' economies are not predominantly based on producing physical products such as cars, but on offering services instead. However, the distinction between what constitutes a product and a service is becoming increasingly difficult. Most physical products come with a certain level of service attached, usually at least at the point of exchange, i.e. the provider, such as a hospital, city or retailer, provides a service in making the product available at a place and time that is convenient for customers. Likewise, services often come with at least a little bit of physical product attached to them, although this can be fairly minimal, such as a paper slip that gives the details of a bank transaction. Other products are composed of fairly equal levels of tangible product and intangible service. It is therefore best to think of a continuum of products, ranging from nearly entirely tangible at the one extreme and nearly entirely intangible at the other extreme, with various combinations of tangible and intangible between these two poles. Figure 5.1 shows a number of products and services in different places along the tangible–intangible continuum.

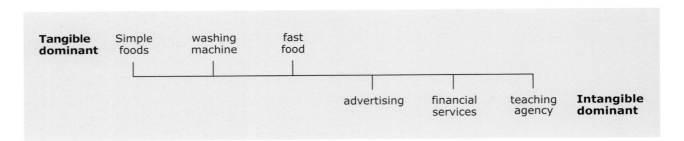

Figure 5.1 The tangible–intangible continuum

This tangible–intangible continuum is important as it shows that what we typically think of as physical goods usually have some service or intangible element attached to them. As a manager you will need to consider the extent to which your organisation's offerings are products or services, as the marketing of products and services is different to some degree. Once you have considered this you should then think about how best to allocate your available resources to support the exchange offering.

If your organisation is involved in some aspect of service offering then it is important to understand how a service differs from a product and the implications of this. The following list identifies how a service differs from a product:

Intangibility The purchase does not result in the ownership of anything (unlike a product where there is physical evidence that one has exchanged something).

Perishability Services cannot be stored as they are produced at the point where the customer buys them. A haircut needs to be produced with the customer present; it cannot be produced in advance and stored for when the customer comes in. This creates possibilities for inconsistency in terms of delivery and quality, and also makes productivity more difficult to measure.

Variability Services tend to be unique in that they are provided specifically for individuals or organisations as they demand the service. This means that the quality of the service is likely to vary with every encounter with a customer.

Inseparability The service cannot be separated from its provider. Services are innately linked to the individual who provided them. To stay with the above example, the haircut one receives at a particular hair salon is far more dependent on the skills and diligence of the individual hair dresser than on the salon as a whole.

Owing to these four differences between products and services, the latter can present a number of problems in terms of differentiation (no service encounter is exactly the same), quality (linked to the previous point) and productivity (how to assess how efficiently a service is being delivered). For example, a wages department in an organisation may use computers to organise payroll administration, reducing problems of differentiation, quality and so forth. Where a fast-food organisation may train its employees to offer a standardised 'meet and greet the customer' service, this may not be possible for a charity which requires volunteers to collect donations from a shopping centre because different volunteers may have different ways of approaching people for a donation. And because they are volunteers an organisation may find it more difficult to make them undergo training or conform to particular ways of doing things.

Table 5.1 illustrates these differences further:

Table 5.1 Problems in differentiating services

	Differentiation	Quality	Productivity
Intangibility	Because it is not possible to see, touch or taste services, in a competitive market it becomes more difficult to differentiate between the marketer's own offering and those of competitors. However, in a not-for-profit setting it may be important to make the different providers' services as identical as possible. For example, in the UK every public ambulance service must reach the patient within a set time period.	It is harder for marketers to manage quality when they are providing something whose quality is hard to measure due to its intangibility.	Intangibility makes this harder to measure and if you cannot measure well, how can you control well? (This assumes that the organisation has given the task of control to managers or marketers.)
Perishability		Because services cannot be stored, this requires that they be produced as and when they are needed, this makes quality assessment more expensive and difficult.	Because services cannot be stored, this limits the productivity of the organisation. The fire department hopes not to have too many fires to put out at the same time.
Variability	When for-profit, it is easier to differentiate between your service and your competitors' if your staff provide a consistent, homogeneous level of service; if they do not, comparisons are more difficult to make.	This is difficult to maintain because service quality is variable between employees of the same organisation and also the same employee may offer different service quality at different times.	Some staff can be productive and others may be unproductive.
Inseparability	When the customer has choice, because services are produced and consumed simultaneously, this makes it more difficult for customers to compare them.	This requires quality assessment to be undertaken on a more frequent basis than would be the case with the production of products.	Because the delivery of services is inseparable from employees, this affects the quantity of services which can be delivered per employee, or at any one time.

Services and resolving variability

The greater the variability there is in how a service is delivered, the greater the need for the manager to try and control this service variability. How service variability can be managed is further complicated by varying levels of customer demands and the ability of the organisation to supply the desired service. For example, a museum may get lots of school students arriving late morning (as this allows the students to be collected from school and taken to the museum). The problem for the museum is trying to manage large numbers of school pupils in the museum, along with allowing other members of the public to enjoy the museum. This type of service problem is one that all service organisations may face (regardless of whether they are profit, non-profit or internal customers). There are a number of ways in which managers can try to manage the demand for a product or service in order to make sure that the organisation is able to meet demand and to supply the level of service needed. For example, suppliers of electricity often try to manage demand in such a way as to even it out and make the costly building of new power stations unnecessary, or at least delay it. They may do so by trying to reduce demand generally, for example, by giving people advice on energy-saving or introducing high prices for electricity. They may also try to even out demand over time, for example, by offering cheaper prices for electricity consumed at night (when demand is generally lower) in order to use their generating capacity better.

To manage your customers' demand for your service you may consider the following actions:

- encouraging people to use your service during non-peak times (through advertising, communicating with your customers)

- create a reservation system, where customers can reserve the service they need; this will help to avoid queues of customers

- if possible try and alternate the price of your service, with high peak service times charged at a higher cost then lower peak times

- computerise, where possible, as much of the service delivery process as possible.

Just managing the level of demand for your service may still require you to try and adapt the supply of your organisation's service. An organisation can manage its service supply levels through asking the following questions:

- Are there ways in which you can get your customers more involved in the service delivery process to make it easier for your organisation?

- Can employees be trained and empowered to do more than one aspect of the service delivery?

- Can the service delivery process be further computerised to increase service delivery efficiency?

- Is it possible to employ part-time staff during busy periods?

The extent that you and your organisation will be able to manage the demand and supply of services will be dependent upon availability of resources, the organisation's willingness to change, employees not resisting change and being supported, and so forth.

Building and sustaining quality in service provision

Services differ from products because of four unique characteristics: intangibility (you cannot see or touch a service), perishability (services only last for as long as the service is being provided), variability (as services require a large human input quality becomes an issue) and inseparability (the service cannot be separated from the service provider). Each of these characteristics will have a direct effect on service quality, which we define as an ongoing process by an organisation to building and maintaining customer relationships through assessing, recognising and meeting customers' implicit and expressed needs. Unlike a product, which can be mass-produced often using machines, services often require a high level of human input to achieve a high level of quality. This human input may range from personal interactions with customers while providing the service to simply supporting the processes involved in delivering the service.

Services' unique characteristics ensure that no two service encounters can ever be the same. This inability to replicate the same service encounter has important consequences for customers' expectations of the service and how the organisation delivers it. Organisations providing services, more so than those providing physical products, need to ensure that each service encounter achieves the highest level of quality possible. You may not have overall responsibility for service delivery or quality standards but you will have an influence on how your organisation's services are delivered. For example, if you work in human resource management you may want to empower your employees to make immediate, low-cost decisions that will improve the service experience for your department's customers.

Although service quality can be assumed to refer to a whole organisation and its interactions with its consumers, it can also refer to individual managers and their own customers. For example, a finance manager may be required to provide numerical data to other departments to help their decision-making processes. Service quality then becomes important to both the organisation and individual employees.

Service quality is often considered essential to an organisation's continued growth and prosperity and many organisations consider it essential that all their employees understand this. Yet how can an organisation, regardless of whether it is an international airline or a local, community-based museum, ensure that they maximise their service quality? Several models have been developed to help managers improve their organisation's service delivery and quality. The most popular of these is SERVQUAL (Parasuraman, Zeithaml and Berry, 1985, 1988). Although originally designed in the 1980s, SERVQUAL is still considered relevant in the twenty-first century owing to its ability to identify five gaps in service delivery that can lead to service failure. Parasuraman, Zeithaml and Berry (1985, 1988) argue that if an organisation can assess its service delivery on each of these five gaps, then it will be able to improve its service quality.

These five gaps are shown in the following SERVQUAL model and will be explained in greater depth below.

Let us now look in more detail at the quality gaps identified in the model shown in Figure 5.2. How do these gaps arise and what can managers do to close them?

Gap 1: The consumer expectation–management perception gap

In this gap, managers may not understand what consumers expect, or want, from a service. Consequently, decisions regarding how to design the systems to deliver the service, allocation of resources needed to provide the service, and prioritisation of what aspects of the service are important to customers

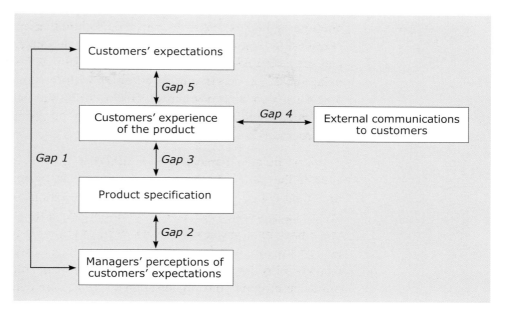

Figure 5.2 The quality gaps model

(Source: Parasuraman, Zeithami and Berry, 1985)

will not reflect actual consumer requirements. For many services – such as education, healthcare, financial and travel – customers require and expect to be able to speak to a knowledgeable individual, with good communication skills, who can answer queries and suggest solutions to problems. For example, a judge in a court of law refers an individual to an assessment centre for a comprehensive assessment – psychiatric, educational, family and medical – before making a sentencing decision. The managers of the assessment centre consider the quality of the reports to be the most important aspect of the assessment. However, the customer – the judge – looks for promptness, and the clarity of the recommendation and of the various options. The managers fail to understand the benefits sought by their customer and deliver what the judge takes to be an incomplete report because it does not set out the recommendations sufficiently clearly for the judge. This gap can by closed if managers correctly identify the predominant customer expectations for their products or services. Yet a general trend in service industries is to reduce the amount of personal contact available, which will only widen this service quality gap further.

Gap 2: Management perception–service quality specification gap

Even when managers are aware of what consumers expect of a quality service, managers are not always willing or able to provide these features in the service specification. For example, priorities of cost reduction in a large bank will result in branch closure and staff reduction in favour of call centres, even when managers may know that these will adversely affect the quality of the service experienced by consumers. In the court example, those who carried out the assessment were not sure what the managers had agreed to do for the court, that is, exactly what should be in their report. Organisations can close this gap by ensuring that the internal specification for the production of goods and services meet the intended concepts. This requires good communication between all those involved. However, many decision-makers, particularly in public services, are prevented, by resource constraints, from offering the service levels that they know consumers want. Consider the example of a national mental health organisation deciding to create a drop-in centre in a particular town for young people to visit for mutual support and to socialise. However, the drop-in centre was located in a commercial area of the town where young people rarely go, because a supporter of the organisation had offered accommodation at a reduced rent.

Gap 3: Service quality specifications–service delivery gap

This gap can be seen when a product is not delivered as specified. There are many reasons why this can happen. Perhaps demand has been greater than anticipated, or perhaps resources are constrained. It should be remembered that it is the customers' experience of the product that is important. This can be affected by many intangible factors – the way a product or service is delivered – which can be especially important in service delivery. In the court example, such a gap would exist if the assessment centre had indicated that a psychiatric report would form part of its report, but then omitted it because the psychiatrist failed to supply it in time. Another example would be where a human resource department must offer professional and personal development training for all its organisation's employees but the department has insufficient funds to offer the comprehensive service required by the organisation. Managers can close this gap by checking whether products and services are delivered according to the specifications. These checks allow managers to detect specification inconsistencies in the products and services delivered.

Gap 4: Service delivery–external communications gap

This gap can be seen when managers or organisations cannot deliver what they promise. Consumer expectations are determined to some extent by the organisation's communications, for example, advertising and publicity messages. However, the service delivered may fail to match that promised for a number of reasons, such as a breakdown in communication between employees delivering the service. It is also possible, of course, that the actual service delivered could exceed that promised, although this probably is less likely. In the court example, the court service used the assessment centre based on the centre's promise that it could produce comprehensive reports. The centre's failure to include one aspect (the psychiatric report) because of its dependence on an unreliable external provider meant that it failed to deliver what it had promised. In effect, this gap means that the actual products and services delivered differ from what has been communicated or advertised. The problem is often due to managers and organisations building up unachievable expectations in the customers' minds. Managers and organisations can close this gap by ensuring that the promises made to customers about products or services can be delivered.

Gap 5: Expected service–perceived service

Often referred to as the service/quality gap, Gap 5 is the culmination of the other four gaps and describes the quality of the service as perceived by the consumer. The premise is that if consumers' perceptions exceed their expectations, then a high-quality service is experienced; conversely, when expectations exceed perceptions, poor consumer-perceived service quality will result. Consequently management must close Gaps 1 to 4, so that consumers' perceptions are at least equal to their expectations. Customers' expectations are affected by their own experiences, the recommendations of others and the claims of suppliers; customers' experiences are determined by their perceptions and not by those of the supplier of a product or service. It is essential, therefore, for managers to see things from their customers' standpoint. In the court example, after failing to deliver in Gap 4, Gap 5 would be revealed if the assessment centre found that it began to receive less work because it had not lived up to the court's expectations and, as a result, acquired a reputation for poor quality.

The gaps above are not mutually exclusive and one gap might cause the occurrence of another gap. For example, Gap 3 (actual products or services are not delivered according to their specifications) might cause a gap between the actual products or services delivered and their image conveyed to the external market (Gap 4).

Of course, it is not possible to say that in *all* circumstances customers will not be satisfied with a product of apparently inferior quality. Sometimes people will forgo quality – and nonetheless be satisfied by products or services – in order to save money or to buy simpler products for environmental reasons. For example, someone may forgo the services of a personal trainer when joining a health and fitness club in order to save money; a supermarket customer may buy smaller and misshapen vegetables because they are locally grown and have not been transported long distances.

However, SERVQUAL as a management tool has been criticised. For example, it assumes that customers evaluate service quality by comparing it against what has been expected and this may not always be the case. Buttle (1996) has argued that no evidence exists to suggest that customers judge service quality in terms of expectations or perceptions. However, these criticisms should not detract from what is potentially a very effective management tool for monitoring how an organisation or a manager deals with their customers.

Customer satisfaction, service failure and service recovery

Unlike products, which can be mass-produced and standardised to be identical, services' reliance on human input ensures that no service encounter between an organisation/manager and their consumers can ever be identical. Although organisations and managers can strive to make their service delivery as similar as possible and improve service quality, through models such as SERVQUAL, there will be times when the service quality experienced by consumers will simply not be good enough. When this occurs it is often referred to as a service failure. A service failure can range from relatively simple problems, such as a person not having their meal delivered at the same time as their friends' in a restaurant, to more irritating issues, such as waste collection from a housing estate leaving loose rubbish on the streets or an airline having to cancel a flight on service grounds. In these instances, it is essential that the organisation and their managers attempt to solve this situation by ensuring consumer satisfaction; how this is achieved is called service recovery.

For service recovery to occur the organisation and its managers must develop a strategy that addresses service failures. These strategies may be based on experience of previous service failures or simply 'what if...?' scenarios where possible service failures are identified and solutions are planned in advance of them actually happening. Ultimately the aim of service recovery is not to deliver the service but to ensure that the consumer is satisfied that their experience of a service failure has been resolved. This could include apologising to the individual whose meal did not arrive with their friends' and offering a free dessert, ensuring that street cleaners are quickly deployed to collect loose rubbish from streets or an airline offering additional free tickets for a journey on their network owing to a flight being cancelled. Ensuring service recovery works may involve employees being empowered to make decisions and undertake initiatives which can help the customer, even though such initiatives may not be included in that employee's job specification. To take initiative, employees must also be motivated enough to care about the customers they are charged with looking after.

Introducing a service recovery strategy is resource intensive for managers to implement. Yet to what extent should managers try to achieve service recovery? After all, it is highly unlikely that 100% of your customers will be happy and the cost of resolving any service failure should be in proportion to the potential loss of profits. One possibility is to use perceived justice. Applying each of these three dimensions of perceived justice listed below may help managers to assess the extent to which they are able to and have achieved service recovery:

- Distributive justice: to what extent was a fair level of compensation for the service failure offered to all customers?
- Interactive justice: how fairly was the customer dealt with by the organisational staff dealing with a service failure or a complaint?
- Procedural justice: how fair was the process used to solve the customer's experience of service failure?

Building good marketing relationships

In any organisation, not all customers can be considered equals in terms of how big they are, their demands and so on. Certainly, market segmentation provides a means to identify which existing and potential customers a manager and the organisation should focus on. However, even within these segments different customers will be considered more important than others. As a manager it is important to allocate your resources in the most effective and efficient way and decide whom you should focus your attention on. This is an aspect of relationship marketing.

Relationship marketing describes the need to 'establish, maintain and enhance relationships with customers and other partners at a profit, so that objectives of both parties involved are met' (Grönroos, 1994). In the simplest way of looking at exchanges in the for-profit sector, there are two ways in which they can be undertaken. At one extreme we have what are referred to as 'transaction' based exchanges: here, buyer and seller simply exchange products and goods for money and at the end of the exchange there is very little likelihood that they will do business with each other again. A one-off purchase from a mobile snack bar at the annual fun fair could be an example. The two parties do not need to trust each other as they immediately see what each side is getting in the exchange, and after all if they have never met before and are not likely to do so again, what basis for trust could there be? In the not-for-profit sector an example of a transaction marketing exchange could be when we see a collection box for a charity of whose activities we know little; we have many coins in our pocket today, so we put some in the box.

At the other end of the continuum are very long-term exchanges with external and internal customers. These are exchanges that will perhaps span many years, they may well involve people making promises to each other and they will likely require substantial levels of trust. Such long-term exchanges are often referred to as being 'relationship-based'. Building long-term relationships with customers is considered to be particularly important in many professional service organisations, such as law or accountancy firms. But long-term external buyer-seller relationships can also exist in the non-profit sector. For example, people who give regular donations to their favourite charity.

It is therefore important for you and your organisation to decide what kind of relationship you need to have with your customers. Table 5.2 provides a means of identifying different types of relationships, which can be applied to both profit and non-profit organisations, as well as to internal customers within the organisation. (When you use the table you should define the term 'profit' in terms of your organisation's needs, i.e. a charity may define profit as number of donations received.)

The table identifies relationship levels into five categories:

Basic This is a simple transaction, the product/service is exchanged with no follow up.

Reactive An exchange occurs and the customer is encouraged to contact the organisation if they have any problems or questions.

Accountable The organisation contacts the customer shortly after the exchange to ensure that the customer is happy. The opportunity to ask the customer about how their product/service exchange could be improved is taken at this stage.

Proactive The organisation contacts the customer from time to time to inform the customer of new products/services/information about the organisation that may be useful to the customer.

Partnership The organisation works closely with the customer to deliver better value.

Table 5.2 Relationship levels as a function of profit margin and number of customers

Number of customers	High profit margin	Medium profit margin	Low profit margin
Many	Accountable	Reactor	Basic
Medium	Proactive	Accountable	Basic
Few	Partnership	Accountable	Reactive

(Source: Kotler *et al.*, 2005)

For example, local government operates a system managing a city centre. Their customers would be local shops, shoppers and so forth. From a profit perspective, local government has a duty to ensure the shopping area is clean, smart and attractive to shoppers. If this isn't achieved then the shop owners will not get people shopping. In this sense, the profit margin is high because of the importance of keeping the shops and shoppers happy, as well as the need for the high profile of having an attractive city centre. If we apply the table then we can argue that local government has a lot of customers (many) and a high profit margin (getting people shopping in the city centre). The table indicates that the local government should pursue a relationship one of being accountable, i.e. seeking information on how it can improve the shoppers' experience.

However, there are two significant criticisms of this table that are important from a manager's perspective. First, the table categorises customers at one moment in time and makes no assumption that customers can grow in size and importance over time. This criticism is particularly relevant to organisations that aim to build up a long-term relationship with their customers, even though they are not particularly important at this moment in time. For example, charities often aim to get customers who make small donations to move on to donating more regularly and then on to larger sums and so forth. We can show this in Figure 5.3 which illustrates the donor pyramid, which provides a means to which charity donors can be seen to move from 'incidental givers' who give whenever they want, to leaving a legacy in their will.

(The downward arrows indicate that a charity should never be complacent and that 'regular donors' if they do not get enough attention can return to being 'incidental donors'.)

The second criticism of Table 5.2 is that it does not take into account the cost and profit generated from developing a relationship with a group of customers. For example, a large group of highly profitable customers may not require or want a relationship with your organisation. Attempting to make a relationship with these customers may ultimately be counter-productive. Instead, it is possible to categorise customers on the basis of the costs and subsequent profit that a relationship would generate. This is shown in Figure 5.4.

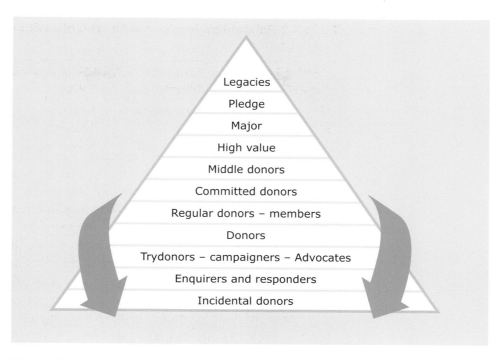

Figure 5.3 Donor pyramid for the twenty-first century

(Source: Elischer, 2008)

Figure 5.4 Comparing customer relationship revenues with relationship costs

(Source: amended from Kotler, *et al.,* 2005)

According to this figure, the extent that you as a manager or your organisation should enter into a relationship is determined by the type of customer you have. These can be categorised into four groups:

Sleeping giants These customers generate a lot of profit but are undemanding and do not necessarily want a relationship.

Power traders These customers provide a large amount of profit but are demanding in their needs.

Pets These customers produce a small amount of revenue and have no real need for a relationship with you or your organisation.

Delinquents These customers provide little profit but are the most demanding in their needs for a relationship.

As a manager the most difficult group to deal with is the 'delinquents'. In some instances you will not be able to remove these customers and you will have to deal with them. In these instances, opportunities should be provided to allow them to access products/services that are less likely to upset them. If this is not possible then as a manager you simply have to accept that they exist and find ways of coping with their behaviour.

The relationship quality checklist

Often managers feel that the marketing relationships in which they or their organisations are involved are not working as well as they could do. To help assess why marketing relationships might not be working as well as expected, a relationship quality checklist can be used. This consists of a number of questions that allow managers to determine the extent or depth of a relationship:

- Which stakeholders am I considering and ignoring here?
- How risky is the exchange? Or what promises (if any) are involved in undertaking the exchange?
  - In what ways is the exchange intangible?
  - How much do the stakeholders have at stake?
- What types of trust are necessary for the exchange to take place?
- How much trust is needed for the exchange to take place?

Answering the above questions in some detail will give managers a better understanding of the nature of the marketing relationships in which their organisation is involved, as well as helping identify any areas that might need attention.

References

Buttle, F. (1996) 'SERVQUAL: review, critique, research agenda', *European Journal of Marketing*, vol. 30, no. 1, pp. 8–32.

Elischer, T. (2008) *2008 Expedition: Rediscovering and climbing the donor pyramid* [online], Think Consulting Solutions, http://www.thinkcs.org/downloads/ThoughtPiece08.pdf (accessed 4 June 2009).

Grönroos, C. (1994) 'Quo Vadis marketing? Towards a relationship marketing paradigm', *Journal of Marketing Management*, vol. 10, no. 5, pp. 347–60.

Kotler, P., Wong, V., Saunders, J. and Armstrong, G. (2005) *Principles of Marketing: Fourth European Edition*, London, Prentice-Hall.

Parasuraman, A., Zeithaml, V. A. and Berry, L. L. (1985) 'A conceptual model of service quality and its implications for future research', *Journal of Marketing,* vol. 49 (fall), pp. 41–50.

Parasuraman, A., Zeithaml, V. A. and Berry, L. L. (1988) 'SERVQUAL: a multiple item scale for measuring consumer perceptions of service quality' *Journal of Retailing,* vol. 64, no. 1 (spring), pp. 14–40.

Chapter 6 The marketing mix
Coordinating the marketing mix

A customer's perception of an organisation and the products/services it sells consists of a collection of interconnecting actions and thoughts. These may be based on the customer's previous experience of exchanges with that organisation, other people's experiences or, more importantly, what the organisation specifically tells us about itself. It is this last point that is the basis for this chapter, where we explore how product, price, place and promotion (the 4Ps) are coordinated to form the marketing mix. The chapter therefore begins with the notion of the marketing mix, followed by a more in-depth look at each of its four components.

In this chapter we shall review the marketing mix not only from a profit, non-profit and public sector perspective but also from the personal perspective of a manager. All managers can learn how to market themselves better regardless of whether they want to achieve promotion, move to new employment or simply want to be seen as the best person to do their existing job.

The marketing mix refers to the controllable aspects of an organisation's operations which can be coordinated to satisfy its targeted segments. Although different authors have offered various lists of what constitutes the traditional marketing mix, it is commonly defined as consisting of: *product*, *price*, *place* and *promotion*. These components are then coordinated to send a consistent message to existing and potential customers. For example, for a profit-orientated organisation the price charged for a product will reflect the benefits a customer receives from actually consuming the product and the convenience of the place from which it can be bought; and it will be supported by the image that the promotion of the product presents, that is, what the customer can expect to experience from consuming the product.

Product

A product can be defined as anything that can be offered to a market to satisfy a want or need (Kotler, 2000). What is important to note about this definition is the satisfaction of needs. Customers do not normally buy a product because they want to own it – they buy it because of the need it fulfils. People do not want washing machines for decoration or the satisfaction of owning them (at least not normally); they want them to wash their clothes. What they are really buying is a means of getting their clothes clean. It is important to realise this as it helps managers to define what other products and services they are competing against. So, if your organisation manufactures or sells washing machines, your competitors would include dry cleaners, for example, not just other manufacturers or sellers of washing machines. The way we use the word 'product' here is not limited to physical products but also includes services, as well as the following less obvious examples of marketable products:

- experiences, such as the experience of seeing wild animals on an organised trip
- events, such as concerts
- persons, such as politicians marketing themselves to voters
- places, such as a city marketing itself as a tourist destination
- organisations, such as a public sector organisation trying to build up a positive image of itself among the citizens it serves
- ideas, such as an environmental pressure group promoting the idea of conserving energy.

As a manager you may have little or no input into decisions about your organisation's product offering. Indeed your organisation's product offering may have very little in common with those sold by a profit-orientated organisation. The purpose of this section, therefore, is not to examine in any depth the various aspects of what constitutes a 'product' within the marketing mix but to explore how organisations decide what type of product they should offer. Complementing this, we shall consider the role of product from the perspective of you, the manager. You may be involved in providing a product or service, whether directly or indirectly, to your external or internal customers. The aim of this section is to help you evaluate what product you offer and whether you should continue to do so.

Products, their features and benefits

Any product, whether a physical good or a service, and whether provided by a commercial, non-profit or public sector organisation, should be assessed in terms of its features and benefits, in order to ensure that it is providing what a customer wants or needs. Three different levels of a product can be considered, as shown in Figure 6.1.

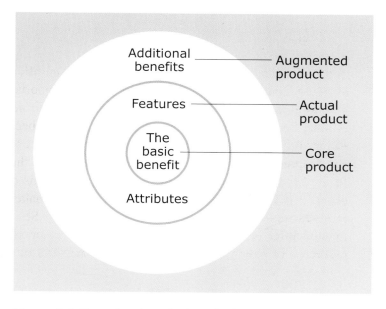

Figure 6.1 Three-level product analysis

The *core product* describes the fundamental reason for wanting to buy the item or use the service. This is often a generic description of the core benefits of several products or services in the same category. For example, the core benefit of a savings account is that it is a safe place to keep money that is not needed immediately.

The *actual product* describes the key features a customer expects from a product. These are often the minimum required for a product to have any chance in a competitive market. The actual features of a savings account might be access conditions, rate of interest and number of branches of the bank or savings institution.

The *augmented product* features additional benefits and customer services that have been built around the actual product. These are often added to differentiate a particular product from other offerings. These extra benefits are unlikely to be the main reason for purchase, but may be the reason for choosing one product over another. For example, a customer might choose a particular bank because it provides user-friendly internet banking.

The product life cycle

We begin our evaluation of what product to offer by introducing the concept of the product life cycle (PLC).

The PLC assumes that all products go through a standard set of stages, over a period of time. This is based on the realisation that most products and services have a limited life span (although some are sold for very long periods of time, spanning several decades). During the life span of a product, sales and profitability levels are not constant. Rather, it is normally expected that sales, and profits made from these sales, grow slowly initially, then hopefully grow rapidly for some time until sales eventually level off and decline. This is illustrated in Figure 6.2.

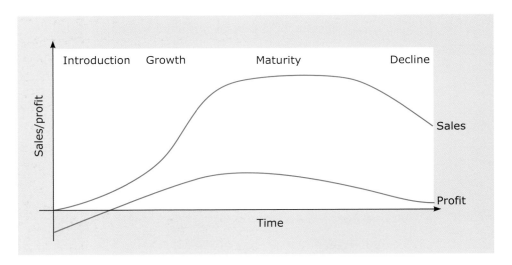

Figure 6.2 The product life cycle

The PLC allows managers to understand what marketing mix strategies need to be applied during a product's life span. These actions can be summarised as follows.

Introduction Low market awareness of the product ensures that sales are low. The organisation will focus its efforts on increasing marketing awareness through promotion or lower prices, for example.

Growth Customer demand sees sales of the product rapidly rise and the organisation begins to see a profit being made from the product. However, strong competition ensures that profits remain low as the organisation spends money trying to increase the product's sales.

Maturity At this stage product sales have reached their peak and the organisation's emphasis now moves to maintaining these sales levels. This can be done through price reductions, amending the existing product and increasing advertising, for example.

Decline The product has now reached the end of its life and the organisation will keep it alive merely to make a profit from it. Once the product is no longer profitable it will be allowed to die.

Besides allowing managers to determine how the product and its related marketing mix should be developed, the PLC concept also introduces the idea of profitability and market share. As a manager you may be required to categorise the products you offer your customers in terms of the PLC, profitability or market share. While the PLC is relatively simplistic in how it can be applied, it does force the manager to consider what products they are offering their customer.

Does the notion of the PLC have any value for people working for non-commercial organisations? It does to the extent that anything which is offered for exchange will go through a period of introduction, when others have to be convinced of the value of what is being offered, a period when the new product, service or idea is taken up by increasing numbers of people and also a stage when it becomes less popular and alternatives are sought. These phases of growth and decline will be influenced by wider political, economic, social, and technological changes. For example the ways in which various health services are provided have changed over the years, not only due to technological changes (different treatments), but also because of economic factors (increased wealth or pressure on governments' health budgets).

Product portfolio analysis for profit-orientated organisations

Profit-orientated organisations have a variety of tools for evaluating their product offerings and consequently making more effective decisions. We do not have the space to explore all of these tools, so we shall focus on one called the Boston Consulting Group matrix (BCG matrix). The BCG matrix provides a means for deciding how an organisation should allocate its resources amongst the different brands or businesses that it owns. The BCG matrix recognises that managers can take into account a wide variety of factors, and this makes managerial decision-making very complex. In order to simplify that complexity the matrix requires managers to look at only two factors. The first factor is *market share*, which reflects the money being generated by the product and can also be a proxy for the amount of power the product or brand or business has in the market-place. The second factor is *market growth*, which reflects how fast the market in which the business, product or brand is competing is actually growing. Market growth has a number of implications. Two important ones are: competing in growing markets absorbs resources, and whether or not a market is growing also demonstrates whether there is long-term sales and profit potential.

Using these criteria, the BCG matrix allows for products to be classified into four categories, as shown in Figure 6.3.

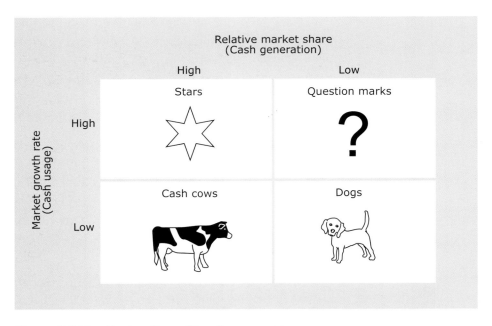

Figure 6.3 The Boston Consulting Group matrix

(Source: Kotler and Armstrong, 2004, p.47)

The matrix assumes that products will begin as 'question marks' before becoming 'stars', then 'cash cows' and finally 'dogs'. As the matrix allows for more than one product to be included, it is possible for an organisation to have products in all of the boxes. Let us now explore each of these four categories.

Question marks This category refers to products that have low market share but exist in a high-growth market. Typically these products have been launched recently and aim to capture a larger market share some time in the future. However, their recent launch into the market means that they have low levels of customer awareness and overcoming this requires a considerable financial investment.

Stars These are products that have a high market share in a market with a high growth rate. However, although products in this category generate a lot of money it is spent on maintaining market share in response to high levels of competition.

Cash cows All organisations need at least one cash cow in their product portfolio. These products have a high market share in a low-growth market, ensuring they are highly profitable. The important point is that this money is used to finance other products in the portfolio, that is, the question marks, stars and dogs.

Dogs A product with a low market share in a low-growth market needs constant money to support it and rarely produces any profit. Ideally, the money used to sustain a 'dog' product should be spent elsewhere in the matrix and therefore products in this category should be discarded.

Each product included in the matrix can be represented by a circle, with the size of the circle indicating the product's importance to the organisation. What does the BCG matrix look like for an organisation that has several products? An example is shown in Figure 6.4.

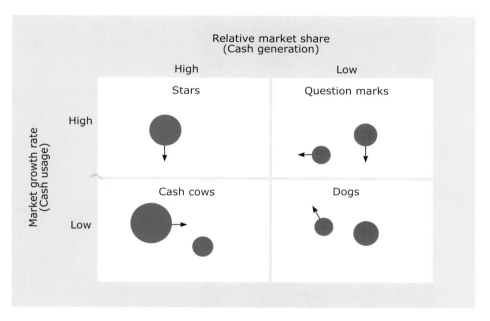

Figure 6.4 A completed BCG matrix

(Source: Kotler and Armstrong, 2004, p. 47)

In this example, the organisation has two products which are considered 'question marks'. The arrows indicate that at least one of them is expected to develop into a 'star' product but the other is likely to fail and go straight to being a 'dog' product. The organisation's single 'star' product' is pointing towards becoming a 'cash cow'. This is acceptable as one of the two 'cash cow' products is moving towards the 'dog' category. Finally, although there are two products in the 'dog' category, the organisation may discard only one of them. Why? Simply because one of the products is moving towards the 'star' category. One reason for this happening is that demand for the product is increasing because it has suddenly been discovered by the market.

You may be wondering how the BCG matrix helps you as a manager if you are not in marketing. By replacing 'market share' with 'professional skills' the BCG matrix allows you to identify management skills areas which may need developing. For example, if you are a manager in human resource management (HRM) you may consider that your skills include employment law regarding older people. However, if your organisation has no older employees, then this skill could be identified as a 'dog'. If you believe that counselling skills are a growing part of HRM but you have not been trained in counselling, then you might categorise these skills as a 'question mark'. The issue for you is then to develop these skills further through additional support, such as training, even though the training will cost money.

Product portfolio analysis for non-profit and public sector organisations

As we have seen, it is possible to reconceptualise the BCG matrix to suit non-commercial contexts. However, some managers in such sectors may still have problems with taking this approach, whether for philosophical or practical reasons. The framework described below is tailored to the needs of non-commercial organisations. In addition it may be of use to people in commercial organisations working in roles that are not directly customer facing or working for parts of the business whose performance cannot easily be measured in financial terms. Depending on the situation facing individual managers this may complement the insights offered by the BCG matrix or it may be seen as a substitute.

To help public sector and non-profit managers make decisions about product offerings, Sargeant (2009) has proposed a non-profit analysis matrix (NAM), which can also be applied to public sector organisations. Unlike the Boston Consulting Group matrix, the NAM encourages managers to view service offerings in terms of external attractiveness versus internal appropriateness, and hence decide which services they should offer. The non-profit analysis matrix is shown in Figure 6.5.

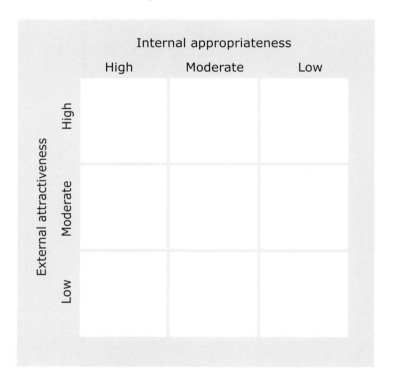

Figure 6.5 Non-profit analysis matrix

(Source: Sargeant, 2009)

From a non-profit perspective, external attractiveness refers to how likely a potential service offering is to raise funds or attract other support for the organisation. While non-profit organisations are not motivated solely by funding concerns, managers need to be realistic and assess whether a new service is likely to be positively supported by the public in terms of funds received and wider public approval. The same argument can be applied in the public sector. Here also, one way in which external attractiveness may be reflected is wider public approval, and in organisations dependent upon public approval (such as voters in the case of local government), product/ service decisions may be influenced by external attractiveness. Alternatively, from an individual manager's perspective, you need to consider if offering a particular product/service is likely to achieve the outcomes you seek, such as wider approval and increased customer satisfaction.

Internal appropriateness refers to the extent to which the proposed product/ service can actually be delivered by the organisation. Sargeant (2009) suggests that a number of components may need to be considered, including whether the organisation has the expertise, personnel, skills and other resources to undertake the proposed product/service. Again the same considerations can be applied to the public sector. For example, should a local government body undertake or propose certain projects? Alternatively, as a manager, are you able to provide the resources to deliver the products/ services you want?

Once the external attractiveness and internal appropriateness of a proposed activity (say Activity A) have been determined, the activity can be placed onto the non-profit analysis matrix, as shown in Figure 6.6.

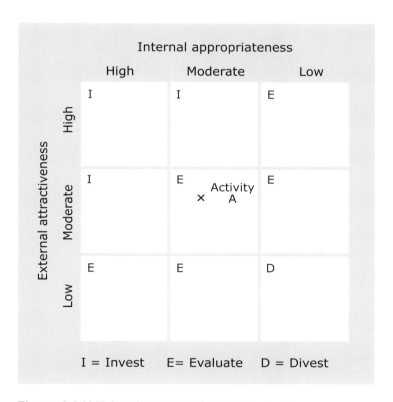

Figure 6.6 Utilising the non-profit analysis matrix

(Source: Sargeant, 2009)

In Figure 6.6 the scores for external attractiveness and internal appropriateness place Activity A in the middle of the matrix. How can we use the matrix to decide whether the organisation should undertake Activity A? You may have noticed that each box in the matrix has been given a letter code of D, E and I.

D – Divest This refers to activities that have low external and internal attractiveness to the organisation and, therefore, should be divested.

E – Evaluate This refers to activities that have moderate external and internal attractiveness. The organisation will need to investigate further whether or not it should undertake this activity.

I – Invest This refers to activities that have a high external and internal attractiveness. The organisation is highly likely to undertake any activity that falls into this category.

You should note that this analysis can be done not just for a single activity but for numerous activities at the same time. In other words, the non-profit analysis matrix could show many activities that the organisation is undertaking at the same time. The matrix allows the organisation to evaluate which activities it should continue to invest in, and question whether it should continue or undertake individual activities or discard them. This matrix offers an alternative to the Boston Consulting Group matrix discussed earlier. Equally importantly, it provides a model that public sector organisations, non-profit organisations and managers within them can apply to the products and services they provide and to themselves. While the matrix has been developed for non-profit organisations, it can also be used for activities in commercial organisations that are not directly customer facing or whose success cannot be measured in financial terms.

Pricing

In marketing, price is defined as the value attached to an exchange between two or more parties. It is typically expressed in financial terms, that is, money. However, price does not necessarily have to refer to financial value but can be identified with emotional costs, time costs and opportunity costs what you could have done if you had not undertaken that exchange. (These are discussed more fully below. For example, someone who helps a charity is incurring an opportunity cost in that they could be using their time for a hobby instead.)

Although as a manager you may not be directly or solely involved in establishing the prices for your organisation's products/services, it is important to understand the role of pricing. In terms of the marketing mix, the price charged for the product/service offering must reflect the other aspects of the mix and the wider positioning of the product/service in the market. For example, a high price must be justified by a high-quality product/service. It should be noted that price is the only element of the marketing mix that brings revenue into the organisation; the other elements all represent costs.

Pricing and profit-orientated organisations

We start with external customers and for-profit organisations. This section will be brief because usually price setting is done by specialists in the marketing and finance functions of the organisation. In establishing the price for a product/service an organisation needs to consider a number of issues:

Internal factors These are the organisation's costs of producing and delivering the product/service, marketing strategy and marketing objectives.

External factors These are aspects of the price that are unique to the nature of the market in which the organisation competes and other environmental factors that the organisation may or may not have control over. For example, marketers of commodities such as coffee are affected by the weather in Brazil when setting their prices.

Product life cycle Which stage in the product life cycle the product/service is at will affect the price. For example, during the introduction stage a high price may be used to increase cash flow and recover research and development costs.

Positioning How is the product/service positioned in the market? Is it seen as top of the range or merely as a commodity? Is it seen as a status enhancer?

Customers' and potential customers' expectations Customers might be prepared to pay more (or less) than organisations think.

Competitors' prices and offers Pricing must be realistic and that includes offering value in comparison with competitors' offerings.

Price sensitivity Some markets are more price-sensitive than others. A high price may denote high quality or status, or it may simply deter people from buying a product/service.

Once these questions have been considered an organisation can then decide how it is going to calculate its prices. There are three approaches the organisation can use:

Cost-plus pricing A profit margin that reflects the organisation's marketing objectives is added to the total cost of producing the product/service.

Demand-based pricing A price is established based on demand from the market. This is not easy to achieve and relies upon market research, managerial experience and previous pricing decisions.

Going-rate pricing Pricing that reflects what the competition is charging and therefore aims not to disrupt the market through creating a price war with the competition.

Pricing approach refers to the different methods that can be used in order to actually set prices. Once the organisation has decided what pricing approach to use, it must then decide what its pricing strategy should be. Pricing strategy refers to how much to charge for a product/service and will ultimately be determined by three key influences:

- organisational objectives
- the other elements of the marketing mix
- what price the market is willing to pay (demand) and what the organisation is willing to supply (supply).

You may feel that there is some overlap between the approaches mentioned earlier and the influences mentioned above. This is not really the case. For example, demand-based pricing is an approach and refers to the idea that the firm should look at levels of demand and supply in order to set prices (as opposed to its costs, for example). However what price the market is willing to pay is an influence, because it will determine the *level* of the prices charged.

Once these influences have been recognised an organisation will be able to develop its price strategy. A simple way of deciding what price strategy to pursue is to consider a price that reflects the quality of the product/service offering. Identifying the quality level of the product/service is a good starting point. (Some judgement is involved in deciding what constitutes a high or low level of quality in any particular market.) Organisations use a variety of price strategies, which can be summarised as follows.

Premium pricing The organisation charges a high price for a high-quality product/service.

Penetration pricing A deliberately low price is charged for a product/service with the aim of temporarily increasing demand in order to gain market share. This is particularly common when a product/service is first introduced to the market.

Economy pricing The organisation charges a low price to reflect the relatively low quality of the product/service offering.

Price skimming A high price is charged initially in order to gain a small market share typically from those customers who are willing to pay a high price in order to have the product/service early; for example an individual may want to enjoy the cachet of being the first in their social circle with a new product. An organisation may believe that it will enjoy a competitive advantage by being the first to buy and use a new technology. Various telephone operators around the world effectively paid Apple in order to have the exclusive licence to sell iPhones on their networks. In turn they attracted consumers willing to pay relatively high prices for the iPhone's functionality and aesthetics. The price is then typically lowered in stages to gain the custom of various other market segments which are not willing to pay the same high price but may be willing to wait a little longer for the product in return for a lower price. This type of strategy is often used with cultural products, such as books and music CDs, where a much higher price is charged when the product is first launched than, say, 12 months later.

Psychological pricing This strategy is commonly found in most shops and petrol stations. Rather than charge £10 for a product/service, organisations charge £9.99 instead. Although the price difference is merely one penny, the belief is that in the customers' minds this is a fundamentally cheaper product/service and, therefore, they are more likely to purchase it.

Price discrimination This can be either legal or illegal depending on how it operates. Legally, price discrimination is operated to manage demand for certain products/services. For example, a train ticket costs significantly more during peak times than during off-peak travel times;

or the unit cost of a product bought in bulk works out cheaper than buying singly. Illegal price discrimination takes place when an organisation (typically one that dominates the market, i.e. it is said to have monopolistic powers) charges different prices for the same product/service to different people for its own reasons. Illegal price discrimination tends to be rare.

Loss leading pricing This is another pricing strategy favoured by supermarkets. Typically a product is sold at below cost value, that is, at a loss; a good example is milk sold by supermarkets. The low cost of a product that customers regularly buy encourages them to use that supermarket. However, once inside the supermarket, customers typically buy other products/services whose profit is greater than the loss made from the one loss leader product. The same principle applies in other types of organisation: some firms may offer relatively low prices to their customers initially, but that may simply be to get 'their foot in the door' and establish a relationship. You may find that telephone companies or those supplying electricity and gas, where they operate in competitive markets, may offer people low introductory prices in order to encourage them to try the service.

Pricing and public services

In the case of public services the issue of deciding upon a price is complicated by vagueness in determining what constitutes a cost. For example, it might be difficult for a doctor to convince a patient that it is worth travelling to a regional hospital – a journey of perhaps two hours, rather than 20 minutes to the local hospital. The doctor would try to convince the patient on the basis of the wider range of treatments available, and hence the greater likelihood of a speedy and successful treatment. For their part, the patient might consider the additional time required off work, the extra petrol, and the fact that they are known in the local hospital, are acquainted with its system and processes, and feel comfortable there.

For a service provider also, costs are complicated. Public services are funded by governments using taxpayers' money. Should the pricing for a service reflect commercial rates or should it be subsidised to achieve other government objectives? For example, offering nicotine patches free of charge to people trying to stop smoking is a cost to the service provider. However, if the person stops smoking there will be no need to treat them for smoking-related diseases in 20 years' time and this will be a cost saving. The consideration then becomes a political one – how best to meet the needs of customers, while satisfying the needs of other stakeholders such as the government.

Pricing and non-profit organisations

Often, non-profit organisations are partly funded by government grants in exchange for providing socially desirable services. In this case, cost and pricing considerations are generally not very different from those for public sector organisations. Similar considerations apply when funding is raised mostly from donors, although the understanding of what the organisation supplies in return for these funds may be less clear or formal. In some instances, non-profit organisations may not receive (sufficient) funding from government and donors and instead may have to charge a price for their services. For example, a charity may raise money for its cause by organising special events, with the profit from the event going to the charity. This may raise certain ethical issues, such as what price should be charged. Would a high price for a charity event prevent people from a poorer socio-economic background from participating? One approach to pricing for non-profit organisations has been proposed by Rentschler *et al.* (2007) who investigated pricing for entry into a museum. While museum entry is free in some countries, in others an entry price has to be charged. From their study of American museums, Rentschler *et al.* (2007) suggest four different pricing strategies that can be applied.

> *Utilitarian strategy* The museum charges a low entry fee to broaden access to a wider variety of people but this does not necessarily raise much revenue. It therefore tries to raise revenue through other means, for example by mounting exhibitions showing well-known artists or collections and charging high entry prices to these. In the UK the British Museum has at least one 'blockbuster' exhibition a year, often charging £7 or more per person for entry. The high price is not necessarily intended to control demand but is more likely aimed at maximising revenue.

> *Integrity strategy* This is a combination of increasing the number of people visiting the museum, while also increasing revenue. It aims to balance two very separate but conflicting needs (access versus the need to raise income). Examples include trying to encourage repeat visits (such as reducing the price for the second and third visits) or including additional benefits with the price being charged, such as money-off vouchers for the museum shop or café.

> *Idealist strategy* The emphasis here is not on widening access or raising revenue, but instead on preserving the museum's collections. Pricing is set so that the maximum amount can be raised to make sure the collections are preserved.

> *Access strategy* This strategy is used by museums that believe that their mission is to broaden access and entry to the widest range of the population possible. The drawback to this approach is that it can become more difficult to maximise profits which can be used to reinvest in the museum; also a low price may communicate to the market that the museum contains little of value and worth seeing.

Rentschler *et al.* (2007) suggest that, as far as the USA is concerned, museums tend to adopt either an access or an idealist pricing strategy, with utilitarian and integrity strategies being little used.

We can illustrate these different pricing strategies in Figure 6.7.

Finally, in some instances, a service may be offered where there is no visible price paid or required. For example, recycling plastic bottles does not have any cost to the recycler. Or does it? In economics the term 'opportunity cost' (mentioned earlier) refers to cost as the loss incurred for not doing something in favour of something else. If a person wanting to recycle their

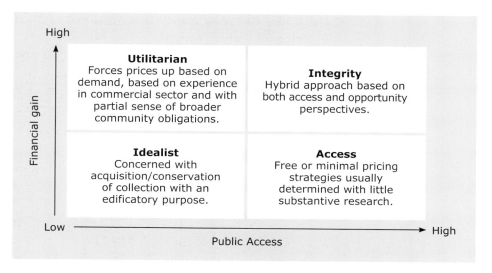

Figure 6.7 Approaches to museum pricing

(Source: Rentschler *et al.*, 2007)

plastic bottles has to take them to a local recycling point, then the costs involved could be: driving the car to the recycling point (cost = cost of driving the car + time taken) or walking (cost = time taken) and storing the plastic bottles at home until you are ready to recycle them (costs = storage required for the plastic bottles, cleaning the plastic bottles of contents to avoid them producing a smell during storage, etc.). The cost of recycling plastic bottles then becomes more apparent and it may be cheaper to simply throw the plastic bottle in the rubbish bin (which incurs no cost in terms of car, time for the individual, or storage, but has a cost in environmental terms).

Place

This section looks at the way in which customers access the products and services they want. Place is important because organisations can develop excellent products and services and price them appropriately, but if they are not then offered at a place which is convenient to potential customers, people are less likely to buy the product or use the service.

Although place in the marketing mix is concerned not only with how a product is distributed but also with how it is presented at the point of sale, here we shall focus on how products are distributed and how conflict can arise from this distribution process. A discussion of distribution within the marketing context usually assumes that channel intermediaries are external to the organisation, since such intermediaries lie between an organisation and its final customers. For example a medical products manufacturer may be able to sell direct to hospitals. However some hospitals have long-term contracts with distributors and in order to reach these hospitals the manufacturer will have to use the distributors as intermediaries. This would be an example of a single layer. Where the manufacturer needed to sell to consumers, they may need to use distributors to get their products into retail stores, which would then sell the products to consumers: this would be a channel with two layers.

As we will see from the ideas that are discussed below, distribution can be just as relevant to an individual or department dealing with others within the same organisation. The fundamental issues of adding value, incurring costs, managing risk and power arise in a variety of situations. Nevertheless, the use of distributors does involve giving them control of some marketing activities. For example, to a large extent the ways in which a product is promoted within a store will depend on the store owner.

Let us start, as usual, with external customers. Organisations producing a product may use other intermediaries to distribute their products on their behalf. Indeed, even the largest producers would find it difficult to purchase an entire dealer network. Furthermore, most producers would not find it economic to have retail outlets selling only their own products. Manufacturers, therefore, are willing to give up some control over their product marketing to allow them to gain wider distribution of their products in the market-place.

Figure 6.8 highlights the various layers of intermediaries in different distribution channels.

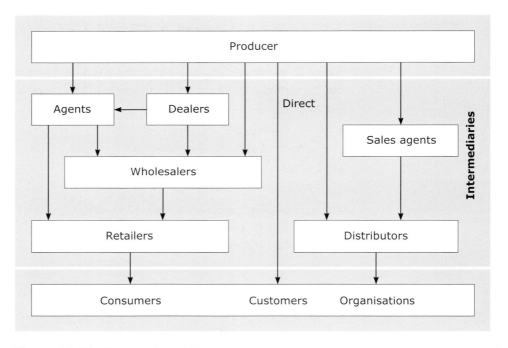

Figure 6.8 Distribution channels

A simple channel ('direct') There is a direct relationship between the producer and the final customer/consumer. Such a channel is usually characterised by relatively low prices for the final consumer, but the level of benefits received can be lower as well. For example, instead of being able to compare different brands in one retail store, the consumer may have to visit or call lots of different manufacturers in order to find out prices and specifications. Take the case of Dell (the computer manufacturer), which sells direct to the public: in order to assess how good their offering is, you need to search for information yourself as there is no independent salesperson in a retail outlet to advise you.

A multichannel distribution A wholesaler and retailer, and possibly other intermediaries also, are involved. These organisations can save the final consumer time through reduced travelling and fewer phone calls. They can also provide information and, in the case of supermarkets, allow customers to buy a lot of different products and brands in small quantities – supermarkets buy those goods from manufacturers in very large quantities that would be impractical for the consumer to purchase. Of course, retailers and wholesalers make additional charges for the services they provide, but consumers often find that they are worth it.

Since services are perishable and inseparable from the service provider, the distribution channels available to providers of physical products are not always practical. As the service cannot be separated from its provider, the service provider needs to be near its customers; an example is a bank that locates its branches in city centres or other large population areas. Although public sector organisations such as hospitals follow a similar approach to commercial service providers, the notion of distribution is more difficult for non-profit organisations. Typically, non-profit organisations such as charities exist in two markets: the donor market where the charity raises revenues (from resource providers) and the customers that the charity aims to serve. A presence is often needed in both markets.

Sargeant (2009) argues that, for non-profit organisations, deciding where to locate themselves becomes important from both the resource providers' and the consumers' perspective. For resource providers, location is important because:

- Many non-profit organisations rely upon volunteers and therefore need to be located near to these volunteers.

- If a non-profit organisation is seen to have a local presence then it may find it easier to raise donations.

- Accessibility to resource providers also needs to be considered, with as wide a distribution of the organisation as possible. For example, a charity may locate donation boxes as widely and intensely as it can in a certain location.

For resource customers, location is important because:

- Customers of the non-profit service may have mobility problems, and therefore it is essential for the organisation to locate itself as closely as possible to its resource customers.

- A non-profit organisation will want to be located where it can have the greatest reach and distribution among its resource customers.

Managing channel conflict

Regardless of whether a product or a service is being delivered, or whether the organisation is non-profit or profit-orientated, channel conflict will arise. Channel conflict refers to a situation where the interests of people or organisations in the distribution channels differ. Conflict arises because of the interdependence between people and organisations involved in product distribution and the different objectives or aims that they want from the exchange. The idea of channel conflict need not be limited to organisations distributing their products but can also be applied to any manager performing their job. As a manager you are responsible for delivering a product or a service and this is likely to involve you in engaging with other people either in the production of that product/service or in its delivery. Opportunities for channel conflict are high and the following discussion on what causes this conflict is as relevant to an individual manager as it is to an organisation.

Berman (1966), although writing in the 1960s, provides what is still an important and highly relevant insight into what causes channel conflict. He identifies causes of channel conflict as arising from:

Communication difficulties Channel members may be unable or unwilling to talk to each other, which has a negative effect on how the product/service is delivered.

Perception differences Different channel members may have different perceptions of what is needed to deliver the product/service.

Expectation difference Channel members may have different expectations of what is required of them and what the customer requires.

Role incongruities Channel members are not aware of their roles, either through lack of communication or lack of clearly defined job roles.

Resource scarcity In some instances channel members may be competing for limited resources. For example, two managers in the same organisation may be arguing over how organisation finances are allocated between them.

Domain disagreements Channel members may feel that other members are infringing upon their responsibilities in making decisions.

Goal incompatibilities Channel members may have very different goals. For example, a manager might want to achieve maximum customer satisfaction while the finance department insists that this increases costs and reduces the organisation's profits.

How to resolve channel conflict largely depends upon the nature of the conflict itself. Like any conflict, channel conflict can be resolved only through more effective communication: either or both of the parties will have to take responsibility for what the manager/organisation has done to reduce or enhance the conflict, and find common shared concerns and issues from which to build a resolution.

You should note that channel conflict becomes less likely if the organisations involved engage in relationship marketing. Since relationship marketing aims to develop a long-term, trust-based relationship between organisations in the distribution channel and their customers, opportunities for conflict are reduced. Regular communication encourages problems to be resolved before they become conflicts. However, from a manager's perspective, channel conflict may still be an ongoing daily problem.

Promotion

Organisations need a way to communicate what they are offering to their customers (whether they are internal, other businesses or end customers). To achieve this, organisations undertake promotion. The term 'promotion' in marketing covers a wide variety of activities, including those below.

Advertising This refers to any non-personal, paid-for communication, where the firm promoting the message is clearly identified. It can be television advertising, banner advertising on websites and advertising in magazines and billboards, among others.

Sales promotion This aims to encourage purchasing by offering potential customers an incentive, usually to make a purchase sooner than they otherwise would or in larger quantities than they had originally intended. Examples include: price discounts for buying more, money-off vouchers and free gifts. As you can see a feature of sales promotion is to alter the *value* being offered to the customer. Sales promotions can be another way of giving the customer a price reduction. This means that they need to be used selectively because otherwise they can 'cheapen' the image of the product or service.

Public relations These are unpaid communications, used to build relations with an organisation's publics. The latter can include customers, but the term 'publics' also refers to other stakeholders such as government and local communities. Public relations campaigns can involve, for example, generating news stories about an organisation's activities and achievements. These may be published by newspapers and magazines as news items (rather than advertising) and may even be more effective than advertising because of the higher levels of credibility that editorials have compared with advertising (people are more likely to believe newspaper reports).

Publicity This is similar to public relations except that an organisation cannot control the information that is generated about it because the information has come from the public domain.

Personal selling Promotion is undertaken through face-to-face contact between the seller and the potential customer. This can be very expensive compared with other methods in terms of the cost per sale and is usually used for products and services that are relatively expensive, such as cars. However, personal selling is effective where the marketer needs to overcome customers' objections. For example, a car salesman may be able to convince a potential buyer that their brand has various advantages over competing brands. Personal selling is also very commonly used in business-to-business marketing.

Telemarketing Potential customers are contacted via the telephone.

Direct mail Potential customers are targeted by sending them personalised mail.

Trade fairs or exhibitions The organisation has an opportunity to demonstrate its product/service to a collection of potential customers.

Point-of-sale displays A branded stand, display or equipment is located near a cash till. This is very popular in food shops, for example, where the name of a cold drink manufacturer is clearly visible on refrigerators.

The reasons why an organisation undertakes promotion activities are varied:

- to change attitudes (beliefs) or behaviours
- to increase sales
- to encourage potential customers to try a product/service
- to create awareness about a product/service
- to inform the market about a feature of a product/service
- to remind the market that a product still exists
- to reassure potential and existing customers about a product/service
- to create an image of a product – product positioning.

As it is impossible to explore the full range of different features of promotion in this chapter, we will focus on a particular aspect of promotion with reference to the communication model shown in Figure 6.9.

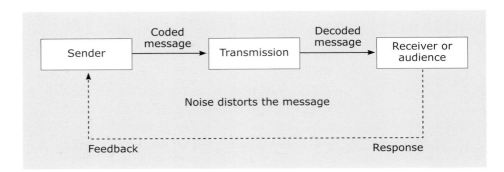

Figure 6.9 A simple communication model

(Source: based on Shannon, 1948, pp. 379–423)

Using this model we can explore how an organisation communicates with its desired audience. This audience may be the customer or a market segment that is being targeted about a behavioural change. We can explore this communication model through the example of a chocolate confectionery bar, the Mars bar.

Sender The organisation decides it needs to communicate a message to achieve a desired outcome. For example, Mars Inc. may decide that Mars bar sales have been falling and they need to increase the sales.

Encoding The desired communication message is now encoded in a style that allows others to understand the message. For example, Mars Inc. has developed a television advertisement that shows young people working, going to the gym and then eating a Mars bar. The advertisement closes with the same young people dancing in a night club with the slogan 'A Mars a day helps you work, rest and play'. The message here is that a Mars bar gives you energy to get through a hectic day.

Transmission The encoded message is now communicated to the targeted market segment. In our Mars bars example this would include television advertisements being aired during programmes that the targeted segment is most likely to be watching.

Decoding The target market segment now decodes the message to try to understand it. In our example Mars Inc. will be hoping that the advertisement is now decoded so that the target market segment recognises that 'a Mars a day, helps you work, rest and play'.

Receiver The final stage of this model involves the receiver responding positively to the decoded message. For example, Mars Inc. would hope that, after seeing their advertisement, people will go out and buy a Mars bar.

Feedback Any communication sent out requires feedback to be gathered. This may involve actually asking people if they have encountered the communication and/or if they actually responded to it. Mars Inc. may simply measure feedback by assessing whether, following their advertisement, sales of Mars bars have gone up.

Applying the different stages of our basic communication model appears to be simple enough, except for one problem – the issue of noise. Noise represents anything that interferes with the communication process and stops the intended audience understanding the message as the sender intended. Returning to our Mars bar example, noise in this communication process may simply be people walking away from their television when the advertisement appears, people talking to others when the advertisement appears, shops selling Mars bars not making them prominent enough for potential customers to see, and so forth.

This basic communication model can also be applied to communications between individuals. How you communicate internally within your organisation and externally with your customers will all fall within this model. For both a manager and an organisation, the aim in communication should be to ensure that your message does not get drowned out by noise.

While we have discussed promotions mostly in the context of commercial organisations so far, non-profit and public sector organisations also use similar techniques to promote their organisations and the services they offer, or in order to encourage people to behave in a particular way. Non-profit and public sector organisations rarely use price promotions, not least because they often do not offer their services for money, but all the other promotion tools listed above are used in some way. For example, a charity wanting to increase donations might advertise on national television or through billboards; it might employ staff who approach people for donations in public places (personal selling); it might encourage newspapers or other media to report on its activities and the needs of the cause it is promoting (public relations/publicity); or it might employ any of the other common means of reaching its intended audience.

Sustainability and the marketing mix

Marketing often has significant implications for sustainability, and the marketing mix is related to many of them. This topic is mostly considered in terms of commercial marketing, where the idea of green or sustainable marketing has been popular for some time. However, non-profit and public sector marketing activities are also concerned with sustainability, as it is equally important to consider the sustainability of the products or services offered by organisations in these sectors.

Sustainability of products

The first question to ask is whether the product or service itself is sustainable. Peattie (1992) distinguishes between *truly sustainable or green products*, which contribute to the improvement of society and the environment, and *relatively green products*, which are less environmentally harmful or more sustainable in other ways than comparable competitive products. Organisations offering environmental clean-up services, for example, could be said to be offering a truly green product. Locally produced and marketed organic foodstuffs might also fall under this category if all attempts are made to eliminate environmentally harmful substances and processes from production and distribution. However, truly sustainable products are rare because they are often not economically viable (not enough customers are willing to pay the full price they would entail), or because no fully sustainable product alternative is available.

Services typically have lower environmental impacts than physical products but their impact is not zero. Peattie (1992) argues that a service can make contributions to sustainability by:

- directly contributing to environmental or social improvement, e.g. waste management services
- preventing or reducing environmental or social damage, e.g. local government planning control
- helping other organisations to become more sustainable, e.g. provision of environmental or sustainability audits
- being provided by an organisation with an improving environmental or social performance or one that is better than the competition.

Pricing and sustainability

Pricing generally has fewer direct sustainability implications than other components of the marketing mix but appropriate pricing can help support the sustainability of the marketing mix in general. For example, by pricing more sustainable products to be within the reach of most customers, the general uptake of such products can be increased.

Place and sustainability

Place and distribution are increasingly considered to have significant implications for sustainability. One of the most obvious concerns is the physical transportation of goods. Often, products sold in one place have been produced in and transported from other locations, sometimes over considerable distances. The carbon dioxide emissions from transportation are a highly significant contribution to greenhouse gas emissions associated with climate change, and the pollution and noise associated with heavy road and air traffic are important local sustainability issues. The sustainability implications of distribution are particularly significant where this transportation takes place over large distances and by air or road. 'Food miles' have become an important consideration in many people's consumption decisions. There is a significant segment of consumers who try to buy food that has been locally produced and not transported by air or road over long distances.

Waste is another sustainability issue related to distribution channels. Because products are often stored in wholesale and retail stores for considerable periods of time, there can be quite a lot of waste of perishable goods, such as food items. An issue that is perhaps more significant is the question of what happens to physical products at the end of their useful life. Some countries, for example Germany, have passed legislation that requires retailers and manufacturers to take back empty packaging for recycling. There are also moves to require manufacturers to make their products fully recyclable and take them back at the end of their useful life. A car manufacturer, for example, would take back old cars when they are no longer workable or roadworthy, and would recycle their parts.

Sustainability and marketing communications

Marketing communications can also promote sustainability, by enabling organisations to differentiate themselves from others on the basis of their environmentally friendly behaviour. Many organisations spend considerable effort and expense on communicating sustainability messages. The uses of promotional tools for sustainability include the following:

- commercial organisations promoting environmentally friendly products and services

- government and non-governmental organisations communicating sustainability messages, for example by trying to get people to use their cars less

- organisations putting out positive messages about their own sustainability.

There are, however, also a number of ways in which marketing communications can contribute negatively to sustainability problems. Marketing, and marketing communications in particular, is often accused of promoting excessive materialism in society by encouraging people to consume more and more, beyond their real needs. This is thought to lead not only to a wasteful use of natural resources (e.g. raw materials, energy, landfill space) but also to growing dissatisfaction where people are constantly striving for lifestyles that they can often not easily afford.

The attempts of commercial organisations to promote themselves as sustainable organisations or providers of sustainable goods and services have also been criticised as amounting to little more than 'greenwash'. A few well-chosen 'environmentally friendly' products and corresponding advertising messages are deployed to give an organisation a green image and thus attract environmentally conscious consumers, without fundamentally addressing unsustainable production and distribution processes or wasteful use of resources.

References

Berman, B. (1966) *Marketing Channels*, New York, Wiley.

Kotler, P. (2000) *Marketing Management: The Millennium Edition*, Upper Saddle River, NJ, Prentice Hall International.

Kotler, P. and Armstrong, E. (2004) *Principles of Marketing* (10th international edition), Upper Saddle River, NJ, Prentice Hall International.

Peattie, K. (1992) *Green Marketing*, London, Pitman Publishing.

Rentschler, R. and Hede, A. (2007) *Museum marketing: competing in the global marketplace*, Amsterdam, Boston, Butterworth-Heinemann.

Sargeant, A. (2009) *Marketing Management for Non-profit Organisations*, Oxford, Oxford University Press.

Shannon, C. E. (1948) 'A Mathematical Theory of Communication Part 1', *Bell Systems Technical Journal*, 27, pp. 379–423.

Chapter 7 The extended marketing mix for services

The nature of services and the marketing mix

Services are uniquely different from products in a number of ways. These differences can be summarised as:

Heterogeneity The service received by one customer is usually different from that received by another customer whereas products are usually identical if they have come off the same production line.

Perishability A service lasts for only as long as it is being delivered; once this has been done the service will no longer exist.

Intangibility Services cannot be assessed for quality before they are delivered because they cannot be seen, tasted or felt.

Inseparability The service cannot be separated from the organisation or person delivering it.

The unique characteristics of services ensure that the traditional marketing mix (or '4Ps', i.e. product, price, place and promotion) may not be entirely applicable to the marketing of services. After all, services are often delivered by people and the traditional marketing mix fails to recognise the importance of people. Booms and Bitner (1981) addressed this criticism by proposing an extended marketing mix for services to include three additional elements – *people*, *process* and *physical evidence* – which take into account service characteristics. Managers can manipulate these additional elements to develop more effective services for customers.

As a manager you may not have much input into how your organisation delivers services and you may question the relevance of the services marketing mix to your job. However, the extended marketing mix is relevant to all managers simply because your job role ultimately involves you in delivering a service. The services may be provided to internal or external customers no matter what type of organisation you work for.

People, process and physical evidence

The three additional elements of the marketing mix are considered in more detail below. As you should note they are used in order to deal with the specific characteristics of services. For example because services are intangible, organisations sometimes need physical evidence (attractive surroundings) in order to give customers more confidence in making a purchase. Because services are variable, organisations may need to pay attention to 'process', in order to make sure that quality levels are consistent. And because services are inseparable, organisations will need to invest in people, in order to make sure that customers' expectations are met.

People

Regardless of whether someone is a channel intermediary, manager or member of staff, an individual has a crucial impact on the way in which the service is delivered and consequently how it is perceived and evaluated by the customer. So for the manager it is important to encourage everyone involved in the service process to ensure that the service delivered is the best it can be.

Heskett *et al.*'s (1994) research, although published in the 1990s, is still relevant for today's manager. They identified that a manager can achieve service quality through their employees by considering the following:

- workplace design – ensure that the place where employees deliver the service is a pleasant one
- job design – ensure that the job is designed to motivate employees
- employee selection and development – recruit only employees who complement your organisation and match your customers' needs
- employee rewards and recognition – reward and recognise good practice from your employees
- tools for serving customers – provide your employees with the means to serve and solve customers' problems.

The authors argue that implementing these points will lead to employee satisfaction, resulting in high employee productivity and retention. The outcome of this, in turn, will create external service value, customer satisfaction and loyalty, which will lead to increased revenue growth and profitability for profit-oriented organisations, and achievement of non-profit aims for other organisations.

Ensuring that employees are supported is only one aspect of the people element within the extended marketing mix. Another aspect is the need for employees to be supported through effective leadership. As a manager you should offer effective leadership, which Zeithaml and Bitner (1996) summarise as:

- creating a service vision – tell, share and demonstrate the vision you have for how you want the service to be delivered
- synthesising the vision – ensure that the way in which you communicate your vision is consistent
- clearly articulating the vision – make sure that you do not allow others to block or hinder your communication
- promoting commitment to the service vision – create and ensure opportunities to promote your service vision
- implementing the service vision – ensure that you actually implement the service vision.

However, providing effective leadership with the aim of delivering better quality services is not without its problems. All organisations are under pressure to cut costs, become more efficient and so forth. In particular, any manager attempting to improve service delivery may encounter difficulties connected with the changing nature of some service jobs and employee satisfaction, the practice of empowerment, and staff incentive schemes based on customer satisfaction. We shall now discuss these issues.

Employee satisfaction and the nature of service jobs

Referring to opportunities to enhance employee satisfaction assumes the potential for job enrichment, employee involvement, and so on, but the trend in many service industries is towards 'routinisation' of tasks and a 'production line' approach to service. The growth in call centres, for example, where strict controls often focus on cost and efficiency (the number of calls made, time spent) offers little in the way of job satisfaction.

Empowering service employees

Empowering employees entails sharing information about the organisation, offering rewards based on the organisation's performance, and giving employees the power to make decisions. Empowering employees involved in service delivery offers benefits from a customer-service perspective. Many stories of poor service revolve around the way in which customers are transferred (often by telephone) along the hierarchy, with growing anger at each repetition of the story, only to find eventually that the one person who could make a relevant decision is not available, maybe because they are on a customer service training 'away day'. Immediate and effective resolution of customer problems is essential to good service. The dilemma here for management is to what extent decision-making should be devolved to the service encounter. Enthusiastic employees, driven by the vision of customer satisfaction and delight, could create problems for the organisation with other stakeholder groups such as shareholders or funding bodies. Striking a balance between the economic costs of providing additional service and/or recovery and the resulting customer benefits, on an individual encounter basis, is difficult. It requires training, confidence and experience; and it is likely to result in some mistakes. In this context 'service recovery' refers to bringing the quality of the service back to the level initially promised to customers.

Incentive schemes based on customer satisfaction

Some organisations attempt to encourage their employees to strive for customer satisfaction through monetary incentives, but do they deliver customer satisfaction? Critics of this approach argue that such incentives lead to short-term changes, manipulation of information and conflict between employees. One approach to resolve this problem is to ensure that incentives and other rewards are closely aligned with the main performance indicators of the organisation (i.e. customer satisfaction) and discourage the unethical behaviour associated with selling products or services that people do not need, typically found in sales-based incentives.

People in non-profit organisations

For non-profit organisations, such as charities or museums, the people aspect of the marketing mix becomes more complicated. Unlike a profit organisation which may offer extensive training to standardise service delivery, non-profit organisations often rely on volunteers. The use of unpaid volunteers by non-profit organisations raises wider issues of service quality, delivery and perception of the organisation. For example, in the UK many charities raise funds through volunteers collecting financial donations in city centres or through selling donated goods in local shops owned and run by the charity itself. The use of volunteers allows members of the public to engage with the charity; however, a negative experience with a volunteer may create a negative image for the organisation itself. Yet training volunteers may be costly and time-consuming, when many volunteers offer only a few hours a week to help out. The extent to which a non-profit organisation needs or wants to train its people to ensure a better service delivery may depend on how important volunteers are to the organisation. If an organisation views its volunteers as its representatives then greater emphasis needs to be placed on ensuring the right level of service delivery.

Determining what type of training to offer volunteers may largely depend on a number of factors, such as how long they plan to work for the organisation, the training costs involved and so forth. Another determinant of the type of training offered may be the reasons why people volunteer to work for non-profit organisations. According to Fenton *et al.* (1993) volunteers' motivation to work for a non-profit organisation can be categorised as:

> *Demonstrative motivations* Volunteers are motivated by the belief that working for a non-profit organisation will lead to external praise from other people.

> *Social motivations* Volunteers are motivated by a need to support the non-profit organisation but also welcome the social interaction that working for the organisation offers, i.e. meeting other people.

> *Instrumental motivation* Volunteers are motivated by a need to help others who are less fortunate than themselves; this reason is less likely to be stated than the previous ones.

Although these reasons are applicable to volunteers, it is important to recognise that in any organisation employees will be working for different reasons. Volunteers or employees can be trained to deliver good-quality services by drawing upon what motivates them in their job. For example, in a non-profit organisation a volunteer with social motivations could be trained on how to improve their social interactions with donors. This would motivate the volunteer as it allows them to have greater engagement with donors. It also may help the non-profit organisation to increase its donations by having a more motivated volunteer.

A manager of a non-profit organisation that relies on volunteers may be faced by a problem that managers in commercial organisations are unlikely to encounter to the same extent – exceptionally high levels of staff turnover (the rate at which existing staff leave over the year and need to be replaced). Retention of volunteers (or staff) is essential, if only to maintain service delivery. It therefore becomes important to understand why volunteers are likely to leave. Wymer and Starnes (2001) have identified a number of reasons why volunteers leave non-profit organisations and in many respects the same reasons, to varying degrees, can be applied to commercial and public sector organisations. These reasons are:

> *Unrealistic expectations* The volunteer is asked to perform certain jobs that they did not expect to do. Unrealistic expectations lead to the volunteer becoming demoralised and if this is not addressed the volunteer will leave.

Lack of appreciative feedback from clients and co-workers Volunteers expect some positive feedback from their co-workers and the organisation itself. If they do not get this feedback they will become demotivated.

Lack of appropriate training and supervision If the volunteer does not feel supported by the organisation in how they perform their duties they will become demotivated.

Excessive demands on time Some volunteers expect to work for fewer hours than are required or find the times they do have to work conflict with their other commitments.

Lack of personal accomplishment The reasons for joining the non-profit organisation may not be met (or may not have been realistic), which again causes the volunteer to become demotivated.

Burnout/emotional exhaustion Volunteers may find the reality of working for a non-profit organisation very different from their original expectations, which may lead to heightened levels of anxiety or emotions. The response to emotional exhaustion is for the volunteer to leave the non-profit organisation.

Fear of liability Some volunteers may feel that they are personally liable for their actions and the wider implications this has on the charity. This means that if they make a mistake, it is the volunteer who is sued, rather than the organisation. This can lead to the emotional exhaustion noted in the previous point.

Stigmatisation If the non-profit organisation serves an unpopular or politically sensitive cause, such as an AIDS charity, then volunteers may feel that long-term volunteering for that organisation may have negative consequences on their personal life. For example, if the volunteer works for an AIDS charity other people may automatically assume (possibly wrongly) that the volunteer's motivation arises because they have AIDS themselves.

Differences between volunteers and full-time staff Volunteers may feel they are less valued by the non-profit organisation than full-time members of staff, become demotivated and leave.

Process

Process involves 'the actual procedures, mechanisms, and flow of activities by which the service is delivered – the service delivery and operating systems' (Zeithaml and Bitner, 1996). The process may be complex, and therefore providers must arrange help. For example, the furniture retailer IKEA provides a description of the consumer selection and purchasing process in its catalogue; colleges provide new students with existing student 'helpers' as they negotiate the registration procedures; hospitals and leisure facilities provide helpful signage. Also, if use of the service involves computers, customers will need effective education in the technology.

Physical evidence

During the service process the consumer often encounters a variety of physical or tangible evidence. This includes:

- the appearance of staff (which can provide important indicators and messages about professionalism, approachability and cleanliness)
- logos, signage, graphics and correspondence
- the physical environment or 'servicescape'.

Zeithaml and Bitner (1996) describe how elements of the servicescape that affect customers include both exterior attributes (such as signage, parking, landscape) and interior attributes (such as design, layout, equipment and décor). Servicescape design has received increasing interest in recent years. The Cooperative Bank, for example, introduced an innovative branch design onto the UK high street by employing designers and adapting ideas from fashion retail outlets. The ambience of the service environment – music, smells, colour schemes – influences the mood of customers, their perceptions and their consequent behaviour. The layout influences the degree and nature of social interaction and conveys messages about status and the consumer's role. It is now a feature of the retail bank layout, for example, that some customer-contact staff will sit with the customer, rather than speaking from behind a security screen. Solicitors are now more likely to sit at a table with their clients, rather than behind a desk.

References

Booms, B. H. and Bitner M. J. (1981) 'Marketing Strategies and Organization Structures for service firms' in Donnelly, J. H. and George, W. R. (eds) (1981) *Marketing of Services*, Chicago: American Marketing Association, pp. 47–52.

Fenton, N., Golding, P. and Radley, A. (1993) *Charities, Media and Public Opinion*, Loughborough University, Department of Social Sciences.

Heskett, J. L., Jones, T. O., Loveman, G. W., Sasser, W. E. Jr and Schlesinger, L. A. (1994) 'Putting the service profit chain to work', *Harvard Business Review*, March–April, pp. 105–11.

Wymer Jr, W. W. and Starnes, B. J. (2001) 'Conceptual Foundations and Practical Guidelines for Recruiting Volunteers to Serve in Local Nonprofit Organizations: Part I', *Journal of Nonprofit & Public Sector Marketing*, vol. 9, no. 3, 63–96.

Zeithaml, V. A. and Bither, M. J. (1996) *Services marketing*, New York, McGraw-Hill.

Chapter 8 Managing marketing information

The importance of information

How does an organisation and its managers know whether they are achieving customer satisfaction? This is an important question as measures to increase customer satisfaction generally cost time, effort and money, and organisations have to work with limited resources. Organisations therefore need to gather marketing information in order to assess, for example, customer satisfaction and the needs and expectations of existing and potential customers. This information can come from various sources, such as sales records, customer complaints, or the experience of sales people and other customer-facing employees. Much can also be gathered informally, by keeping well informed of customer trends, for example through the media. The most formal way of gathering marketing information is to undertake marketing research. Marketing research is a set of techniques for collecting, analysing and interpreting data, which is used as input in management decision-making processes.

Marketing research supports and helps the manager to assess situations and make the most appropriate decisions. Note that marketing research does not provide the right decisions – it merely provides information to support the manager's decision-making. A good example comes from the 1980s when the Coca-Cola Inc. spent hundreds of millions of US dollars in redeveloping the taste of Coca-Cola to increase its market share. All the marketing research indicated that the new Coca-Cola flavour was popular, which encouraged the company to start selling it. The result was a financial and marketing disaster, with sales rapidly falling and customers protesting about the new flavour. What went wrong? The problem was that the marketing research did not ask people 'If Coca-Cola were to change the flavour of the cola drink would you still buy it?' The answer would have been 'No' as it turned out that Coca-Cola's customers have an emotional attachment with the brand, but nobody had thought to ask the question. It is important to understand that marketing research is a tool to help solve a problem, not a solution in itself.

Marketing research is used for a wide variety of reasons. These include the following:

- The cost of making a wrong decision is generally much greater than the cost of doing marketing research to confirm or disprove a manager's arguments.

- When competition is fierce, it is crucial to track changing trends in the market-place and competitors' activities by providing systematic feedback information. This helps organisations to counteract existing and potential competition and position their products and services strategically.

- Managers need to substantiate their proposals regarding products, ideas or marketing programmes with relevant data before taking them to top management for approval.

- New products/services launched in the recent past have not been successful and the reasons need to be investigated before any future products can be launched.
- Changes in customers' behaviours need to be monitored.
- Measuring customer satisfaction can help retain customers.

Marketing research should not be seen as exclusively for marketing managers but a tool that all managers can use within their organisation.

Types of marketing research

Secondary and primary research

Most managers will typically experience two categories of marketing research:

- secondary research – looks at secondary data, i.e. data that has already been collected for purposes other than the specific marketing problem
- primary research – looks at primary data, i.e. data that is collected exclusively by the organisation for the specific purpose of addressing the marketing research problem.

Secondary research (also called 'desk research') involves collecting and analysing data and information that is already available to organisations. As the data is already available, organisations tend to undertake this type of marketing research first. The advantage of secondary research is that it is less costly, quicker to obtain, and provides information that the organisation would not otherwise have the time or the resources to gather. Managers may decide to use secondary research before committing financial resources to primary research, or they may use secondary research only.

Secondary research data may be available internally (e.g. sales data, customer complaint levels, financial data, sales reports, management reports) or externally (e.g. marketing intelligence reports such as those from Euromonitor, Economist Intelligence Unit publications, government publications, information from trade/professional bodies, and a wide range of databases).

Primary research, in contrast, is 'made to measure', meaning that it is either collected by the organisation itself or is outsourced to a marketing research agency. The benefits of primary research are that the data gathered specifically addresses the marketing research problem, is based on current information, and tends to have greater validity than data collected through less specific, secondary research. Primary research is, however, a time-consuming and expensive method, and is undertaken only if secondary research findings do not provide an answer to the marketing problem.

The differences between these two types of research are summarised in Table 8.1.

Table 8.1 A comparison of primary and secondary research

Data collection	Primary data	Secondary data
Purpose	For current marketing problems	For more general marketing problems, e.g. scanning and monitoring the marketing environment, exploratory research before primary research is commissioned
Process	Designed specifically to address a particular marketing problem	Often quick and relatively simple to obtain from databases, publication bulletins, government publications, etc.
Cost	High	Relatively low
Time needed	Long	Short time needed to gather and disseminate research findings

Qualitative and quantitative research

A further distinction can be made between qualitative and quantitative research.

Qualitative research typically involves questioning a relatively few marketing research participants. The main purpose of qualitative research is to get useful insights, ideas and opinions from respondents in their own words. The results from qualitative research will be represented in the form of words, for example people's own stories about how they select and use products, or the emotions they attach to particular possessions, or the motivations behind choosing one brand over another. Qualitative methods used by marketing researchers include:

- focus groups
- personal interviews
- projective techniques.

Focus groups

Focus groups involve a moderator who introduces a topic for discussion to a group of participants and who then conducts the entire meeting in an unstructured and natural fashion – in the style of a group of friends meeting up for an informal discussion. The moderator introduces the topic, and the group discusses the topic openly and freely in an informal way. Sessions normally last from one to two hours. The moderator's primary task is to observe and/or record the participants' reactions and to keep the discussions focused on the topic given.

Focus groups are popular with marketers because they are cheap, quick and easy, as all you need is a moderator, six to ten people, a topic and sometimes a two-way mirror. (This allows observers other than the moderator to monitor reactions, behaviour, and body language in the group situation. The window is blanked out from the group's view, but observers can see through the window mirror.)

Focus groups can be used in a variety of ways, such as for gaining insights into consumer acceptance of a new product idea or packaging, identifying criteria that eshoppers use in evaluating websites, or observing reactions to a change in organisational direction.

Personal interviews

Personal interviews involve an interviewer asking a single participant a variety of questions in order to identify underlying motivations, beliefs, insights and feelings on a particular topic of interest. The interview is conducted in a relaxed and natural fashion. Thus the difference between focus groups and in-depth interviews is that the latter takes place on a one-to-one basis. Typically an in-depth interview may take 30 minutes to one hour. The interviewer encourages the participant to talk freely about their perceptions, attitudes, motivations, feelings and so on towards the topic that is being discussed. Probing by questioning is the key to uncovering hidden issues in the mind of the participant.

Projective techniques

In projective technique research, participants are asked about their perception of a particular topic in an indirect way, sometimes without the exact nature of the research being made clear. In contrast to the first two, direct, methods, projective techniques are conducted to encourage the respondents to project their motivations, beliefs, behaviours and attitudes with regard to the issues of concern, for example by thinking about products as people or animals and describing what kind of person or animal they would be, or by interpreting pictures of other people engaging with the type of product or situation of interest.

Often, in projective techniques, the participants are asked to interpret the behaviour of others rather then to describe their own behaviour. In interpreting others' behaviour the respondents are, in a way, analysing their own behaviour. For example, consider a university wanting to broaden its appeal to a wider group of people. It has identified low socio-economic group males as its target group and decides to use projection techniques to gather their opinions. It achieves this through showing participants pictures of males similar to themselves but based at the university. This approach will allow the participants to identify themselves with the males in the pictures and then comment on them.

The advantages and disadvantages of these three qualitative research methods are presented in Table 8.2.

Table 8.2 Key data collection methods used in qualitative research

Method	Focus groups	Personal interview	Projection techniques
Basic characteristic	Direct communication without physical presence	Interviewee is questioned on a one-to-one basis by the researcher	Participants are asked to describe how someone else may feel towards a product/ service
Advantages	Quick, inexpensive, and has national coverage capability. Response rate is moderate	Extremely flexible, allowing the participant to discuss their own thoughts, and allowing for greater depth to answers	Encourages participants to talk about what they really think, as they believe they are talking about an imaginary other person
Disadvantages	People cannot always express their thoughts or one individual may dominate the group discussion	Interviewer and interviewee can create a bias, e.g. encouraging the interviewee to give particular, favourable, answers or saying what the interviewer wants to hear	It can be difficult to keep participants focused on the topics being questioned

Quantitative research

A key limitation to qualitative research is that findings are limited to the sample who were studied. It is not possible to generalise the findings beyond the sample to a wider population. In contrast, quantitative research allows the researcher to identify, with a given level of certainty, an answer that is more representative of a larger population. It does so through the use of numerical data that can be analysed using statistical techniques. A typical form of collecting quantitative marketing data is the use of questionnaires, which can be administrated by asking people directly (personal interviews), by posting them to participants (mail surveys) or increasingly by using the internet (online surveys). The advantages and disadvantages of the last two methods are shown in Table 8.3.

Table 8.3 Key data collection methods used in quantitative research

Method	Mail survey	Online survey
Basic characteristic	Self-administration without physical presence	Direct communication without physical presence using the internet
Advantages	Participant anonymity leading to a high level of participant responses, good geographic reach, respondent convenience, and low cost	Cheaper and quicker than traditional alternatives. Can be less intrusive and more convenient for people and organisations to respond to, partly because online surveys offer 'real-time' feedback and the anonymity of the internet. It can encourage more frank answers to open-ended questions because of participant anonymity. It is also easier to manage such answers – which can be forwarded directly by email to the relevant manager. Finally, it is efficient in capturing specific target groups such as online buyers, and regular web users
Disadvantages	Highly standardised, inflexible, time-consuming, and has a low response rate	Online surveys take longer to complete and resistance to switching to a new survey method can create different response patterns, so new data is not strictly comparable with what had been elicited from previous surveys using older methods, such as postal surveys. Potentially high rejection rate due to information overload from the internet

Designing a valid questionnaire ensures that it can measure the specific issues that the marketer is interested in. As a manager you may be required to understand the findings that a questionnaire has revealed but you will rarely actually have to write one, as the design and administration of market research is typically handled in the marketing department of larger organisations, and is often contracted out to market research agencies by smaller organisations. However, it is beneficial to learn the stages a questionnaire goes through when being designed, both in case you need to do so yourself on some occasion and in order to understand and sometimes steer the process if undertaken by others. These stages are shown in Table 8.4.

Table 8.4 Stages in designing a questionnaire

Stage	Description
Specify what information is sought	The questions should relate closely to the marketing research problem and the questionnaire should be tailored to meet the information requirements. The quality and completeness of responses are important for achieving successful outcomes.
Determine type of questionnaire and method of administration	Questionnaires typically use structured questions referring to 'the degree of standardisation imposed on the data collection processes'. This means that questions asked will involve rating scales, such as 1–5 or 'strongly agree' to 'strongly disagree'.
Determine the content of individual questions	The content of individual questions needs to be relevant to the marketing research problem.
Determine the form of response to each question	The options will include, for example, whether a rating scale is to be used (as described above) or whether a simple 'yes/no' option will be adequate.
Determine the wording of each question	The wording of questions needs to be clear so that respondents understand the meaning of words or phrases. Questions should not be worded in such a way that they are biased. Leading questions, i.e. those which direct respondents towards a specific answer, should also be avoided. For example the question 'All right-minded citizens of this local authority think that we should protect the environment. Do you?' guides the respondent to say that the environment should be protected.
Determine the question sequence	Questions need to be presented in a logical flow so that respondents do not become confused with what the questions are asking. You should always leave more sensitive topics such as personal details until the end of the questionnaire.
Determine the physical characteristics of a questionnaire	The presentation of a questionnaire should always be attractive and appealing to the eye. Often it includes the company's brand logo and an image which conveys the theme of the survey. The length of the questionnaire also needs to be considered. A lengthy questionnaire can cause boredom and often respondents will reject participation in a lengthy survey.
Re-examine the first seven stages and revise if necessary	Ensure the questionnaire design is 'fit for purpose'. It is rare that a 'perfect' questionnaire is designed at the first attempt. The first draft may include ambiguous questions, or some double negatives, or leading questions, or may be too vague in addressing the marketing research problem.
Pre-test the questionnaire and revise if necessary	Pre-testing a questionnaire on a small sample group can help eliminate errors, especially how participants interpret questions. This will help reduce sample error (i.e. rejection rates by respondents) and misinterpretation of questions.

For most managers who do not work in a market research department, the most important of these stages is the fourth stage 'Determine the form of response to each question'. This is because you are most likely to be concerned with how the questions are going to be answered.

When designing a questionnaire you need to ask yourself how you want the questions to be answered. You may want a simple 'yes' or 'no' tick box but you might also want your participants to provide some indication of how closely they agree with your question. Getting participants to express the extent to which they agree with a question requires an answer style that goes beyond a simple 'yes' or 'no'. The following types of question response are most commonly used.

Likert scales These ask respondents to rate the extent to which they agree with a given statement.

An example is given below.

Choosing a school with good academic credentials for my child is highly important to me.

1	2	3	4	5
Disagree strongly	Disagree slightly	Neither agree nor disagree	Agree slightly	Agree strongly

Multiple-choice questions These ask respondents to tick those answers, statements or other items that apply to them (asking them to tick either one or several boxes).

An example is given below.

The following aspects of choosing a school for my child are important to me (tick all that apply):

☐ within walking distance from home

☐ good social and after-school activities

☐ a friendly and supportive atmosphere

☐ my child can make friends there

☐ good academic credentials

Semantic differential scales These are quite similar to Likert scales but are constructed slightly differently. Respondents are asked to rate their attitudes to a particular subject by choosing a point between two opposing statements.

The following is an example.

Schools are there...							
... to teach academic knowledge	7	6	5	4	3	2	1 ... to develop children's abilities holisticially

Open and closed questions

It is important to recognise that different types of marketing research use different types of question. For example, qualitative research questions designed to elicit a maximum amount of information, perceptions and views from participants in focus groups or in-depth interviews need to be different from the kinds of question that will elicit useful quantitative data for statistical analysis.

The most customary general distinction between types of question is that between open and closed questions.

Open questions are designed to arrive at respondents' own views, in their own words, and to get them to talk freely. The interviewer therefore needs to be careful not to indicate the answer in the question already (e.g. 'would you agree that ...?') and to avoid questions that can be answered in single words or very short sentences (e.g. 'do you like this product?', or 'where do you normally go shopping?'). Questions should be non-leading (e.g. 'what are your views on ...?') and give respondents scope to answer (e.g. 'tell me what you like or dislike about this product.' or 'tell me something about where you do most of your shopping.').

Closed questions, on the other hand, are designed to elicit short answers along preconceived lines, such as asking people to rate something on a Likert or semantic differential scale, getting them to tick one or several boxes in a multiple-choice question, stating how many times per day/week/year etc. they do something, or what quantity of product X they typically buy.

Choosing respondents and gathering data

Sampling

Once a manager or their organisation has decided whether they are going to use quantitative or qualitative research, the next question to consider is 'Exactly whom do we ask?' In an ideal world it would be great to ask all the people who are in your target market or segment, but this is usually impractical as there are too many people and it would therefore be too expensive. Instead, a manager could choose a sample group, a subgroup of members drawn from the population. The results from the sample can then be used to draw conclusions about the wider population. Sampling is an essential component of survey research and can be justified when:

- It would not be practical to collect information from every member of the population each time there is a need to conduct research, because the cost would be prohibitive.
- There is no need to survey an entire population, because sufficient accurate information can be obtained from a sample.

The most common forms of sampling are:

Probability sampling A form of sampling in which all members of the population have the same chance of being in the sample. Forms of probability sampling are:

- random sampling – members of the population are chosen at random to be sampled
- stratified random sampling – the population is first divided into subgroups according to criteria relevant to the research, such as age, gender or income group. Members of each subgroup are then chosen at random.

Non-probability sampling A form of sampling in which not all members of the relevant population have an equal chance of being in the sample. This is often done for convenience, when it would be too difficult or expensive to choose a probability sample. Forms of non-probability sampling include:

- convenience sampling – the researcher samples those members of the relevant population that are easiest to reach
- quota sampling – the relevant population is divided into subgroups according to appropriate criteria, such as age, gender, income; a predetermined number of people falling into each of the subgroups are then selected.

Samples need to be chosen to match the purposes of the research. For qualitative research it is not usually important to have a randomly chosen sample, as the sample will be relatively small and thus no statistical generalisations about the whole population can be made in any case. If, on the other hand, an organisation wants to be as certain as possible about, say, the proportion of the entire population that is likely to respond positively to a new product, a random sample will normally be chosen.

Gathering data

Gathering data from a sample group is not simple and is often complicated by various problems that emerge during the data collection. You may or may not be responsible for marketing research data collection, but when implementing a marketing research study in the field (the term used to mean you are gathering data from your chosen sample group), you should consider the following points:

- Ensure that the people collecting the data have detailed field instructions. The collectors will know what they need to do and there will be consistency.

- If you are posting out questionnaires you should monitor who is responding and at what rate. This can be done by placing a coded number on the questionnaire for each individual in your sample group. This is essential to identify whether or not subgroups in your sample are responding. If not, you will need to send out more questionnaires and encourage the people concerned to participate.

- What reward are you offering people to participate in the research? You could offer a financial reward but this may introduce a bias in your research results.

- Have you provided support mechanisms for your market researchers in the field? For example, suppose a mental health charity is investigating the experiences of people with mental health difficulties who are undergoing hospital treatment. Gathering this data may be emotionally upsetting for the marketing researchers as people with mental health difficulties are more prone to poor service from hospitals. In such instances, all marketing researchers in the field should be offered some form of support such as counselling.

Critiquing marketing research

One of the challenges facing managers is related to marketing research reports commissioned by the organisation or bought from an outside agency (secondary data). It is often necessary to read such reports and then assess their implications for the decisions the manager has to make. There are a number of important issues involved here.

- Such reports can be relatively long and will cover a number of different areas. The manager has to identify the issues that will be most relevant to their needs.

- The manager has to understand the information presented, assess the implications and identify a course of action.

- The manager also needs an awareness of the insights and limitations of the research methodologies used since this will have an impact on the significance and relevance of the findings.

- All of this usually has to be done in a relatively short time frame.

As a manager you may have sat through marketing research presentations given by your colleagues or professional market researchers and thought to yourself 'How do I know what they say is actually true?' Many managers are often sceptical of marketing research results, partly because they might not understand them, but also because they feel that the results just do not seem right. The saying that 'There's lies, damned lies and then there's statistics' is often used by people to criticise marketing research results. As a manager you need to know how to critique marketing research, even if you are not in marketing. Emory (1976) identified four aspects of effective research design that can be used to critique the effectiveness of marketing research (as well as other types of research): objectivity, practicality, reliability and validity. We shall review each of them now.

Objectivity

In conducting any marketing research, the researcher should not allow their own biases, such as what they believe to be the right interpretation of the data, to influence the research findings. Researcher bias is particularly evident in qualitative research, where participant narratives need to be interpreted. This problem can be addressed through 'triangulation', where other related groups (such as a panel of experts) are used to provide their own interpretation of the data. If this has not been done, then as a manager you could criticise how the marketing research results are being interpreted.

We touched on bias in Table 8.2. Possible sources of bias in data are:

Hospitality bias The respondent may not be truthful or may try to impress the researcher by giving answers they believe the researcher wants to hear.

Interviewer bias The researcher's prejudices, their background and the assumptions they make based upon ethnic, national or language differences, racism, etc. may have an effect.

The setting of the interview It may be too formal to encourage intimacy in responses or too informal to encourage adequate responses.

Practicality

The practicality of a research design is about how convenient, economic and interpretable it is. The issues of practicality and its implications are primarily concerned with research feasibility and the consequences for the quality of the data collected and the subsequent analysis. Practicality does not aim to prevent marketing research from being undertaken, merely to encourage the researcher to understand the limitations of their research.

For example, at a hospital the human resource director wants to ask all their employees what they think about their working conditions. While this idea sounds good, the hospital employs over 3,000 people and the cost and time of implementing a questionnaire would not be practical. Instead, a smaller study using a smaller, representative number of employees would make more sense.

Reliability

Reliability is predominantly applied to quantitative studies, where the extent to which the quantitative research tool delivers consistent results is important. For example, a questionnaire that has been used in one sample group would be considered to be reliable if it produced similar results for another, similarly composed sample group, and vice versa. This would indicate that the questionnaire produces consistent results and therefore is reliable.

Validity

Validity relates to the extent to which research findings accurately represent what is really happening in the given situation, and can be categorised as either external validity or internal validity. External validity is concerned with the problems of collecting data and internal validity refers to the researcher's ability to attribute observed effects to what is being investigated rather than to other factors. However, qualitative and quantitative research methods have different approaches to how to achieve validity in their research.

Marketing research ethics

Although marketing ethics applies to all aspects of marketing, it is particularly relevant in marketing research because marketing research actively involves the collection of data from individuals, often on sensitive topics. Indeed given the importance of validity that we have seen above, it is important to recognise that the best way to ensure that data has validity is to win the trust of the various stakeholders involved in the research process. In primary research, participants must feel 'safe and secure' when engaging with marketing researchers so that they answer truthfully and accurately. Clearly, the way marketing research is conducted and the reasons for doing it can raise numerous questions about how data is collected. Therefore, when collecting data from participants you should consider the ethical concerns listed in Table 8.5. These apply to all data collection and not just marketing research.

Table 8.5 Ethical issues in marketing research

Participants' rights	Explanation
The right to privacy	No information about the participant should be distributed, made available to others or presented in such a way that the participant can be identified. Doing any of these activities is unethical
The right to safety	Participants should not be asked for information that is likely to have a detrimental effect on their safety. For example, conducting research into alcohol consumption amongst people who have an alcohol problem would raise serious ethical issues
The right to know the real purpose of the marketing research project	Participants are entitled to know exactly what their data will be used for in the marketing research project. If they are not told, then this could be seen as exploitative and, therefore, unethical
The right to the research outcome	In marketing research on a sensitive topic, once the data has been analysed and is ready for publication, participants are entitled to see what the analysis says and, within reason, challenge it. If participants are excluded from this process, then this will raise ethical issues
The right to decide whether to answer a question	Some research questions may be seen as too personal by participants and, therefore, participants have the right to refuse to answer the question, without any detrimental consequences

Reference

Emory, C. W. (1976) Business Research Methods, Homewood, USA, Richard D. Irwin.

Chapter 9 The marketing plan
Uses of a marketing plan

The culmination of a marketing manager's year is the writing and delivering of the marketing plan. This plan sets out the aims and objectives that the marketing department wants to achieve over a specified period of time. It also stipulates the actions that will need to be carried out to achieve these aims and objectives, as well as specifying the targets that these actions will subsequently be assessed against. It is this last point that often has the most effect on managers within an organisation as marketing departments argue that marketing should be an organisation-wide activity.

A marketing plan has a number of different uses and a number of different audiences. Central to marketing planning is the need to facilitate the change process that an organisation goes through over a period of time. As marketing plans tend to cover a period of one year, the plan will aim to address problems from the previous year and how they will be addressed in the coming year. Doyle (2000) argues that marketing planning plays an important role in creating and sustaining customer satisfaction. This links into a number of other aspects of marketing, such as customer satisfaction and marketing relationships with stakeholders, who may be customers, shareholders or wider publics.

In large organisations, a marketing plan is used to convince internal stakeholders (and some external stakeholders, e.g. banks) that the plans for addressing the needs of external stakeholders are reasonable and resources should be allocated to them. In smaller organisations, a marketing plan is often used to convince external stakeholders who provide finance that the plans for addressing the needs of customers are reasonable and should be funded. Looked at from the perspective of exchange, a marketing plan can be understood to refer to the acquisition of resources from one party so that value can be added and exchanges undertaken with another party. Given this role, it should be clear that a marketing plan itself is a 'selling device'; it is used to sell the marketing ideas of the people writing it to resource holders and to others in the organisation who need to carry out actions in order to make the plan happen. Looked at from this perspective, the marketing plan material itself can be regarded as the *product*, aspects such as the clarity of the writing as *promotion*, and the targeting of the correct people for reading it as *segmentation*. Making the plan easy and clear reduces the time and effort required to read it.

As we have seen in previous chapters, all organisations can have a role for marketing activities. The difference between them is that their objectives may well be different: for some it will be the improvement of profits; for others it may be maximising the number of taxpayers who are served; for yet others it might be increasing the size of donations received. Of course it can be tempting to set objectives that are too ambitious, unrealistic and unachievable. In addition to over-promising it is also easy to under-deliver if the resources necessary for achieving those objectives are not available.

Putting a marketing plan together requires a number of different skills. The marketing plan demonstrates the technical skills and knowledge of the person/team who has produced it. After all, if the plan has limitations, is not well thought through, and does not demonstrate knowledge of the market being addressed, internal and external stakeholders may have little confidence that the team will be successful in actually delivering to the plan. Writing and developing the marketing plan also tends to incorporate all levels of an organisation, often transcending an organisation's marketing department. For example, it may include input from human resource management, operations management and finance, amongst others.

Marketing planning is an important management tool because it forces the person who is putting it together and other people involved in preparing it to match the organisation's marketing objectives with the tasks that are necessary in order to achieve them and the resources that will be required in order to undertake those tasks. This process means that there are clear costs for the organisation attached to any promises that are made to a stakeholder, and this reduces the possibility of over-promising. This process encourages the use of SMART objectives, allowing subsequent performance to be measured and remedial action to be taken where necessary.

Unless you are the marketing manager of a commercial organisation, it is unlikely that you would have sole responsibility for writing a marketing plan. However, you may well have an input into the marketing planning process in a number of ways:

- providing input based on the knowledge and expertise of your area of the organisation
- undertaking various forms of marketing research, including secondary and primary data collection
- analysing secondary data such as previous sales figures by region or product/service, analysing customer complaints, etc.
- measuring which aspects of the previous marketing plan were achieved, and why, and if not why not
- liaising with and supporting other members of the marketing team in writing the new marketing plan.

Doyle (2000) argues that an advantage of marketing planning for an organisation is that it encourages a balance 'against the tyranny of accountants'. By this the author means that it provides a formal process by which objectives other than costs are considered. Another advantage is that marketing planning forces the organisation to assess its performance and the reasons for this performance. However, this does not mean the marketing plan is not without its critics. It has been argued that marketing planning:

- uses valuable resources that the organisation would be better off using to fight its competitors
- creates a false sense of security because the organisation relies upon its marketing plan and fails to be more proactive in responding to changes
- has tended to merge into wider organisational strategic planning in many organisations, creating tensions with other departments who feel that the marketing department has too much power within the organisation.

What goes into a marketing plan?

A marketing plan consists of a sequence of information that enables the reader to quickly assess what the plan is about. In many instances the summary may well determine for the reader whether or not they need to read the plan in any further detail. For this reason the summary needs to be clear and succinct, and should be written bearing in mind that it needs to tempt the reader to read further.

Table 9.1 Contents of a generic marketing plan

Section	Description
I Executive summary	
II Marketing objectives	The marketing objectives and how these will be reached
III Situation analysis	Company analysis
	Customer analysis
	Competitor analysis
	Collaborators
	STEEP analysis
	SWOT analysis
IV Market segmentation	Segmentation process and rationale; identifying segments that have been targeted
V Marketing strategy	Product
	Price
	Place
	Promotion
	People
	Process
	Physical evidence
VI Short- and long-term projections	Sales and market share projections
VII Monitoring and evaluation	How the marketing strategy's performance will be monitored and evaluated
VIII Conclusion	A conclusion to the report
IX Appendices	For example data analysis that is used to form the short- and long-term projections

The *marketing objectives* identify what the organisation wants to achieve and should be written in SMART terms. The plan should indicate how these marketing objectives were derived.

The *situation analysis* attempts to explain what is occurring in the organisation's internal and external environments and how these have led to the previously stated objectives.

The analysis will cover a variety of topics including:

- analysis of customers and competitors (have they changed, how and why?)
- the internal and external environments (STEEP, i.e. social, technological, economic, environment and political; and SWOT representing the organisation's strengths, weaknesses, opportunities and threats); particular attention should be given to how STEEP and SWOT have affected the organisation and how they may or will affect it in the future.

The next section deals with *market segmentation*. This describes which groups of individuals or organisations the plan suggests should be targeted. The text should be supported with sufficient data to justify the choice of the proposed segments.

Marketing strategy (often called the marketing mix) makes up the major part of the plan, dealing with how and when the strategy will be implemented to achieve the marketing objectives; this is often referred to as the tactics. This section will also develop the means by which the product/service positioning will be achieved. The marketing strategy often covers the 7Ps: product, price, place, promotion, people, process and physical evidence. As with the previous sections, the key considerations here are: first, whether the marketing strategy reflects the previously stated aims and objectives and, second, whether these aims and objectives are consistent with the description of the marketing environment. If they are not then the marketing strategy may not achieve the marketing objectives.

The feasibility of the marketing plan is then demonstrated through its *projections*, which are based on the material presented so far. They may include projected sales figures, customer complaint levels, queuing times – simply anything that the marketing objectives aim to address.

The next part of the marketing plan is *monitoring and evaluation*. As the marketing plan aims to use the organisation's resources (money and labour), there needs to be a way of monitoring the plan's performance. This is often done by means of future forecasts and by stating the method by which actual performance will be assessed against the earlier marketing objectives. People can sometimes be inclined to produce plans that are overly conservative but success is determined by how close the forecasts are to actual performance, so forecasts should be as realistic as possible.

The final part of the marketing plan is to offer some *conclusions* to the report. This section may include an assessment of the strengths and weaknesses of the proposed plan of action, and what its wider implications are.

Reference

Doyle, P. (2000) *Value-based Marketing: Marketing Strategies for Corporate Growth and Shareholder Value*, Wiley, Chichester.

Introduction to Chapters 10–19

Does your mind go blank when people start talking about 'fixed assets', 'income and expenditure', 'value for money', 'the accounts' or 'the bottom line'? How do you regard requests from your finance department or accountant about expenses vouchers, spending forecasts or variances from (perhaps inaccurate) budgets, reported in (possibly incomprehensible) monthly budget reports? Are these requests less important than achieving some task in which money seems to you to be an incidental, if unavoidable, aspect? Well, do not worry. That is fairly common amongst managers. It is quite usual (and reasonable) for people to regard the management of financial resources as a means to an end and not an end in itself, even though you will probably have financial targets to meet as well as other objectives.

Part of the reason for this reaction probably lies in the organisational reality that securing, managing and accounting for financial resources have often been largely the preserve of finance and accounting specialists. These experts tend to surround themselves with complex professional concepts, documents and jargon. They may seem to have privileged access to senior managers. They apparently work to undisclosed rules and impossibly short timescales. They often do not tell you things you need to know, or at least not in a form you can readily understand. They may regard managers as ill-informed or positively unhelpful when it comes to agreeing budgets and measuring their activities against financial constraints or targets.

This is to paint one picture, perhaps extreme, from a range of possibilities. However, it highlights the common perception that financial management and accounting go on 'somewhere else' in an organisation, and that concern with financial processes and information is not the primary responsibility of ordinary managers. This book has a very different perspective. An organisation will rarely achieve its objectives unless all its managers understand the relationship between what they do and the impact it can have on financial results. Yet because of the customs, practice and terminology of the financial community as it generates financial information, it is often difficult for managers to understand this relationship. Hence this book, with its aim to help you understand how financial information is compiled and how you can use it.

This material can only be an introduction to the subject. So our focus is on highlighting some of the main ideas that underpin the structure of financial information and on giving you some practical examples of their impact. But we need to start by making sure you appreciate your own role and responsibilities and their relationship with financial matters.

Chapter 10 The need for financial information

The importance of financial information

Managers may complain about the financial information they are expected to use and in some cases generate. However, Example 10.1 illustrates the consequences of a complete lack of it. Jonathan cannot make a fully informed decision and the organisation is not in effective control of its costs.

Example 10.1 Whose money is it anyway?

Jonathan had been with his organisation for about three months. He was employed by the training department to develop leadership courses for senior managers in three divisions.

He had done well in determining the needs of the organisation and its managers during his first three months in the job; now he needed to start developing courses and looking for resources. He had found a computer simulation that addressed some of the core skills that managers in the organisation needed, but it seemed expensive. He went to his team leader, Michelle, to discuss the budget for this project. He explained the course he wanted to develop and shared his concerns about the cost. Jonathan asked: 'If you could tell me last year's budget for senior management training courses, it would really help me make some decisions.'

Michelle laughed and said, 'Never mind the cost. Our budget is paid for by head office at the moment.'

'Meaning what?'

'It means that we don't have to worry much about our costs. Head office is doing very well and has lots of money. It covers just about everything we ask for these days,' Michelle explained. 'I'll check to see how much we forecast for this project. I think it was about €20,000, but I'm not sure. In the meantime, just do what you think is right and don't get hung up on the budget.'

Financial information is important to managers and stakeholders in assessing the activities and performance of organisations. Financial information can play a role in helping an organisation with:

- managing cash, liquidity and solvency
- controlling its activities
- planning
- decision-making
- performance measurement
- resource allocation.

Managers may be directly affected by financial matters such as:

- targets set for them to achieve
- spending limits constraining their activity
- ability to recruit and train staff
- ability to invest in new assets
- incentives established in monetary terms.

There is a perception that financial information is mainly concerned with calculating a profit figure. However, what represents financial success is dependent on the objectives of the organisation. It may be that financial information is needed to assist managers to:

- provide a quality service to the public within a financial constraint
- raise sufficient funds to carry out charitable tasks
- remain solvent
- make a profit
- provide value for money to the taxpayer.

Consider how you and your work group are expected to contribute to the financial wellbeing of your organisation. The commonest ways members of an organisation typically contribute to its financial health are listed below. Which of them apply to you?

- improving productivity
- reducing costs
- staying within budget
- meeting sales targets
- purchasing goods and services that increase efficiency
- hiring staff whose benefit to the organisation will be worth more than the cost of employing them
- evaluating the cost-effectiveness of results
- making proposals to improve performance
- constructing plans
- reporting on what they have done.

However, it is often difficult to connect the financial implications of what you do with the financial performance of your organisation or department as a whole. The connection between what you do and your organisation's collective achievement is made by the ways financial information about your activities is combined with that of others and presented to senior managers. In all but the smallest organisations, these connections are usually performed by financial specialists who use financial information systems and work within recognised financial frameworks. Your work affects theirs', but in ways that may not be very clear to you. Managers may find that they are impacted on in a number of ways. Financial controls such as budgets may limit the amount and timing of resources available to them and may also limit the way in which financial resources are spent. Managers' performance is often at least partly judged in financial terms and how well they have managed their budgets, even where managers may not particularly view their roles in the organisation in these terms. Although a good performance management system would include both financial and non-financial aspects of performance this still has a financial element to how well a manager is perceived to be performing. This is why we are going to explore these financial frameworks and the way they affect you.

Financial stakeholders

The stakeholders in an organisation may be interested in financial aspects of an organisation's performance and management. In particular, they will be interested in how an organisation's performance is likely to impact upon them. Other people have a stake in and use for the financial information that results from what you and others do in your organisation. The way in which financial information is used and compiled into financial reports and statements is heavily influenced by perceptions of what these users need and expect. Table 10.1 summarises stakeholders' main needs from and interests in an organisation's financial information.

Typical internal stakeholders with financial information interests include managers and employees, and also the board of management directors or, in the not-for-profit sector, bodies such as school administrators, the board or management committee, elected members of local government, and so on. Some of these management bodies may include stakeholders whose position is difficult to determine in terms of whether they are internal or external, such as non-executive directors or trustees. Some other groups may also be hard to define in these terms, for example self-employed staff on short-term contracts, volunteers and trade union officials. Similarly, elected members of local government from opposition political parties and those whose parties are in power have different interests in a local authority's financial information.

Typical external stakeholders include customers or clients, those owners or shareholders who do not play a part in governing or managing, lenders, financiers and guarantors, suppliers of goods and services, donors, government agencies and local communities. Other groups that may be interested in your organisation's financial information include competitors, pressure groups, the media and the general public.

Different stakeholders may wish to consider financial information available to them from slightly different perspectives. For example, employees may be interested in the stability of their employer in terms of risk to their jobs but may also look at the profitability with a view to pay expectations/negotiations. Also, suppliers may wish to assess the creditworthiness of their customers. Are they likely to have the ability to pay their debts when they fall due and are they financially stable such that the business relationship is likely to last. Customers may wish to assess the profitability to see if there may be room for movement on pricing and, again, be interested in the financial stability of the organisation as a way of judging the reliability of future supply. A shareholder may want to consider the likely returns and risks associated with investing in an organisation. Fund providers such as governments and charitable donors may want to consider the stewardship of their funds – has the money been spent wisely and in line with the objectives of the organisation.

Table 10.1 Stakeholders' financial information needs and reasons for them

Internal	Main external	Other external
Managers	*Owners/shareholders*	*Government agencies*
• Planning, controlling, decision-making and stewardship (safeguarding assets)	• Calculating returns if investing capital	• Taxation
	• Holding managers to account for financial (and/or other) performance	• Informing regional and national economic development, competition, regulation and/or employment policies
• Internal controls		
• Context for their own remuneration		
Employees	*Lenders/financiers*	*Local communities*
• Future job prospects	• Repayments and interest on loans or investment*	• Source of local employment, or of local pollution or congestion
• Comparison with conditions in other organisations		
Management board/ governors	*Suppliers*	*The general public*
• Responsibility and accountability to stakeholders for financial performance	• Likelihood of being paid	• Context of employment or environmental concerns
	• Future growth/ survival prospects	• Public sector organisations' use of tax
	Customers/clients	*Competitors*
	• Prospects for the organisation remaining a supplier	• Knowledge to inform their own strategies
	Donors	
	• Cost-effectiveness	

*In the private sector, money for interest or repayment comes mainly from sales or revenues, whereas in the public sector it comes mainly from taxation. Because of the legal constraints on what public sector organisations can do, and the near certainty of their taxation income, these organisations often attract very good credit ratings and so can borrow at competitive interest rates. Voluntarily sector organisations may have less certain sources of funding and therefore may have difficulty in securing loans. In all cases, lenders will be looking at the available information to make a judgement about an organisation's financial stability.

Perspectives of financial information

Accountants generally do an excellent job of convincing us that financial information about or within an organisation is valid, accurate and 'true'. But to understand more about the financial frameworks that are the background to the picture that accountants paint of an organisation, you need to appreciate that these frameworks require judgement and choice. The frameworks that shape the financial information you receive as a manager may not be as scientific or objective as they seem.

Think about the transactions and activities you (or your organisation) is involved in, for instance receiving money from someone for a service. You may want to record the money received and the financial value of the effort – the cost – that was incurred in providing that service. You may regard the money received as exactly representing your effort, and the cost of it as greater or less than this amount. Whether or not you are happy with the result of the transaction will depend on your objectives when you entered into it, and on whether you were able to conduct the transaction in the way intended.

That all seems very reasonable. But already we have adopted a number of conventions or perspectives. For example, we are focusing on money as the means of measuring what has happened. Even if you do not put a monetary value on your effort (although time usually does cost money), you will probably want to record the monetary cost of any transactions you have with others when buying materials needed for the transaction. The convention of *money measurement* is fundamental to financial information. It is a *convention*, a *choice*. It may be a good choice, and it may be difficult to think of an alternative way of recording the transaction, but it is still a choice. The convention of money measurement means that it is easy to show things in financial reports and accounts that are already expressed in terms of money, such as an invoice. It also means that people interested in monetary returns, such as the shareholders we mentioned in the previous section, are likely to want records kept in a way that enables them to calculate this return. But it also means that it is more difficult to include things whose monetary value is less clear, for example the value of the environmental damage done by an oil tanker disaster. We look further at this and some other conventions later.

Measuring things in terms of money is not the only convention used when compiling financial information. One of the most important is the choice of what is known as the *accounting entity*. The entity, such as a firm, is the thing that is accounted *for*. Examples of other accounting entities are projects, not-for-profit organisations and governments. This is another convention, about the need for boundaries between different entities to which income and costs are attributed.

In management, it is usually the organisation that is thought of as the entity, that is, the basis of financial information. But what exactly is an organisation? In what way do organisations really exist? Groups of people working together in a formal way for some common goal are taken to be an organisation. But it is an abstraction, something to believe in because it is useful.

It is easy to think you know where an organisation begins and ends. But in these days of autonomous divisions and franchises, outsourcing, supply chain management, inter-organisational partnerships and joint ventures, the boundaries of organisations are less rigid and visible and more extensive, complex and variable. Consider, for example, The Open University (The OU). The OU has a central campus in the UK located in Milton Keynes but there is also a regional and international structure to its course provision. This involves many partnerships with international educational providers. These partnerships are in the development and delivery of its courses. A key element of its delivery is its associate lecturers (tutors), many of whom are only part employed by the University and have other main employers. The students who study with the University or its partners are directly or indirectly customers but also often future tutors. The OU is not alone in developing a complex structure to try to best achieve its goals. Yet financial information is still thought of as information about an organisation, or at least about an accounting entity within it. Financial information is one of the main ways in which organisations are made meaningful. It is tidied up into totals that neatly fit the entities to which they relate, when in reality the boundaries between those entities may not be clear or unchanging.

So it is important to realise that, instead of being an unambiguous reflection of reality, like a mirror, financial information is much more like a complex painted picture, with many rules and conventions invented for convenience and consistency. Accountants, a bit like artists making a drawing, choose how to represent a three-dimensional world in two dimensions. There are many different ways of doing this.

You need to be able to appreciate the way in which the financial picture of an organisation is built up, the financial frameworks that underpin it, before you can usefully make sense of it. So we move now to one particular way of representing organisations and show how this is related to the financial frameworks in use.

Financial pictures of organisations

If we accept that financial frameworks are ways of drawing pictures of organisations in financial terms, what exactly are we trying to draw? In financial terms, an organisation can be pictured as a series of resource flows, beginning with the initial flow of finance to get it going. The reasons for its existence and its sources of funding can be major influences on the kind of financial information it produces.

There would be very different sources of funds if you were (a) starting a commercial business, (b) initiating a voluntary organisation or (c) setting up a new public sector service. There would be differences in both the possible sources of start-up finance for each of the three activities and any additional sources from which additional and ongoing funding might come when the venture is up and running.

- For a commercial business, you might invest some of your own money as capital, persuade others to invest capital as shareholders, and/or borrow money from a bank.
- For a voluntary organisation, you might seek government grants, sponsorship and donations from organisations and individuals.
- For a public sector service, the host public sector organisation might well provide funding, as might central government, from taxation revenues.

The same financial sources may, of course, continue to be used once the venture is up and running but this is not always possible. The providers of start-up finance might start to ask awkward questions if you keep going back to them for additional funds. They might like to know whether you have generated the sales and profits you claimed you would when persuading them to invest in you. They might also like to know whether you have delivered the services they funded you to provide. Additional and ongoing funding might come from the following sources:

- For a commercial business, the shareholders and banks would expect their financial input to enable it to produce goods or services – outputs – that are sold at a price greater than the cost of providing them. Thus the business generates profits – its own source of additional financing.

- For a voluntary organisation, while the initial funders would not expect it to generate its own profits, it would increasingly be expected to actively raise funds from a variety of sources: the public sector, commercial lenders, corporate sponsors and/or individual donors. It may also generate ancillary income from commercial activities (such as sales of greetings cards). If it generates more income in a year than it spends, it has more to spend in the following year.

- For a public sector operation, there would be similar expectations that it would broaden its funding base and generate ancillary income from charges. Public services need to justify their consumption of public money, either for one-off capital projects (new buildings, equipment, etc.) or for annual expenditure on running the services.

Whatever the sector, managers who want money for resources – inputs – need to show how that money will be used to deliver outputs. Are they the outputs the organisation needs? Are stronger cases for being given scarce resources being presented by other managers? Plans, justifications and costings are required, and these need financial information that can be widely and easily understood.

Chapter 11 Budgets for planning and control

The function of budgets

Budgets are the short-term quantification of an organisation's longer-term plans. In essence, a budget contains a list of an organisation's (or part of an organisation's) planned expenses and revenues, that is, the money it is expected to spend and receive. Budgets should be more than mere forecasts of what is expected to happen as they include an element of what the organisation wants to achieve. Budgets are often expressed in financial terms but may also include non-financial elements. They form a key element of organisational planning and control.

Budgets can communicate to managers how much resources are going to be available to them and this can determine staffing levels and what activities can be carried out and which there may be insufficient funds for. Budgets may also provide an indication of what is expected from a manager in terms of performance and a basis on which (at least in part) to judge their performance. Budgets should also be related to the organisation's goals and indicate to managers their individual role in achieving organisation-wide goals. Budgets are also important in coordinating the activities between departments/managers.

A commercial organisation may budget for output levels with a view to increasing its profitability. However, budgets are not just for commercial organisations. A school might have to budget for such things as staff salaries and training, books, maybe even to build a new classroom to try to make the best use of its funding. A hospital's budgeting may determine the staffing levels and availability of medicines etc., which in turn could influence the amount of care available to patients, so that it is seeking to find the best ways of allocating the resources available to it. A voluntary (charitable) organisation may seek to use its budgets to try to make best use of the funds available to it.

Managers frequently complain about the budgeting process and how it may be unfair or constrains their activities. A manager might question the need for budgets: 'Why do we have to spend so much effort on our budgets, isn't it the actual results that count?' But without a budget a manager may be unaware of what their spending authority is, not know what is expected of them in terms of production or sales levels, or lack coordination with other parts of the organisation. It would also be difficult to measure their performance or operate a reward system. The organisation may also find it difficult to predict solvency problems, that is, problems that arise when at some point in time the organisation does not have enough money available to pay its bills and other expenses.

Organisations use budgets in different ways as part of their planning, information, performance measurement and control systems. There is more to budgets than simply monetary targets – budgets become more meaningful when understood in the context of an organisation's objectives, management culture and people. Budgets are practical financial expressions of the operational aims of an organisation. They express the planned and then the actual costs of the resources (inputs) that are consumed by parts of organisations, and in many cases also the planned and actual values of their outputs. These operational aims need to connect to organisations' wider objectives. Budgets, therefore, need to be understood in relation to organisations' objectives. Managers frequently experience budgets within organisations in terms of constraints, spending limits and targets (both financial and non-financial). For example, a departmental manager may have a budget which would effectively be an authorisation to spend up to certain amounts in particular areas. A sales manager's budget may be a target of how much an organisation is aiming to sell. A production manager's budget is likely to include aspects covering the amount of production anticipated and expenditure levels in order to achieve this output. A not-for-profit organisation, such as a voluntary organisation/charity, may have a budget detailing what level of funds it anticipates raising and the ways in which it is planning to spend these funds. A government department may be allocated a set amount of funds and it would need to budget for how to use these resources in the forthcoming period.

Many organisations and managers use budgets to plan, monitor and control the use of their resources. Budgets help managers to assess their own performance, and help organisations to assess the performance of their managers and of the teams, projects or sections that they manage. Managers need to be able to work with budgets and to interpret budget statements.

A typical budgeting process would have the following steps:

- setting objectives for a period within an overall plan
- scheduling the activities and quantifying the resources needed to achieve those objectives by means of a budget
- action
- monitoring feedback and control.

Budgeting is part of the control process in organisations: the 'control loop' of setting objectives, planning and implementing tasks, monitoring progress, reviewing results and adjusting tasks, as shown in Figure 11.1.

The stages of the budgeting control loop are as follows:

- At stage 1 the organisation's objectives need to be established.
- At stage 2 the ways in which these objectives are going to be addressed are established and the short-term quantification of this is the budget, that is, what needs to be achieved in the next year to work towards our longer-term objectives. It should be noted that it is not always easy to plan accurately even a year ahead.
- Stage 3 is the comparison of actual results to the budget to see how successful or otherwise we have been. This needs to take into account the economic and competitive conditions under which the performance has taken place.
- Stage 4 is the point at which control takes place, as here we have the corrective action based on our monitoring. It may be that we are satisfied by our performance and no action is necessary however often we may have areas of concern. This corrective action may be in the form of

trying to be more effective in the achievement of our goals, or we may realise that in fact our objectives were unrealistic given the economic and competitive conditions and may wish to revise them.

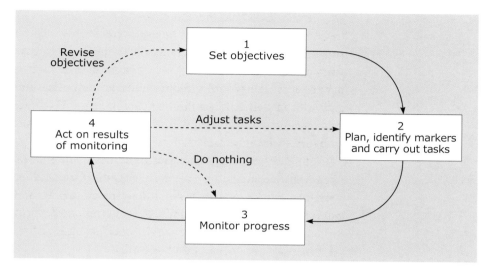

Figure 11.1 The control loop

The functions and possible benefits of budgets

Budgets have the following five functions.

Planning and setting objectives

Organisations have strategic objectives. Resources, quantified in money terms, are made available to their managers to undertake activities that enable goods and/or services to be delivered so that they can advance towards their objectives. For any given period, budgets express the resources to be used and the outputs to be achieved within it. Detailed budgets are generally prepared to cover a limited period, usually a financial year, subdivided for control purposes into shorter periods. These shorter periods are commonly 12 monthly periods, or 13 four-week periods, or even weekly should such detail be necessary due to seasonal factors. Some organisations may have greater sales in summer months such as hotels and other organisations which cater for tourists. Agricultural organisations' outputs and incomes may occur after harvests yet their expenditure may occur throughout the year. The whole budgetary process facilitates planning. Plans need targets and budgets if they are to be implemented; budgets for the short term enable long-term objectives to be implemented. Budgets are thus key planning and forecasting tools.

Controlling and monitoring

Budgeting enables you and other managers to obtain regular information about results. This feedback element provides a control facility. A budget controls the internal operations and activities and the individual departments and sections (the budget centres) of an organisation. By the continuous comparison of their results with the budget, managers can regularly judge their performance; deviations from budgeted performance will be highlighted, explanations will be obtained, and corrective action can be taken. If the budgeting system does not indicate that something is amiss, the managers will assume that the enterprise is on course and that no corrective action is called for.

Communicating

Control loops do not work unless people know their role in them and have sufficient information to monitor activity. Budgets are one means by which staff can know what is and is not important in their organisation and in their part of it: through them they know what they can and cannot spend on activities; through them they can know how well they are doing. Budgets, and arguments over their size and detail, can also be a means by which staff can communicate upwards in an organisation about the needs and realities of front-line activities. Some organisations feature staff participation and a bottom-up approach to budget setting and management. Other organisations have more top-down cultures and systems. All budgets indicate what is expected of people.

Coordinating

Many organisations have budgets for lots of different departments, teams and activities. Some of these depend on one another. Budgets are one means of achieving a coordination between the resources, outputs and targets of different parts of a whole. They can even facilitate 'goal congruence', whereby all parts of an organisation work towards the same ends; there should be a consistency between the aims of individual managers and departments and the aims of the organisation as a whole. In budgeting, the operations of different individuals and departments should be coordinated in the context of the objectives of the whole organisation. The procedures used to formulate the budget must therefore provide mechanisms to resolve conflicts of interest between departments, which may have mutually contradictory plans. Individual departmental budgets are consolidated into an overall so-called master budget for the organisation as a whole. This gives an indication of our expectations for the organisation's performance in terms of profitability and cash flow (i.e. the movement of money into and out of the organisation) but also an opportunity to make sure individual budgets are synchronised, so that purchasing budgets relate to production plans (budgets) which relate to sales budgets.

Motivating

There are few things as demotivating as being set up to fail, for instance by setting staff targets that are unachievable with the resources available. Conversely, achieving or exceeding the specified targets within or under budget can be one of the most motivating work experiences. So, as well as providing clear communication about the expectations of staff, the setting and management of budgets can be an important influence on their motivation.

Criticisms of budgeting

While in theory budgets have important functions within an organisation, in practice their implementation can be problematic. Although a stated aim of budgeting is motivation of managers and staff, in practice budgets are often found to be demotivating and lead to dysfunctional behaviour. Managers can find the experience of preparing budgets laborious. Budgets can be demotivating to managers if their perception is that they are:

- unfair/inequitable
- outdated
- too constraining
- too difficult.

Hope and Fraser (2003) have criticised traditional budgeting and introduced the concept of 'beyond budgeting'. This suggests that organisations should abandon budgets altogether and replace them with a more adaptive and flexible approach. They see budgets as top-down constraints on managers which take up management time and reduce their ability to be flexible and innovative because they are tied to constraining financial targets. Fixed financial budgets are replaced by relative and self-imposed key performance indicators, including non-financial indicators, and managers are measured in terms of their success in relation to these. For example, a marketing manager may be assessed in terms of market share, a personnel manager in terms of staff retention and a research and development manager in terms of the number of new products brought to market. Higher levels of expenditure may be acceptable if greater success is being achieved. For example, the research and development manager may be allowed to spend more in order to develop more products, so that expenditure is measured relative to what is being achieved, not a fixed budget that could constrain or delay the manager from developing some products.

Budgets and planning

The link between budgeting and long-term planning

Budgets should be related to the achievement of the long-term objectives of an organisation. Longer-term plans relating to strategic goals should be broken down into shorter-term budgets indicating what each element of an organisation should attempt to achieve and what resources will be available to them to achieve its goals. A starting point in budgeting should be to focus on what is it that the organisation (or a manager's part of the organisation) is trying to achieve. A budget should be more than just forecasts in that they comprise an element of intent or goals in the targets they set.

The pyramid of purpose

Budgets should help organisations achieve their goals and objectives in relation to their mission. They share out the scarce resources among the day-to-day activities at the bottom of the 'pyramid of purpose' (see Figure 11.2), for which targets need to be achieved so that the organisation can attain its medium- and longer-term goals.

The pyramid of purpose illustrates the idea that there is a broad strategic purpose for the organisation as a whole, but that this needs to be supported by a series of sectional aims (which may be divisional and then departmental aims in some larger organisations). The arrow on the right-hand side of the figure illustrates how the organisation's purposes vary according to the level

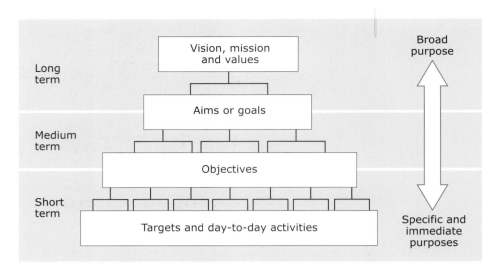

Figure 11.2 The pyramid of purpose

of management, and also represents a timescale. Senior managers need to think and plan for the long term, pursuing a broad strategic mission. For front-line managers the timescale becomes shorter and the objectives become more specific. They should, however, relate to what needs to be achieved in the short term to contribute to the organisation achieving its overall goals and objectives. For this reason the pyramid of purpose is sometimes also referred to as the 'cascade of objectives'.

For example, an organisation may have long-term goals but at the operational level line managers' budgets and targets may act as a day-to-day indicator of what they should be doing in order to fulfil their function in contributing to the achievement of the overall goals. A personnel manager may have targets to do with staff recruitment, development and retention that would be important to allow the organisation to achieve sufficient intellectual capital in order to be successful.

Figure 11.3 shows how budgeting links different aspects of an organisation but covers a larger canvas, showing managers and budgets as central to the flow and management of financial information within an organisation. Figure 11.3 also reminds you of many of the other factors that shape what you do and the budgets that affect you (Figure 11.3 illustrates the situation if you were a manager in a large organisation). Note, in particular, the environmental influences (social, technological, economic, environmental and political – STEEP – influences from the *far* environment, and customers, competitors and suppliers in the *near* environment) and the influence of organisational strategy, culture, missions and values on the process.

Setting budgets in the context of how an organisation functions is important because, in isolation, they can help managers achieve budget targets yet not help the organisation. For example, a production manager may wish to maximise output and believe this is in the best interest of the organisation, yet this may be wasteful in circumstances when the organisation is not able to sell all this production. It may end up with high levels of unsold stock. It would be better to have coordination between production and sales managers. If the pyramid of purpose is not functioning properly, you can end up doing the wrong things very well. This can be a frustrating and demotivating waste of your time and effort.

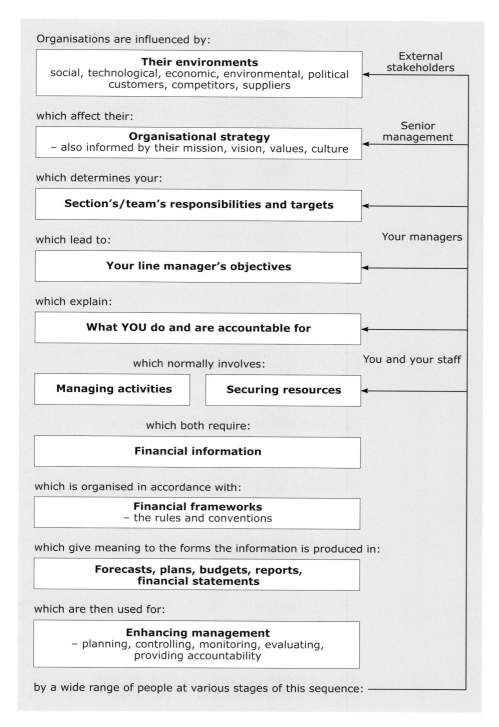

Figure 11.3 You, your budgets and your organisation

Limiting factors

Whatever type of organisation you work in, it is very likely that at least one constraint stops it from achieving easily what it would like to do. In a commercial concern it may be the finite number of its customers, whom competitors are also trying to attract. In a charity it may well be the limited number of potential donors who can be persuaded to part with their money. In the public sector it may be cash limits imposed by the government. In general, demand at required price levels is the limiting factor for commercial enterprises, whereas public and not-for-profit-sector activities are limited by the supply of sufficient resources.

An organisation may have lots of customers or clients and cash; if, however, it does not have enough staff with the right skills or the right equipment it will be limited in what it can do. These limiting factors are a starting point in budget setting. Because there are always limited financial resources, priorities have to be made and sufficient funds allocated to them. Some 'desirable' expenditures become non-essential. If you lack the staff, the machinery, the packaging and the advertising to achieve all your objectives, you will have to decide which of them are the most important to obtain. The limiting factors serve as a discipline when you are setting targets that fit with your organisation's resources and objectives and its environmental context.

The cycle of planning

Having identified constraints as a starting point, we can enter what is often called the *budget planning cycle*. This comprises four broad stages:

- preparation
- collation and iteration
- authorisation
- implementation.

Each of these is considered briefly below.

Preparation

In this first stage all budget holders should consider carefully their targets and their associated resourcing requirements for the next year. This should be within the context of organisational objectives and its strategic plans; if managers of an organisation have no clear idea what it is trying to achieve, there is no clear starting point to its budgeting.

Collation and iteration

The need then arises for collation and checking between budget holders and those responsible for the organisation's finances overall. The total of the individual budget submissions should be consistent with the aims and goals of the organisation. In practice there is rarely a match first time round. Often, the claims of individual budget holders add up to more than the total resources available to the organisation. Iteration needs to take place where managers' budget submissions need to be reworked and resubmitted: this can be frustrating, but it is an essential part of the process. There may need to be more than one iteration of this stage of the budgeting process.

Authorisation

The iterations merge into a negotiation stage, culminating in the final authorisation and approval of a budget that is appropriate and affordable. Negotiation usually takes place between senior managers and individual budget holders. The objective will be to ensure that targets are achievable and the resourcing appropriate.

Implementation

As in the control loop, it is in this stage that activities take place and the resources are consumed. The results are then compared against budgetary targets. Implementation is all-important. It is one thing to set targets but another to ensure that a reporting system is in place to give managers the information they need to monitor progress and make decisions.

Planning for next year may take place many months in advance and be managed by an experienced senior manager.

This stage will normally involve comparing actual results to those budgeted. If there is a difference this is known as a variance. Variances can be both favourable (where the actual is better than budgeted) and unfavourable (also known as an adverse variance – where the actual is not as good as budgeted). For control to take place it is not sufficient to calculate and report variances. Control comes from managers taking timely corrective action in response to the information. Where there is an unfavourable variance this action may be to try to improve efficiency or reduce expenditure. A department may have overspent its budget in March by £10,000, so action may be needed to find out why this has occurred and what, if anything, can be done to prevent such variances in future months. This needs to be proactive and not wait till an even bigger variance has accumulated by the end of the year. Where the variance is favourable no action may be needed but it could be useful to learn from how it had been achieved so that more favourable variances can be achieved in the future.

The time factor

A budget relates to a particular period. The period chosen may depend on a number of factors, such as the nature of the organisation, the length of any operating and/or trading cycles and the feasibility and dependability of forecasting. One year is the most common budgeting period for control purposes: it is convenient for planning and fits with the statutory requirement that companies and public authorities produce annual accounts and reports. For internal control, the year is phased into smaller accounting periods, and, conversely and increasingly, organisations prepare an outline long-term financial plan, which may stretch over several years.

The traditional annual budgeting cycle does have its problems. It can be hard to plan accurately this far ahead and, once set, a budget may become out of date due to economic or competitive pressures. Also, once set, in many organisations the budget acts as a constraint which may limit spending but at the same time constrain managers' ability to be flexible or innovative. New ideas may have to wait for next year's budget but in terms of, say, market pressures or customer expectations, that may be too late.

Many businesses prepare an annual budget, always starting at the same point in the year – say, January to December or April to March. Others have 'continuous' or rolling budgets: as each month (or quarter) is completed, the budget for another month (or quarter) is added to the end so that a budget for a full year ahead is always available. This is, in general, a desirable policy, since it encourages managers to look ahead continuously, discourages short-term budget manipulation and avoids any disruption caused by one major annual budget exercise. But whether budgets are prepared for a fixed period or on a continuous basis, a carefully prepared timetable for all budget activities is essential.

Budgetary procedures and structures

Budgeting is a management function, not simply a financial function. In theory the managers at all levels should have a good understanding of the nature and objectives of their organisation's budget and should participate to some degree in its preparation. Budgeting can be a means to create an atmosphere of teamwork and cooperation.

To facilitate planning and to enable control to be effective, an organisation should ensure that the structure of its budget corresponds with its organisational structure. In this way the budget may be seen as a financial model of the organisation, a model that can be adjusted to show how changes in one part of it affect other parts and final results.

Example 11.1 Tresham Manufacturing

Tresham Manufacturing is a medium-sized company which makes two domestic electrical products. It is organised into four main departments: sales, production, administration, and research and development. Each department has a manager responsible for producing its departmental budget. These budgets are constructed from those of the subordinate sections within their departments.

The interrelationships between Tresham Manufacturing's budgets are shown in Figure 11.4. The budgeting process is informed by the company's stated objectives and policies. A key objective for Tresham is to generate a certain level of profitability to satisfy the demands and expectations of its owners. This requires a certain number of electrical products to be sold. Thus, the achievable level of sales is the main limiting factor behind the setting of the budgets.

In Tresham Manufacturing, as in many commercial organisations, the preparation of the sales budget comes first, because production expenditure cannot be planned until the source of its income has been identified and its amount estimated. There are important exceptions to this. For example, in parts of the construction and engineering industries, where production capacity is the main limiting factor, the *production* budget may be the starting point. Some organisations do not have to base their budgets on the uncertain revenue from their sales estimates. Their income may come from a fixed-price contract or, in public and some not-for-profit services, from some funding source which provides a known level of income. However, income may still be the main limiting factor because ultimately all organisations have to base their expenditure budgets on it.

We now look at what lies behind Tresham's budgets and production plan.

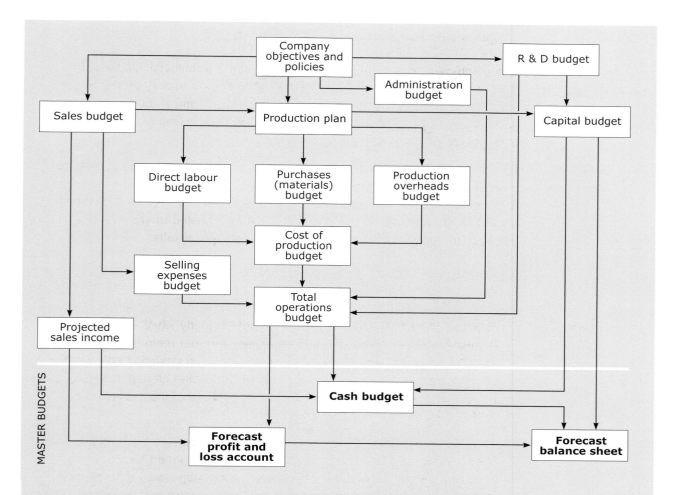

Figure 11.4 The relations between departments and budgets in Tresham Manufacturing

The sales budget

The first part of the sales budget – this should relate to the marketing plan – based on forecast sales volume, is the projected sales income, which should reflect the sales and marketing managers' estimate of several factors. These factors include:

- the effectiveness of marketing
- the size of the markets for Tresham's products
- the forecast growth of these markets
- the selling prices of the products
- the sensitivity of demand to price
- competition from other firms
- the effect of advertising on its market share.

The second part of the sales budget is the selling expenses budget, the preparation of which should also involve the marketing and sales managers; it includes the costs of sales administration, marketing, promotion and any other selling expenses incurred. The sales income less the selling expenses represents the net income the sales manager is committed to generate. (In a not-for-profit organisation, the total income less the costs of generating it is the net income available for pursuing its objectives.)

The production plan

Once the sales budget has been drafted, the production plan can be prepared. Assuming the company has sufficient production capacity and does not buy stock from other manufacturers, the budgeted level of production is calculated as:

Budgeted level of production = budgeted level of sales − any planned reductions in stock + any planned additions to stock

The cost of production budget

Once the budgeted level of production has been established, the production labour budget, the purchases (or materials) budget and the production overheads budget can be calculated. These three components together make up the cost of production budget. The production budget needs to take into account the time taken from placing an order for raw materials until their delivery and then the time taken for manufacture and distribution to make sure not only that we have sufficient production but also that it is timely in relation to sales. This is particularly important when demand fluctuates seasonally.

The capital budget

The production manager will also examine the machinery requirements for the production plan, and may conclude that the replacement of an existing machine or the purchase of a new machine will be necessary − this would be a factor in the draft capital budget. This budget might be augmented by expenditure to improve manufacturing technology and process by the research and development department.

Discretionary costs

Budgets need to be set for the level of discretionary costs such as advertising, research and development, or staff training. Deciding on an appropriate amount of resources to allocate to these areas can be problematic, as the benefits may not be easy to determine and are unlikely to be realised in the same budget period.

The master budget

The master budget is the consolidation and coordination of all the individual budgets, such as the various components of the sales budget and the production budget, together with other budgets, such as the capital budget. All these budgets are combined into three master documents:

- the cash budget
- a budgeted income or profit and loss budget statement
- the forecast balance sheet.

We will return to look at each of these statements in more detail later in this book but they are explained briefly below to help you follow this case example.

The first, the **cash budget**, converts all the activities of the company to cash flows in terms of the balance between all of its receipts and expenditures (usually broken down into monthly or even weekly periods). It is vitally important that Tresham should avoid cash deficiencies, or at least be aware of them in advance, so that loan facilities can be planned accordingly. It is also important that it should be able to forecast cash surpluses which can be invested in the short term to increase its revenue.

Table 11.1 Extract of Tresham cash budget January to April

	January	February	March	April
	£	£	£	£
Opening balance	100,000	120,000	50,000	– 10,000
Receipts	50,000	20,000	30,000	75,000
Payments	30,000	90,000	90,000	25,000
Closing balance	120,000	50,000	– 10,000	40,000

In Table 11.1 the cash budget indicates a potential cash deficit in March and arrangements may need to be made to address this, such as delaying expenditure or arranging a bank overdraft.

The second master budget, a **budgeted income** or **profit and loss budget**, includes all the company's revenues and costs, and indicates the planned level of profit or loss. It is what we expect our profit and loss account to look like if things all go according to budget. This would start with the budget revenue for the whole organisation from which all the organisations budgeted expenses would be deducted to arrive at a profit (or loss).

The third master budget is the **forecast balance sheet**, which sets out to predict what the company's published balance sheet will look like at the end of the period.

The master budgets go to Tresham's board of directors for approval. If the master budgets' figures for profit, sales, growth, the rate of return on capital employed, cash requirements during the budget period and the financial standing of the whole enterprise are satisfactory, it approves the budget.

Tresham is a manufacturing business, and its budget-setting process has distinctive characteristics. But it shows a framework for budget preparation that can be adapted for the different circumstances of many types and sizes of organisation.

Budget procedures – who does what?

The responsibility for the supervision and coordination of the preparation of a budget is sometimes delegated by senior managers to a member of staff called the budget officer. In some organisations the budget officer is directly responsible to them, to ensure independence. The budget officer should not prepare the budget: the function of the position is to provide technical assistance to managers at all levels and to organise the collation of the various budgets prepared by the managers of the various departments. Where departmental managers need information about their past performance, or an analysis of this information in relation to future prospects and objectives, they can seek this information or analysis from the budget officer.

In many large organisations, a formal committee deals with budgets instead of, or to support, the budget officer. This committee may consist of the heads of the main departments together with a senior accountant or the finance director. A budget committee is often very powerful within an organisation, charged with the tasks of coordinating, preparing, authorising and administering its budgets. A budget officer may act as secretary to a budget committee.

Organisations that establish such formal responsibilities and/or structures need to do so in ways that foster rather than inhibit good budgetary practice. This should not deny a senior manager or committee the formal responsibility for deciding the final budget.

An important step is the coordination of draft departmental, sectional or project budgets. Since departments within an organisation are necessarily interrelated, any decision in one area regarding its budget is bound to affect the projected operations and budgets of other areas. Indeed, in many cases, the data from one budget will form the input to another. Ideally, an organisation should examine the effect of every decision on all its sections simultaneously, and IT and spreadsheets have increasingly made this possible. However, not always: frequently a trial-and-error process is necessary. The communication and exchange of information between departments is a feature of the budgeting process and a budget officer may have an important role in it.

Line managers may have a small part in the overall budgeting process but it is an important one in developing the overall budget which needs to combine and coordinate individual departmental budgets into an overall (or master) budget. It is important for budget holders to be aware of the ramifications of budgets that are set, as the budget will be an important aspect of how their performance is perceived and what resources are available to them in the forthcoming budgetary period.

The final stage is reached when each department has finalised a detailed budget which is consistent with every other department's budget and with the organisation's objectives. These budgets may be reviewed by an organisation's governing body (i.e. its board or management committee); if it judges them to be unsatisfactory, the iterative process may have to continue until it feels able to approve them. When, finally, the budget is approved by the governing body, it becomes the operational plan to guide the managers at every level, and it should be altered only with specific approval or according to previously agreed procedures for budget variation.

Organisations may be concerned about the time and other resources consumed by the annual budget-setting process. For many, other important and core activities grind to a halt while much effort is expended – and all on a budget that may well be out of date shortly after the next year begins! Consequently, some organisations have moved away from annual budgeting to quarterly budgeting, reviewed, revised and updated on a quarterly basis.

Reference

Hope, J. and Fraser, R. (2003) *Beyond Budgeting: How Managers Can Break Free from the Annual Performance Trap*, Boston, M.A., Harvard Business School.

Chapter 12 The practical use of budgets

Different approaches to budgeting

There are a number of different approaches to budgeting; there is no single best approach and the different types should be considered in terms of their appropriateness to a particular organisation's needs and circumstances. The methods differ in their complexity and how expensive they are to implement. Some methods are more flexible than others. The choice of which type of budgeting system is employed will often depend on an organisation's context. Factors which will influence the choice of method include the organisation's sector; organisational objectives; volatility of its environment; and the level of control which senior managers wish to impose.

Incremental budgeting

The simplest form of budgeting is to take last year's budget as a starting point and adjust it for things such as inflation. This may be a simple way of coming up with a budget but may not consider the best way to allocate future resources within an organisation. If a manager's natural tendency is to start with the preceding year's figures this could result in a suboptimal allocation of resources, as shown in Example 12.1.

Example 12.1 Fashion plus 5%

Jean works as a distribution director for a fashion designer and clothes manufacturer in Paris. To set its budgets, directors such as Jean have traditionally used the previous year's figures as a base and allowed an amount for inflation. Jean has always taken pride in good budget management and at the year end invariably has 'enough left' for other purposes. Last year there was enough to buy each member of the administration staff a new computer. In addition, no matter what other parts of the organisation do, Jean is well known for achieving the budget agreed. But better use of resources could have been made elsewhere in the organisation.

Limitations of incremental budgeting

Jean's incremental approach to budgeting is widespread and is a natural way of preparing budgets. It is a logical approach to planning for a year, in that it starts with the current or latest year. The approach bases a year's budget on the previous year's actual (sometimes budgeted) figures plus, say, an allowance for inflation, and, perhaps, a percentage deduction to encourage cost reductions. It adds to or subtracts from the previous budget on an incremental basis. The incremental approach has the advantage of being relatively simple and therefore cheap to implement. This is useful for organisations and departments whose activity and resourcing levels do not change much.

However, the major problem with this approach is that where inefficiencies and imperfections have existed in previous years, they are then compounded on a continuing basis into the budgets of future years. Once slack is in a budget it remains there. There is no questioning as to whether resources could be better employed elsewhere in the organisation. Additionally, incremental budgeting does not necessarily take into account any changes to the organisations objectives and/or strategic plans. There is a tendency to have a legacy of doing things the way they have been done and this may not encourage innovation, as the money is not factored into the existing budget.

Zero-base budgeting

Zero-base budgeting (ZBB), sometimes known also as priority-base budgeting, is an approach that seeks to avoid the inherent problems in incremental approaches.

Budget holders are told to forget about last year and the past and to concentrate on next year, to identify their targets and to establish the level of resourcing now required. This does away with the incremental budgeting approach of being based on past spending patterns. Managers have to make the case for all their expenditure.

For example, a research and development manager may have to put in so-called 'decision packages' for the activities they plan to perform. These decision packages are essentially documents setting out the costs and benefits of each activity. The research and development manager's decision packages are likely to include funding for products to be developed but may also include decision packages for other items such as training and development for their department's staff. Each of the decision packages is evaluated and prioritised relative to others in the organisation and funding goes to the decision packages in order of agreed priority. Advocates of this approach argue that it will result in better resource allocation. It is difficult in practice, as there is a tendency for managers to all view their areas as being a priority and it's hard to choose between different areas.

Managers may be asked to prepare budgets for a number of levels of activity, starting at a minimum level of service, then detailing extra resourcing required for higher levels of service. If every budget holder does this, senior managers can then produce a range of activities reflecting their available resources and management priorities. The operation of ZBB in an organisation requires a high level of participation from all its managers, and it is said to encourage a high level of learning and commitment, enhance innovation and responsiveness to change and help managers understand the needs of others.

As in any system of control, it is necessary to gauge the balance between cost and benefit. ZBB can be expensive in terms of management time. On the other hand, such a thorough approach does not need to be applied every year, but can be used in the various parts of an organisation in different years on a revolving basis.

ZBB systems were traditionally most associated with budgeting in public sector organisations but have also been used in commercial organisations, particularly in budgeting for discretionary costs.

Rolling budgets

One problem with budget setting, however it is done, is that changes may take place elsewhere which affect the activity area budgeted for. Ideally, flexibility should be built into the budgeting system to deal with any changes arising. One way of doing this is known as rolling budgets.

Rolling budgets sometimes called continuous budgets stem from the concept of day-to-day management by first-line managers. Budget holders responsible for day-to-day activities should not really need to worry about a full year ahead. The rolling budget argument is that the time horizon for decision-making at the first-line manager level is quite short.

The staff may have a 12-month target, but much can happen in 12 months, and, in addition, activity may be high or low at different times of the year. It is likely that your own organisation, department or section will experience peaks and troughs.

The way rolling budgets work is that they are set every month or three months rather than for a year. They are thus updated much more frequently. Taking a monthly cycle as an example: every month a new budget would be prepared. This may include general plans for a year ahead but much more specific plans for the next month or so. These would be updated each month in relation to organisational circumstances. The benefit is always having a detailed budget that's up to date and a more general budget for 12 months ahead which is rolled forward every month (hence the name). Often under traditional budgeting systems, when you get towards the end of the budget period you only have a couple of month's budget ahead, which may not be enough for some planning purposes such as staffing requirements.

The rolling budget approach avoids the disruption of a major 'big bang' annual budget exercise, and it certainly allows flexibility. Senior management teams often report the advantages of being able to divert resources from one part of their organisation to others without the typical ownership and demotivation problems of other systems. It is sometimes said that rolling budgets require a greater administrative effort, but organisations increasingly use IT systems which allow all managers access to a central site, making regular rolling budgets easier to manage.

Rolling budgets can be particularly useful in times of uncertainty, such as economic downturns, as they allow budgets to be updated frequently.

Fixed budgets

The original or fixed budget set for a forthcoming period assumes a given or intended level of activity and is then compared with actual results. This produces a meaningful difference or variance, in that it is possible to see by how much any under- or overspend varies from the original budget, as shown in Example 12.2. Fixed budgets can, however, make interpreting information difficult, if the actual activity differs from the budgeted activity.

Example 12.2 Eurotraining

Eurotraining was a commercial training organisation based in Italy. The owners wanted it to be profitable and successful and to operate across Europe. For it to do that, however, they had to arrange and run a number of courses, procure and apply resources, incur and control costs, and attract a sufficient number of customers to pay fees. To maintain their business they needed to provide training which enabled delegates to take away the knowledge and skills to improve their performance in the workplace. But it did not happen automatically. There were constraints which had to be taken into account before planning could start. Table 12.1 shows Eurotraining's recorded costs for one of its training cost centres, budgeted and actual, for one month.

Table 12.1 Eurotraining monthly training centre costs

	Budget	Actual	Cost variance	
	€	€	€	
Course materials	2,000	2,250	250	(adverse)
Consultants' fees	10,000	17,500	7,500	(adverse)
Variable course-related consumables	1,000	500	500	(favourable)
Fixed overheads	4,000	4,000	–	

The variances shown do provide some meaningful cost information about deviations from original planned cost – the cost variance – by comparing two sets of figures. However, they reveal nothing about the transformation of inputs into outputs – what was achieved by using resources. Apart from the under- or overspend of money against budget, this statement tells you very little. One problem is that it does not show the budgeted and actual levels of activity (i.e. is the number of courses run or people trained). If it did, you could attach some meaning to the variances calculated, as you would be comparing like with like. It shows the cost for consultants who are paid for each course that they run, at €7,500 more than budgeted, as an adverse (or unfavourable) variance. But what if the activity had increased significantly? You would naturally expect labour costs to go up. The same applies to course materials and variable overheads.

What you need is some indication of the activity levels, both budgeted and actual. If you find that the budget was for, say, 10 courses of 10 delegates each, but that there were actually 15 courses of 10 delegates each, you would expect there to be variances. But to produce meaningful variances you should redesign the statement to enable you to compare like with like, in this case creating a budget for 15 courses. This involves *flexing* the budget. You should never forget that, no matter how well you may plan ahead, reality is unlikely to match your forecast. A well-designed budgetary process should allow you to take account of changes, particularly when you try to measure any financial performance and establish what (if anything) needs to be done. In this context we introduce the concepts of *flexible budgets.*

Flexible budgeting

Flexible budgets reflect changes in levels of activity. During any financial period, fixed cost items, such as rent or insurance, will normally be unaffected by increases or decreases in activity. Other costs may vary in proportion to the level of activity. However, care must be taken in flexing budgets as not all cost will remain fixed for large increases in activity, or vary proportionately to volume. For example, there may be discounts for buying in bulk.

Clearly, it would have been unrealistic to expect the cost of Eurotraining's planned course materials for 10 courses (€1,000) to be the same as that for 15 courses. In flexible budgeting, the cost behaviour of each item is recognised by revising the original budget in the light of the actual level of activity attained. For the purposes of cost control, this provides a meaningful comparison between the actual cost and the budget allowance, which are now both based on the same level of activity.

Example 12.3 Flexible budgeting in practice

In practice, the system can be operated by preparing a series of plans for income and/or costs for discrete levels of activity, say 5, 10, 15 and 20 courses in Eurotraining's case. Alternatively, the budget allowances can be reworked at the end of an accounting period, when the activity level is known.

In Table 12.2 the original budget based on 10 courses shown in Table 12.1 has been 'flexed' to refer to 15 courses. The actual figures and the resulting variances are shown alongside. It is now possible to compare like with like and make the variances more meaningful.

This has advantages when you think about the causes of an overall cost variance. It is sensible to recognise that there are likely to be two main causes:

• a change in activity levels
• spending more or spending less per unit of input.

It would be very useful to know the causes of any variances. By comparing the flexed budget column with the actual column, you are comparing, in activity terms, like with like. Thus, if there is a resulting variance the cause cannot be the level of activity; it must be related to expenditure.

Table 12.2 Eurotraining spend variances

	Original budget 10 courses	Flexed budget 15 courses	Actual cost 15 courses	Variance	
	€	€	€	€	
Course materials	2,000	3,000	2,250	750	(favourable)
Consultants' fees	10,000	15,000	17,500	2,500	(adverse)
Variable consumables	1,000	1,500	500	1,000	(favourable)
Fixed overheads	4,000	4,000	4,000	–	

Thus the causes of an overall cost variance have been identified. One of the reasons may be that a manager failed to control spending. By stripping out the activity differences you are left with what were effectively spend variances on the flexed statement – useful additional information. Table 12.2 indicates that there was a €2,500 adverse (unfavourable) variance for consultants' fees. This indicates that the cost was higher than would have been expected, even after taking into account the change in volume by flexing the budget. In Table 12.3, both the activity and spend variances are shown.

Table 12.3 Eurotraining spend and activity variances

	(a)	(b)	(c)	(d)	(e)	(f)
	Original budget 10 courses	Flexed budget 15 courses	Actual cost 15 courses	Overall variance (a) – (c)	Spend variance (b) – (c)	Activity variance (a) – (b)
	€	€	€	€	€	€
Course materials	2,000	3,000	2,250	250 A	750 F	1,000 A
Consultants' fees	10,000	15,000	17,500	7,500 A	2,500 A	5,000 A
Variable consumables	1,000	1,500	500	500 F	1,000 F	500 A
Fixed overheads	4,000	4,000	4,000	–	–	–

(F = favourable A = adverse)

Table 12.3 shows a sensible layout for providing managers with information about spend variances. The layout could have been adapted to show whatever information the managers felt they needed.

For example, they may have to determine and show the activity variances, that is, the extra cost that would be expected as a result of carrying out more activity than planned. In this case the extra costs that would be expected from running five extra courses.

Management by objectives

The above techniques all provide financial targets but it is possible to also set targets for non-financial aspects of performance. Management by objectives (MBO) defines and analyses the objectives of an organisation in such a way that they become the specific targets of individual managers. If this is successful, goal congruence is enhanced. Within such a framework, or cascade of objectives, MBO facilitates a system of self-control for managers, rather than control imposed from above. It is especially useful for managers who do not need to receive, or are unable to make use of, regular financial reports.

MBO has a number of features:

- establishing a clear, usually hierarchical, reporting and delegation structure
- obtaining a consensus between different levels of management in setting objectives
- seeing budgetary control systems not as constraints, but as guidelines and resource providers to help managers achieve recognised goals
- implementing a measurement and reporting process which involves joint discussion with managers
- regular periodic reviews.

These objectives and measures do not all have to relate to financial targets but can include aspects relating to efficiency and quality of a manager's (or their department's) activities. A research and development manager could have a target for the number of new products developed; a marketing manager's objectives may relate to market share achieved.

Budgets and people

Consider two managers in the same organisation. It is approaching the end of the budget year. One manager has under-spent her budget and one has overspent his. The first manager may wish to spend all her budget in case it is cut back the next year. The second has to reduce spending to minimise any overspend of his variance. Both managers' actions are aimed at achieving a level of spending in line with budget but it is possible the first manager is not making the best possible use of the organisation's resources. And there may be possible consequences to the organisation of the second manager having to delay expenditure.

Consideration of the behavioural aspects of budgeting is crucial in order to understand how budgets actually function in practice. Budgeting should be seen as a behavioural process.

Budgets may not always lead to the optimal allocation of resources in an organisation. The amount of resources allocated to managers may relate to their ability to negotiate rather than where the resources could be best used to achieve the organisation's goals. Managers may seek more resources for their departments than optimal for the organisation as a whole for a number of reasons including: they may have a biased view of the importance of their area; or want their performance to look good; or protect their staff.

The budgeting system can seriously influence the level of motivation and culture of an organisation, because budgets play a central role in:

- assessing how well managers have carried out their responsibilities
- identifying those areas that require corrective action
- motivating managers to achieve their goals
- allocating resources and imposing constraints on activity.

When designing a budgetary system there are two key behavioural considerations: the level of participation and the severity of standards. Allowing managers to participate in the budgetary process can be motivating and can make use of their detailed operational knowledge. However, it can lead to dysfunctional aspects, such as competition between managers for resources and slack being built into budgets. Building in slack means asking for more resources than needed in order to make the budget easy to achieve. In terms of severity of targets a balance is needed. If budgetary targets are too severe it can lead to demoralisation, if they are too lax it can lead to a lack of efficiency.

An understanding and appreciation of the links between budgeting and human behaviour help you to understand more fully the operation of budgeting processes. The budgetary process will be influenced by the behaviour and actions of managers, who are influenced by:

- their individual values, ambitions, fears, ways of working
- the way the group they work with normally expects people to behave, often expressed by the informal approval or disapproval of behaviour
- the organisational structure and cultures that have shaped the ways budgetary processes operate across the organisation
- prevailing patterns of behaviour, trust and efficiency in the society in which the organisation and its staff exist.

It is often argued that the more that staff are involved in budgetary processes, the better the processes work. In practice, there are a number of factors that discourage people from participating in budget-setting and management processes, or that reduce the effectiveness of those processes. We consider eight of these issues.

Lack of influence

If managers cannot influence many of the figures in their budgets, they may find it easy not to take responsibility for achieving budget targets. This applies to both income and expenditure budget items. If most of the expenditure in a budget is on costs for which managers have little or no influence – over the choice of a supplier or over the terms on which goods or services are purchased – then they may resent their performance being judged in relation to expenditure verses budget. Similarly, if managers feel that they have no direct influence over what they sell or to whom they sell it, or on what terms they sell it, then they may resent the income budget's targets.

Building in slack

Most people think it is better to overestimate the amount people will eat in a meal rather than underestimate it: some left over is less of a problem than not enough to eat. So managers may be tempted to exaggerate their expenditure needs and underestimate their income, sales or production targets, so that they are more likely to remain within budget than outside it. 'Slack' is thus allowed for in budgets. Such 'budget games' can be very complex in large organisations and can distort the whole rational model, whereby different levels of management agree on what are fair and appropriate targets and budgets for individual managers and teams, sections or projects. Sometimes managers want the slack to spend on their own pet projects or interests, rather than on those of their organisation.

Fear

Fear is often associated with organisational culture. If staff feel that budgets are being set to test them, that people want to prove them incompetent, wasteful and worse performers than colleagues, they may shy away from involvement in the process. In such instances, managers may prefer to have budgets imposed on them – then they can blame the unrealistic budgets, rather than their own performance against budgets they helped to establish.

Lack of understanding

A worryingly large number of managers are ignorant of their organisation's budgetary systems and accounting figures in general. They may seek to avoid or minimise their involvement in something they do not understand. People may convince themselves that things are more complicated than they are and that this is not what they are good at in management. 'I'm more a people sort of person' is a commonly heard claim. But it's important for managers not only to understand the human element of management but to have a good understanding of figures, costs, financial constraints and targets as well.

Constraint on initiative

Some managers may be 'ideas' people, or risk-taking leaders. The process of formalising targets and reviewing the details of performance can feel like a constraint to them. They complain that the bureaucracy and 'small-minded accountants' of their organisations are stifling innovation and initiative. Such managers can be reluctant to participate in setting and monitoring budgets.

Confused processes

Unfortunately, in some organisations inaccuracy, lateness and a lack of co-ordination between the budgets of different sections may occur. In such cases managers are unlikely to trust the budgets. They do not find budgets provide the clarity, resources and targets they need to do their jobs well. There may be poor communication (whether top-down or bottom-up), leading to misinterpretation, uncertainty and misdirection.

Bitter past experience

There is often at least one manager in any organisation who has failed to achieve budgetary targets in the past, or was set and judged on an unfair budget.

Self-interest

Where individual managers pursue their own aims rather than their organisation's, it is very easy for the whole budgetary process to become corrupted – other managers worry they will lose out unless they behave similarly. Sometimes 'empire building' occurs; managers will add a percentage to their requirements in the light of almost subconscious feelings that a bigger budget makes the budget holder a more important person. As a financial year end approaches, perhaps two months away, a budget holder may find that there is plenty of money left in the budget. Often, this money quickly gets spent, sometimes on unnecessary items and activities. The budget holder has survived quite well on a particular level of spending for ten months and then wastes money. This is sometimes termed the 'hockey stick' effect, for reasons which are apparent from the spending graph shown in Figure 12.1. The curve on the hockey stick may go either way. The downward curve illustrates the situation where the manager has overspent the budget during the first ten months needing to curtail spending until the end of the year to make budget.

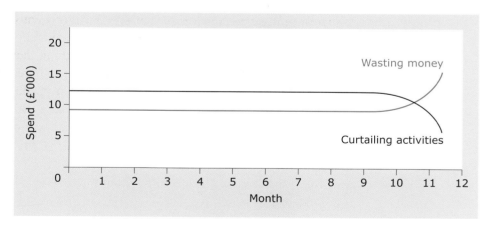

Figure 12.1 The 'hockey stick' effect

Budgets are often linked to reward systems which can motivate managers to achieve targets set. It is important to coordinate these reward systems with organisational objectives so that managers are working towards the goals of the organisation as a whole (so-called goal congruence) and not their individual departments.

Chapter 13 Measuring costs in organisations
Introduction to cost concepts

Much of the financial information you receive as a manager is about costs: how much different resources (such as staff, materials and transport) have cost or are expected to cost; whether the costs for the service, project, unit or organisation you are responsible for are more or less than was expected; how much it costs to undertake specific activities or to provide specific outputs. Important decisions are made on the basis of this kind of information. Behind the cost information that circulates in your organisation and all others are many different approaches to how costs are calculated and expressed. These approaches involve different costing techniques, but all share the objective of giving managers the information they need to make informed and rational decisions. Costing is therefore part of what is termed *management accounting* – where the focus is on information for internal planning decision-making and control. This is different from *financial accounting*, where the focus is on the formal reporting back to stakeholders of the financial position of an organisation. In costing, a number of different classifications or labels are used.

Understanding and classifying costs

To understand cost information you need to understand what the term 'costs' means, and how a knowledge of costs can help you in your role as a manager. Managers and their organisations need cost information for the same core managerial functions as they need other financial information, namely:

- planning – for instance, to know what it is sensible to aim for in future spending
- controlling – for instance, to know which costs are responsible for any overspend, and therefore need attention
- decision-making – for instance, deciding what to charge for different services, taking into account the costs they incur
- stewardship – for instance, being able to account for where money has been spent so that the financial statements presented to internal and external stakeholders show a true and fair picture of the finances of an organisation.

Money, despite its shortcomings, is the most common way of measuring the costs (inputs) of producing goods or providing services (outputs).

Formally, the term 'cost' refers to the amount of expenditure (actual or notional) incurred on or attributable to a specific item or activity. Put simply, a cost is a money-based measure of the resources used in order to generate outputs. Cost information is that which quantifies these resources. However, it is not always straightforward to generate. This is because measuring costs often requires a series of judgements on, for example, the sharing of overhead costs between different products or services.

The cost object

The cost object is whatever it is we are trying to arrive at a cost for. A cost object, depending on the circumstances for which the costing is being carried out, could be such things as the cost of a unit of output, a marketing campaign, to run a department, to build a bridge, to treat a patient or to employ someone. Note, many organisations have cost centres (departments) aligned to managers' responsibilities. A cost centre may be the cost object if you wanted to know the cost of running your marketing department for a month; but not all cost objects are cost centres, such as wanting to know the cost of a particular marketing campaign.

Costs for different purposes

The purpose for which the cost calculation is required can influence the cost approach used. For decision-making we may look at determining extra or marginal costs and benefits associated with the decision. For financial reporting we might want to calculate the total cost associated with running an area of the organisation. These different purposes have resulted in different costing approaches and ways of classifying costs. We start our look at how costs are classified with the important distinction between fixed and variable costs.

Fixed and variable costs

Fixed costs are those which do not change with different levels of activity. Variable costs are defined as those that vary proportionately with the level of activity. Example 13.1 will help you develop this principle into an organisational context.

Example 13.1

Imagine you are organising a one-day festival. You have hired a field from a farmer for €1,000 and have been quoted €1,000 each for the hire of marquees. In addition, each marquee will require an attendant, costing €100 for the day. Controlling the entrance to the field will require two security teams, at €100 each.

Table 13.1 shows the workings for the total cost of the event based on four, five and six marquees. Notice what happens to the average cost per marquee as the number of marquees rises – why does it change?

The calculations contain a number of lessons. First, notice how the average cost per marquee falls as the number of marquees and attendants increases; this is to be expected where economies of scale exist. The greater the activity, the lower the cost per unit. Second, note that the fall is not proportional. The fall between four and five is €60 (€1,400 – €1,340) and between five and six €40 (€1,340 – €1,300). You may not have expected this. The reason is important. It is caused by some costs being fixed and some being variable. The hire of the field stays at €1,000, and the security teams at €200, irrespective of the number of marquees. On the other hand, the costs of the marquees and the attendants vary with the number of marquees hired. Hiring more marquees spreads the fixed costs – gets more out of the costs if you like. Hiring fewer means paying proportionately more fixed costs per marquee.

Table 13.1 The average cost of marquees

Number of marquees	Hire of field	Marquees @ €1,000 each	Attendants @ €100 each	Security teams: 2 @ €100	Total cost	Average cost per marquee (total cost ÷ number of marquees)
	€	€	€	€	€	€
4	1,000	4,000	400	200	5,600	1,400
5	1,000	5,000	500	200	6,700	1,340
6	1,000	6,000	600	200	7,800	1,300

This idea of fixed and variable costs is very important. If you have high fixed costs you need to generate more units of products or services to keep your unit costs down, taking advantage of economies of scale. For example, the average cost of four marquees is €1,400, which is €60 more than for five marquees and €100 more than for six marquees. This is because with a lower level of activity the fixed costs are being spread over a smaller number of units. In addition, there may come a point where, if you hire more marquees, the fixed costs may change and thus no longer be fixed. For example, if you hired ten marquees you might need to hire a second field and pay for more security teams. Similarly, if you had only two marquees you might hire a smaller field and have only one security team.

The distinction into fixed and variable costs is limited in that it is a very simplistic view. In fact, so-called fixed costs are often fixed only within certain limits, which need to be established. In such cases they are sometimes referred to as step or stepped costs. Above a particular limit there may be a need for expenditure on fixed costs to rise. If activity falls, so, too, might fixed costs. In the long run, all costs can be considered variable, or at best semi-variable. Variable costs may not always be proportional to activity. For example, although you currently pay €1,000 per marquee, it may be that a discount of, say, 10% might be available if you were to hire more than eight marquees. In such cases working out the cost becomes more of a challenge. However, despite being a simplistic approach the recognition of fixed and variable costs provides you with a starting point in understanding the overall costs of a particular activity, service or product.

The ratio between fixed and variable costs varies hugely between organisations. For instance, a hospital has to pay wages and salaries, heating and cleaning costs and insurance regardless of how many patients or operations there are on a particular day. Its fixed costs are high, so the more patients, operations or other 'units of service' it can deal with within a particular period, the more efficiently these costs are being utilised. A supermarket has to pay similar costs regardless of how many customers there are or how much they spend. However, by far the biggest component of supermarket costs is the cost of the items that customers purchase. A supermarket's costs therefore vary according to the volume of purchases made. So, as well as needing to keep its fixed costs low and spread over a large number of customers, a supermarket also needs to minimise its main variable costs – the cost of each item it sells.

This relationship between fixed costs and total costs is often referred to as operating gearing or, sometimes, as operational leverage. Having a high proportion of fixed costs is both an opportunity and a threat. It is a threat because those costs have to be covered. Paying for an under-used hospital or supermarket can be an expensive drain on resources. However, high fixed costs can also be seen as an opportunity, because they may reflect an infrastructure capacity that facilitates high volumes of activity. An automated car production facility would have much higher operational gearing than a market trader.

Direct and indirect costs

Costs can also be classified as direct and indirect costs. Direct costs are those associated with a specific activity or output. Direct costs are those that can be directly traced to the cost object. Indirect costs (also called overheads, or burden in the USA) are those that cannot be identified with or allocated to a specific cost object and which therefore need to be shared between different cost objects.

In an organisation how many costs can be directly traced may depend on what you are costing (i.e. what the cost object is). For example, more costs may be directly traceable to a department than to an individual unit of output.

So, in the marquee example, where you were asked to focus on the cost per marquee, the marquee hire and attendant costs were directly attributable to each marquee and were thus direct costs. The field hire and security costs had to be apportioned between each marquee and were thus indirect costs.

In this example, the fixed costs were the same as the indirect costs and the variable costs the same as the direct costs. While this is common, it is not always the case. For instance, the salaries of particular staff can often be attributed directly to a specific unit or activity or output in an organisation. In this case they would be a direct cost and also a fixed cost. To decide which costs are direct and which are indirect, it is necessary to understand the nature of an activity.

Financial recording systems can be refined to allow more costs to become direct costs, so long as the effort is worthwhile. For example, electricity costs may be indirect, but if separate meters were installed in each department of an organisation, electricity could be treated as a direct cost of a department. At one time, telephone costs were usually treated as indirect, whereas now improvements in telecommunications systems allow them to be charged to the specific user departments. To what extent it is worthwhile establishing systems for converting general indirect costs into specific direct costs is a matter of managers' judgement.

Many indirect, less easily attributable costs such as rent, lighting and heating costs are received in the form of large bills for the whole organisation which need to be broken down in order to be charged to individual departments, activities or outputs. In many organisations they are broken down into all three. For instance, the hospital we discussed earlier may wish to know:

- the heating and lighting costs for discrete buildings or departments
- the average heating and lighting costs incurred in each major operation and other energy-intensive activities
- the average cost of heating and lighting per patient treated: if a hospital treats 100,000 patients in a year when it spent £50,000 on heating and lighting, this 50 pence average per patient can be compared with previous years, other hospitals and other costs.

These are all valid reasons for calculating cost information. However, they expose the need for different but fair means of apportioning indirect costs to different units of activity. When people talk about direct and indirect costs, you need to ensure that everybody is clear about which activity area is being referred to. We now consider some approaches to how to apportion indirect costs.

For example, in a training organisation the division could be based on costs such as trainers' fees and printing costs as these are easily identified with specific courses; other costs, such as rent, senior managers' salaries, depreciation of equipment, insurance, and so on, are the indirect ones. In a carpentry business some costs could be easily identified with specific items being produced. In making furniture, the cost of wood and, perhaps, wages would probably be classed as direct costs. Other costs, such as rent, lighting and heating, tools, phone and post are much less easily attributable to each item of furniture. These would therefore be classed as indirect costs.

The way indirect costs are allocated in an organisation can have an impact on how it perceives the performance of its products/services. If allocation of overheads is made disproportionately, then some activities may be judged unfairly in term of cost and profitability.

Contribution

Contribution is primarily used for decision-making and applies the concepts of fixed and variable costs. It is calculated by deducting variable costs from sales revenue, with any contribution firstly having to cover fixed costs and then any contribution over and above fixed costs is profit. When calculated on a unit basis it provides an indication of how much an extra unit of output contributes towards profitability.

Contribution = sales revenue − variable costs

Profit = contribution − fixed costs

Contribution can also be calculated on a unit basis:

Contribution per unit = sales revenue per unit − variable cost per unit

Many managers face decisions for which they need to know the immediate cost implications: squeezing in an extra delivery, extending opening hours, increasing the number of beds in a ward, taking on an extra worker or putting an unused room into operation. Such decisions are based on contribution costing, which is also referred to as marginal costing or variable costing. This is important because many managers at some time face decisions along the following lines:

- What are the marginal (extra) costs and benefits from an extra unit of activity?

- What are the implications if we squeeze in an extra customer or appointment at the end of the day?

- How much extra would it cost to fit an extra student on the course, or a delivery on the van run?

- How many more do we need to sell to cover all our costs (break even)?

One reason for using a contribution approach is the problem of how to allocate indirect costs. Indirect costs (overheads) present challenges when trying to determine the cost of a product or service. The need for judgement in apportionment and the wide range of overhead absorption methods can lead to the cost information produced under that approach being open to question. The contribution (marginal cost) approach seeks to avoid this problem by calculating the contribution made by each product or service towards the fixed costs (and once fixed costs are covered, profit) of the organisation. This approach provides a model for explaining the relationships between price, cost and volume, and for comparing alternative courses of action.

It should be noted that in most countries the regulatory framework for accounting requires the absorption/recovery approach to be used for external reporting purposes. In those same countries most organisations use a contribution approach for internal decision-making.

Example 13.2 illustrates the underlying distinction between absorption and marginal/contribution costing approaches.

Example 13.2 Colours

Colours is an interior design business that offers domestic and business customers consultations on their premises. A designer visits the property, assesses colour schemes for decoration and furnishings, suggests possible options and follows up with a brief written summary of the consultation. Each consultation costs Colours £50 in variable direct costs, that is, these costs relate directly to the consultation and would not be incurred if the consultation did not take place. Colours charge £100 per consultation and plans to provide 1,000 of them to customers in the coming year. Colours' fixed costs, that is those it will incur even if it sells no consultations, are budgeted to be £40,000 for the year.

This example allows us to illustrate the differences between contribution (marginal) costing (using fixed and variable cost analysis) and absorption costing (using direct and indirect cost analysis). Using an absorption approach the company might wish to calculate an overhead absorption/recovery rate for indirect costs of £40 per unit (£40,000 ÷ 1,000 consultations). The results are given in a cost statement as shown in Table 13.2.

Table 13.2 Absorption operating statement

	Average per unit	Total
	£	£
Sales (1,000 consultations)	100	100,000
Direct costs	50	50,000
Indirect costs (overheads) (1,000 × £40)	<u>40</u>	<u>40,000</u>
Net profit	<u>10</u>	<u>10,000</u>

The overhead recovery rate per unit depends on judgements about apportionment and particularly on an estimate of the volume. If there are any estimating errors the £40 figure may, for a whole variety of reasons, be completely inappropriate. Perhaps the company will provide a greater or smaller number of consultations, and/or the actual fixed overheads will be higher or lower than planned, thus invalidating the £40. An alternative approach, the contribution approach avoiding the problems of absorbing indirect overheads, is shown in Table 13.3.

Table 13.3 Contribution operating statement (1)

	Per unit	Total
	£	£
Sales (1,000 consultations)	100	100,000
Variable costs	<u>50</u>	<u>50,000</u>
Contribution	50	50,000
Fixed costs		<u>40,000</u>
Net profit		<u>10,000</u>

The absorption/recovery approach treats fixed overheads as costs of activity and they are thus charged into the activity costs. The contribution cost approach assumes, on the other hand, that fixed overheads are costs that will be incurred during the period in question whatever level of activity takes place. The contribution of £50,000 (1,000 units at £50 per unit) contributes first towards covering fixed overheads and then, if anything is left over, towards profit or surplus. If the contribution is lower than fixed overheads, the amount by which it is lower represents a loss or deficit. Table 13.3 illustrates this, with the contribution being the balance remaining after deducting variable costs from sales revenues. This contribution figure provides sufficient funds to cover fixed costs and so produces a profit or surplus. Of course, if it did not, there would be a loss made on that operation, but less of a loss than if there were no contribution.

The important point is that the contribution costing approach helps to avoid the problems caused by trying to absorb fixed overheads. With a contribution of £50 per unit, we know that each extra unit sold will increase the profit or reduce the loss by £50.

If the company had provided and sold only 500 consultations instead of 1,000 it would not have made a profit, as shown in Table 13.4.

Table 13.4 Contribution operating statement (2)

	Per unit	Total
	£	£
Sales (500 consultations)	100	50,000
Variable costs	50	25,000
Contribution	50	25,000
Fixed costs		40,000
Net loss		(15,000)

The reason for this loss is clearly that not enough contribution (£25,000) has been produced at this level of sales to cover the fixed costs (£40,000).

In the case of Colours, one important thing is to know how many consultations it has to sell in order to 'break-even', that is, to exactly cover all costs. So far you have seen (Table 13.4) that 500 consultations results in a £15,000 loss. We look at how to calculate points at which break-even occurs later, but Table 13.5 shows the level of sales needed to generate an amount of contribution that exactly matches the level of fixed costs.

Table 13.5 Contribution operating statement (3): the break-even point

	Per unit	Total
	£	£
Sales (800 consultations)	100	80,000
Variable costs	50	40,000
Contribution	50	40,000
Fixed costs		40,000
Net profit		0

It can be seen that once the company has succeeded in selling enough consultations to provide £40,000 contribution (i.e. 800 consultations), each extra consultation the company sells will provide £50 contribution to profits (£100 − £50). If 801 consultations were sold the operating statement would read as in Table 13.6. Once the break-even point has been reached and all costs, including fixed costs, have been covered, any contribution generated becomes profit/surplus.

Table 13.6 Contribution operating statement (4)

	Per unit	Total
	£	£
Sales (801 consultations)	100	80,100
Variable costs	50	40,050
Contribution	50	40,050
Fixed costs		40,000
Net profit		50

A practical benefit lies in the fact that in order to calculate net profit or loss (or surplus or deficit) different operating statements do not need to be produced for different levels of activity – all that needs to be done is calculate the sales in excess of the break-even point and multiply the answer by the contribution per unit. Because all the fixed overheads will have already been covered at the break-even level, any contribution from extra units sold above the break-even level must produce profit. With this technique a manager can calculate the effect of different amounts of sales on the profits or surpluses of an organisation.

Managers, therefore, need to know the relationship between each item of sale (or episode of income generation) and the contribution this makes. This is most conveniently represented as a percentage, and is often referred to as the contribution to sales ratio.

In the case of Colours this can be calculated thus:

If sales of consultations rose to 1,500 units, determine the resulting net profit using the contribution to sales ratio of 50% calculated above.

The contribution ratio of 50% tells us immediately what effect on profit a change in sales would have. If sales were increased to £150,000 contribution would increase to 50% of £150,000 = £75,000. With fixed costs remaining constant at £40,000, the net profit would be £35,000, as shown in Table 13.7 (and assuming that the increase in volume remained within the range of capacity served by the fixed costs of £40,000, of course).

Table 13.7 Contribution operating statement (5)

	Per unit	Total	%
	£	£	
Sales (1,500 consultations)	100	150,000	100
Variable costs	50	75,000	50
Contribution	50	75,000	50
Fixed costs		40,000	
Net profit		35,000	

The contribution to sales ratio is a useful concept because it presents a simple and immediate guide to profit or surplus levels. It helps to identify which product or service makes the most contribution and to assess the impact of each product or service on profit or surplus. This is particularly important and useful if an organisation has more than one operation or activity, and not only in businesses such as Colours, which sells directly to customers. Many private and public sector organisations have internal recharging systems: if the business units (or cost centres) within these organisations have a certain level of fixed costs and a volume-related recharging system, some version of the contribution to sales ratio will be relevant. Many educational organisations have their budgets determined, at least in part, by formulae related to numbers of students. Managers can use the ratio to work out the financial effect of admitting extra students.

Operational gearing

This is the proportion of total costs made up by fixed costs. If fixed costs form a high proportion of total costs, and are thus high relative to variable costs, the contribution per unit of output will be greater than if the variable costs are high relative to fixed costs. That is, a product or service with a high proportion of fixed costs is greatly sensitive to changes in volume. Increased volume leads to a disproportionate increase in profit and, conversely, a reduced volume causes a disproportionate reduction in profit. In this sense a higher operational gearing implies potentially greater volatility and thus higher risk. We explore this in Example 13.3.

Example 13.3 Children's Aid

A small not-for-profit charity which helped children who run away from home, Children's Aid, was faced with a decision on how to organise its fundraising. The charity's fixed costs were £3,000 a month.

- In Scenario A, it would contract specialist fundraising agents who would pass 50% of the funds they raised on to Children's Aid. The charity would have no liability for the salaries or expenses of the agents.

- In Scenario B, Children's Aid would do the fundraising itself. Only 20% of money raised would go on variable costs, but Children's Aid would have to employ extra administrative staff costing £3,000 a month.

Under either scenario, Children's Aid anticipated that £10,000 a month would be generated in donations.

Table 13.8 implies there is no difference in the net effect on the charity.

Table 13.8 The impact of cost structures

	Scenario A	%	Scenario B	%
	£		£	
Donations	10,000	100	10,000	100
Variable costs	5,000	50	2,000	20
Contribution	5,000	50	8,000	80
Fixed costs	3,000		6,000	
Funds generated	2,000		2,000	

However, we can see that the greater the proportional fixed costs, the greater the operating gearing. In Scenario A, the operating gearing is 37.5%, being £3,000 (fixed costs) as a proportion of £8,000 (total costs). In B it is 75%, being £6,000 (fixed costs) as a proportion of £8,000 (total costs). Consider how changes in volume impact on the net result in each case.

Scenario B generates a far larger contribution than Scenario A. If donations increase, surpluses will increase more rapidly. If donations fall, however, and Scenario B applies, the charity will lose surpluses more quickly. In Scenario B, the charity has more to lose and more to gain than in Scenario A because of its different cost structure. It will also need to monitor expenditure particularly carefully to ensure fixed costs do not exceed the planned levels.

Another way of looking at this is the degree of operating gearing. This is a useful measure of how a given change in sales/income volume will affect profits/surpluses. It can also be expressed as a ratio:

Degree of gearing = contribution: net profit

For the two scenarios in Table 13.8, the degree of operating gearing will be:

Scenario A 5,000:2,000 = 2.5:1

Scenario B 8,000:2,000 = 4:1

This ratio indicates the effect on overall surplus of various changes in income. As you have seen, the effect of gearing can be considerable and a small change in volume can in some situations produce a large change in surpluses. In Scenario B, for instance, a 5% increase in donations will produce a 20% increase in profits.

Break-even analysis

Break-even analysis identifies the level of activity at which an organisation generates neither profit nor loss, no surplus or deficit. It is designed to show where the value of the inputs equals the value of the outputs. This is generally referred to as the break-even point. The break-even point in units is determined by dividing the total fixed costs by the contribution per unit.

Break-even analysis is a useful tool in risk management as it may be useful to know how far volumes can fall before losses are incurred, or to what level volumes must rise if a product or service is to cover its total costs. Break-even analysis is particularly relevant to not-for-profit operations when managers are planning services designed not to produce profit but rather to cover the costs of providing them.

A break-even point is where an organisation makes neither a profit nor a loss because its total revenue was exactly equal to its total costs at that level of activity. Looking at it another way, its contribution was exactly equal to its fixed costs. This enables us to calculate the break-even point for any operation or activity.

Break-even analysis is an application of marginal costing principles. If fixed costs such as rent, insurance and administration remain unchanged as a consequence of a decision, only the variable or marginal costs (i.e. the extra costs arising from the decision) need to be considered when assessing the comparative costs of alternatives. Provided additional revenue exceeds the additional variable costs, the activities should be undertaken because the organisation will benefit from the additional contribution.

Example 13.4

If fixed costs are £40,000 and contribution is £50 per unit.

$$\frac{\text{Total fixed costs}}{\text{Contribution per unit}} = \text{number of units to break-even}$$

$$\frac{\text{Total fixed costs}}{\text{Contribution per unit}} = \frac{£40,000}{£50} = 800 \text{ units to break-even}$$

That is 800 units would need to be sold in order to break even, as each unit contributes £50 towards the organisation's fixed costs. Each unit sold over the 800 would contribute £50 towards profitability.

Break-even charts

Some managers prefer to work with visual presentations rather than with figures. Cost volume profit relationships can conveniently present the information in chart form, as in Figure 13.1. Break-even charts are an effective way of representing the relationships between costs and income. We illustrate this using the scenario in Example 13.5.

Example 13.5 The concert

Freda Gomez is an impresario. She is currently arranging a concert in the USA. Freda assumes the following:

- customers are prepared to pay no more than $10 to attend the show
- the event will be 'sold out' if 1,000 customers attend
- the variable costs will be $5 per customer
- various fixed costs associated with the event will amount to $1,000
- a one-off insurance payment of $1,000 is needed
- the performers will be paid $1,000 regardless of how many people attend.

Using the above data, Freda can prepare a break-even chart. This will require a graph which shows:

- the sales line (A)
- the variable costs line (B)
- the fixed costs line (C)
- the total costs line. (D)

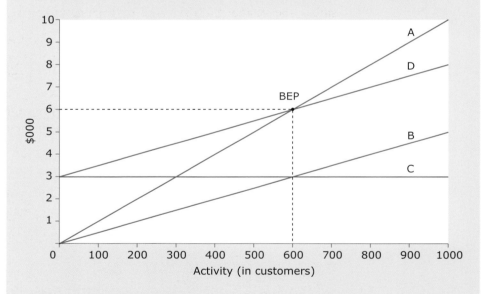

Figure 13.1 The concert break-even point (BEP)

- Line A is the sales line, with zero sales income at zero activity and $10,000 when all the tickets are sold.
- Line B is the variable costs line, with zero variable costs at zero activity and $5,000 at an activity level of 1,000.
- Line C is the fixed costs line, being $3,000 (insurance, various fixed costs and the performers' fee) at all levels of activity.
- Line D is the total costs line. At zero activity the total costs are just the fixed costs of $3,000. They increase by $5 additional cost per customer, so that at the level of 1,000 customers the total costs are $8,000.

Where lines A and D cross is the break-even point (BEP): 600 customers generating $6,000 sales income. Note that the gap between line A and line D increases after the BEP: this is where Freda starts to make more of a profit with every ticket she sells.

The BEP can be checked using the calculation approach you saw earlier. In this case it is:

$$\frac{\text{Total fixed costs}}{\text{Contribution per unit}} = \text{number of units to break-even}$$

$$\frac{\text{Total fixed costs}}{\text{Contribution per unit}} = \frac{\$3,000}{\$5} = 600 \text{ customers to break-even}$$

Margin of safety

Another useful statistic for risk assessment that can be determined from a break-even chart is the margin of safety. This is the gap between the break-even point and the assumed level of activity. For our example, there is a margin of safety of 400 customers (1,000 less 600): activity can fall by this amount before Freda will make a loss. The greater the margin of safety, the smaller the risk. And vice versa, of course.

A break-even chart is an effective way of communicating cost–volume relationships, and changes in those relationships. If you fail to control costs there is a danger that the total costs line on your break-even chart will become steeper – more cost being incurred at every level of output. This will cause the break-even point to shift to the right, meaning more work required before losses or deficits are avoided, and a smaller margin of safety.

Stepped costs

Stepped costs are when fixed costs are fixed only within certain limits of capacity. To undertake much more activity it may be necessary to increase capacity and thus incur more fixed costs. Example 13.6 illustrates this.

Example 13.6

Assuming that Freda Gomez has now ascertained that there is a huge demand for her concert. She feels that 1,500 customers will turn up. While the theatre holds up to 2,000 people, for every 250 customers in excess of 1,000, fixed costs will rise by $500. Insurance costs will also rise, from $1,000 to $3,000 for any number of customers over 1,000. The impact of these stepped costs is illustrated in Figure 13.2.

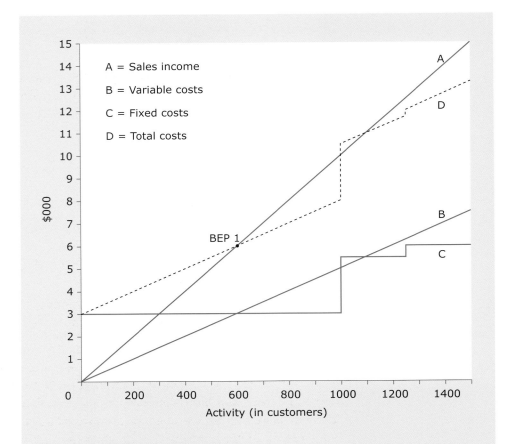

Figure 13.2 The concert break-even analysis (2)

Note that although the break-even point remains the same, there are 'stepped' increases in the total costs line at the 1,000 and 1,250 customer stages that mean Freda is only just making a profit at these points. Her greatest profit is still made with 1,000 customers, because of the increase in fixed costs, particularly insurance, once there are more than 1,000 customers.

Break-even analysis and volume/price decisions

Break-even analysis is especially relevant when there is a need to set prices or charges that are sufficient to cover costs or to deliver a specific profit margin. Example 13.7 illustrates this.

Example 13.7 Pricing snacks

An organisation had a small catering facility. There was a policy that the cafeteria had to break-even in any year. Last year the costs were:

- variable costs per snack:
  - food 45p
  - fuel, etc. 15p
- annual fixed costs:
  - wages £36,000
  - overheads £24,000

The cafeteria had a capacity of 825,000 snacks and 700,000 snacks were sold, at an average price of 72p each.

This year the cost of food per snack was forecast to rise to 50p, fuel etc. to 16p, annual wages to £38,000 and overheads to £25,000.

A good starting point for this type of problem is to calculate the contribution. Last year it was 12p but this year it is expected to fall to 6p per snack. The old selling price of 72p will not give sufficient contribution to allow the cafeteria to break even this year, even at full capacity utilisation. At the costs given it would be necessary to increase the capacity (unlikely, at least in the short term) or to increase prices. Just as we can calculate a break even if we know the fixed costs, variable costs per snack and selling price per snack, we can also calculate a required selling price from an assumed break-even volume. In the revised budget in the third column of Table 13.9 we assume that the manager has been told to break even at 700,000 snacks; this implies a contribution of 9p per snack (63,000/700,000, being fixed costs divided by the number of snacks), which, with variable costs of 66p per snack, implies an increased selling price of 75p per snack.

The first column of figures in Table 13.9 shows that the number of snacks the cafeteria needed to sell last year to break even was 500,000; note that it in fact sold 200,000 more than the break-even level. The second column shows what it would have to sell this year if it charged the same price despite the new costs. The third column shows the position if there was a price increase of 3p per snack: a challenging break-even point of 700,000 snacks. This would mean selling the same number of snacks this year as last despite the 3p price rise.

The cafeteria manager could go on to develop a whole range of different options on which to base a decision. This is using a knowledge of cost information and break-even analysis to make informed decisions. The manager would need to consider carefully the ramifications of changing the price. For example, the increase in fixed costs would impact on the operational gearing and the change in price and variable costs would change the contribution margin.

Table 13.9 Different break-even scenarios

	Last year (actual)	This year (budget)	This year (revised budget)
	£	£	£
Variable cost per snack:			
Food	0.45	0.50	0.50
Fuel, etc.	0.15	0.16	0.16
Total	0.60	0.66	0.66
Selling price	0.72	0.72	0.75
Contribution per snack	0.12	0.06	0.09
Annual fixed costs:			
Wages	36,000	38,000	38,000
Overheads	24,000	25,000	25,000
Total fixed costs	60,000	63,000	63,000
Number of snacks to break even	500,000	1,050,000	700,000

We will be looking at a number of other ways in which managers make use of cost information for decision-making, but first it is worthwhile reviewing the assumptions which often lie behind the reporting of costing information.

Limitations of contribution and break-even assumptions

Break-even analysis and contribution costing models are dependent on assumptions made about actual costs. Assumptions are convenient simplifications which may need to be modified to reflect the circumstances at the time. Key assumptions are that:

- variable costs remain constant per unit or activity
- there is a linear relationship between costs (seen as straight lines on a break-even chart)
- volumes are within the relevant range of capacity (not the case with the cafeteria example)
- there is either only a single product or service, or that the mixture of different products or services remains constant.

We look at each, in turn, below.

Variable costs remain constant per unit

It is normally assumed that variable costs per unit will remain constant throughout the analysis process. This is likely to be an oversimplification, because changes in volume may involve other changes, such as production methods, production efficiency, sales price or sales mix. A particular analysis will apply only to a given set of circumstances. For example, in the Colours case, if the sales price per consultation were reduced, the company might opt for cheaper direct travel costs, thereby reducing the variable costs.

Linearity

The contribution approach assumes that costs and revenues are proportional to output. It also assumes that the unit variable cost and the selling price are constant. This ignores the possibility of bulk discounts given by suppliers at higher levels of output, for example.

Relevant range

This extension of linearity beyond certain constraints was also considered in the cafeteria scenario. We saw then how figures are appropriate only for decisions taken within a relevant range, given that costs will only remain constant within certain parameters. The use of stepped costs may help to meet this criticism of a simple model, as we illustrated in the example of the concert. A production facility may have a certain capacity before more fixed costs are incurred. A volume of production beyond which, new machinery or bigger facilities are needed.

Single product or service, or constant mixture of different ones

This limitation of cost models arises because it is sometimes assumed that the proportion of the different products sold (the sales mix) will follow a predetermined relationship. When there is a range of goods or services, average variable costs and average revenues for the mix may be used, which may be an oversimplification of a complex situation. Averages, of course, can hide a great deal.

In the simple, single product/service organisation, you can look at how profit/surplus changes with the level of output (e.g. calculate break-even point) by calculating the contribution per unit, or contribution to sales ratio, as the case may be. But what happens when there are a number of different products or services, each with a different contribution per unit or contribution to sales ratio? This, of course, is a much more common situation and if cost– volume–profit analysis is to be generally useful, it must be able to accommodate this situation.

The procedure normally adopted is to assume that, as the level of output varies, the 'sales mix' (i.e. the relative proportions of each product/service) remains the same. You can then calculate a weighted average contribution to sales ratio in order to determine the break-even revenue. You do this by calculating the total expected sales revenue, the total expected contribution resulting from this level of sales and then dividing the latter by the former. Finally, divide the organisation's total fixed cost by this figure to find the break-even level of revenue.

Similarly, you can calculate the break-even number of 'units' (in this case the total number of meals) by determining the total expected number of units (of all products/services) and dividing the total expected contribution by this figure, to obtain the average contribution per unit. Dividing the total fixed cost by this figure gives the break-even number of units.

The implication of these limitations is that break-even analysis should only be used with care. However, despite its limitations break-even analysis can be a useful albeit simplistic modelling tool to understand cost and revenue relationships.

Chapter 14 Costing products and services
Charging indirect costs to cost objects

It may be necessary for an organisation's managers to know what accountants call the full cost (or total cost) involved in producing a product (or in the case of service industries, providing a service) for a number of reasons. These include setting selling prices, product/service profitability analysis, business segment performance measurement and cost control.

In this chapter you will see that the main difficulty in determining full product or service costs is estimating the amount of indirect (overhead) resource consumed by any particular product or service. You will also look at the main approaches that are used to deal with the problem of assigning indirect costs to products or services. In considering indirect (overhead) costs, a distinction is often made between common costs and joint costs. Common costs are the costs of resources which are shared by a number of different products. For example, a machine may be used in the production of a number of different products; people in various service and support departments (e.g. production scheduling, stores) may be involved in activities that are consumed by various different products. The problem, then, is to find a way of apportioning these machine or people costs in a way that reflects each product's consumption of these resources. Joint costs are the costs of particular processes that produce (automatically) more than one output (e.g. product). For example, in refining crude oil, various intermediate products are automatically produced as a result of the same refining process. The emphasis in this chapter is on common costs, as this is a more pervasive problem in most organisations – but you also need to be aware of the problem of joint costs, as it may be relevant to your organisation.

Absorbing indirect costs

Under the system known as absorption costing each product, service or activity receives a charge for the overheads that have been incurred by the organisation. The overheads are charged to an appropriate cost object. For example, whereas a hospital may calculate cost per patient day, a transport company may use passenger miles, a plumber may work on a cost per chargeable work hour and the OU may use a course as its cost object. The purpose is to calculate the full or total cost of the cost object including both direct costs and a share of indirect costs.

Example 14.1 showing the manufacture of a simple table in a carpentry business usefully illustrates the complexity of determining costs. This is a manufacturing example, but the principles are the same in all types of organisation.

Example 14.1 Woodhouse Carpentry (1)

Woodhouse Carpentry makes 1,000 of a particular type of table as its only business activity in its first month of operation. The specification details are:

- *Materials required for one table*: one table top is bought in at £20 and four legs at £5 each. Glue is used to secure the legs to the table top. The glue costs around £1,000 per 1,000 tables.

- *Labour costs*: the staff who assemble the tables do not receive a fixed wage; instead, they are paid £20 per table assembled.

Table 14.1 Other cost data

Other workshop costs	£ per month
Supervisors' salaries	20,000
Workshop lighting and heating	1,500
Workshop rent	4,500
Workshop cleaners	2,000
Workshop equipment insurance	1,000
Other organisation costs	**£ per month**
Office lighting and heating	1,000
Office rent	3,000
Office equipment insurance	1,000
Administrator	4,000
Phone, post and sundries	1,000

These costs need to be classified appropriately to establish the cost per table.

First, we identify the direct costs of producing a table. Such direct production costs (sometimes called prime costs in manufacturing) can be broken down into:

- direct materials (the cost per table of the top plus the four legs)
- direct labour (the money paid per table to the assemblers).

There is a case for including glue as a direct material cost in this simplified example where the glue is not purchased for any other activity. However, because glue is the sort of general stock item an organisation might buy for use in a range of activities, we will not classify it as a direct cost. Similarly, there is a case for including the supervisors' salaries as a direct labour cost because they supervise the production of only one activity; again, we will not classify it as a direct cost, because normally supervisors' salaries might cover a range of activities, for each of which you might want to find out the cost. These arguments for inclusion show that costing classification is not an exact science that always involves only clearly right and wrong approaches. It involves judgement of what makes sense for the activities being costed.

Next, we identify the indirect costs of producing a table. Most organisations break down their indirect costs, or overheads, into groups. In this case, it makes sense to consider two groups:

- *production overheads*: (the indirect materials (glue); the indirect labour (supervisors' salaries); and the sundry indirect items connected to the production workshop (light and heat, workshop equipment insurance, rent, cleaners),
- *administration overheads*: (the indirect office and administration costs of running any organisation, in this case the 'other organisation costs').

Many organisations use other groupings, such as sales and distribution overheads, or other titles, such as central establishment charges. Again, what matters is what makes sense for the organisation, to managers and for the activities being costed.

Table 14.2 Cost statement for tables for Woodhouse Carpentry

Direct costs	£	£
Materials		
Tops 1,000 × £20	20,000	
Legs 1,000 × (£5 × 4)	20,000	
		40,000
Labour		
Assembly staff 1,000 × £20		20,000
		60,000
Production overheads		
Glue	1,000	
Supervisors' salaries	20,000	
Light and heat	1,500	
Rent	4,500	
Cleaning	2,000	
Insurance	1,000	
		30,000
		90,000
Administration overheads		
Office light and heat	1,000	
Office rent	3,000	
Insurance	1,000	
Administrator's wages	4,000	
Phone/sundries	1,000	
		10,000
		100,000
Production cost per table (£90,000 ÷ 1,000)		90
Total cost per table (£100,000 ÷ 1,000)		100

In the real world the overheads are not always as clearly identifiable as they are in the Woodhouse example. Take the cost of rent: the workshop rent is £4,500 and the office rent £3,000. How do you know this is correct? The total bill may be £7,500, but on what basis is it divided up (or apportioned)? An equal division might not be appropriate, particularly if the workshop is twice the size of the office. This could apply to other overheads, such as lighting and heating. If costs were apportioned on a different basis, the total cost per table would remain unchanged but the production cost per table would increase or decrease accordingly. Such distinctions may be significant where management responsibilities for cost control are subdivided.

Of course, the production cost per table of £90 remains constant only for this level of activity. This is because some costs (such as materials and production wages) will change directly with the level of activity while others (such as rent) will remain unchanged. This reintroduces the principle of classifying costs not only as direct and indirect but also as variable and fixed, since the latter classification allows an understanding of how total costs vary with changing activity levels.

If Woodhouse Carpentry produced both tables and chairs, it would not only have to decide how much to charge to the workshop as opposed to the other functional areas, it would also have to decide how much each product should be charged for, say, building insurance or rent. There is no definitive means of establishing the precise amount of rent to be borne by each product: the appropriate amount to charge into the unit cost figure as an amount for overheads is a matter of opinion. The terms 'allocation' and 'apportionment' are both methods of attributing overheads to cost units. Allocation is the assignment of a whole item of cost to a single cost unit, and apportionment is the spreading of costs over two or more cost units

Indirect costs are normally accumulated into cost centres. Cost centres are simply functions, locations or activities that act as collection points for costs. We saw this in Table 14.2, with Woodhouse using production and administration areas as distinct cost centres. Cost centres should mirror the organisation of responsibilities within the enterprise, enabling the costs to be monitored for control purposes and compared with the agreed budget. The cost so collected may then be charged to or recovered from products or services. Thus a share of the costs of a number of cost centres may be charged to cost units. The number and type of cost centres will vary from organisation to organisation, depending on factors such as complexity and size.

To illustrate this, we look again at Woodhouse Carpentry, but this time in the context of a more complicated example (Example 14.2).

Example 14.2 Woodhouse Carpentry (2)

Suppose that Woodhouse manufactures tables and chairs in two production departments within the workshop. Thus we have three cost centres (two production, one administration) and two cost units (tables and chairs). Both products share administration facilities. If the task is to work out the costs of both tables and chairs, this means:

- identifying costs that are directly chargeable to cost centres
- identifying overhead costs and finding a way of allocating or apportioning them to cost centres
- charging cost centre costs to the two different products (tables and chairs).

Woodhouse's cost centres in this case are:

- production cost centres
  - table department
  - chair department
- administration cost centre
  - administration section.

To work out the total cost per unit in any given period, we need to identify the costs that can be attributed to each cost centre. This can be achieved in four stages:

1 Certain costs can be identified as relating to a single cost centre. Where there is no dispute about this, they can be allocated as a whole to that cost centre. The direct costs (labour, materials) and some indirect costs (such as workshop cleaning, workshop equipment insurance, and glue) can be allocated in full to the two production cost centres. Some administration expenses, such as the administrator's wages, can be allocated to the administration cost centre. Allocation means that you can relate the expense to a particular cost centre without any further calculation.

2 There are total overhead costs that relate to all three cost centres and should be apportioned accordingly. The organisation's occupancy costs (the rent of the premises, lighting and heating, and so on) would need to be apportioned to each of the three cost centres. The following bases of apportionment are examples of the often somewhat arbitrary methods frequently employed.

Table 14.3 Apportionment of overheads

Overhead	Basis of apportionment
Rent	Area occupied by each cost centre (based on square metres or square feet)
Lighting	Area occupied by each cost centre or number of light fittings
Heating	Space (cubic capacity) occupied, or number of radiators

Other overhead costs incurred would need to be apportioned on bases considered appropriate.

1 The total production overheads often cannot be identified with any particular product and, as in the case of Woodhouse, must be apportioned to the production cost centres as equitably as possible. The basis of apportionment may not produce entirely accurate results, since the process of establishing costs is frequently a matter of judgement.

2 Finally, in order to achieve a cost per unit, the total costs so far allocated or apportioned to the administration cost centre must be reapportioned to the two products. Again, appropriate bases need to be selected and a wholly accurate and fair apportionment is unlikely to be possible.

The overall cost profile will change because the firm is now producing tables and chairs in one workshop. The relevant cost details are:

Table 14.4 Cost data

	£
Tables	
Table tops (each)	20
Four legs per table (each)	5
Wage costs per table assembled	20
Chairs	
Materials for each chair	25
Wage costs per chair assembled	10
Other workshop costs (per month)	
Supervisors' salaries	20,000
Glue for tables and chairs	2,000
Cleaning costs	2,000
Insurance on workshop equipment	1,000
Other organisation costs (per month)	
Rent	7,500
Lighting and heating	2,500
Administration costs (per month)	
Administrator	4,000
Phone, fax, post and sundries	1,000
Insurance on office equipment	1,000

As before, the direct costs are fairly easily identified: materials for the tables and chairs, and the wages that are paid for each table and chair assembled. It is the overheads that, again, present problems. To establish the costs we start by presenting the various costs as shown in Table 14.5. (The intended output is 1,000 tables and 1,000 chairs.)

Table 14.5 Cost allocation

	Costs		
	Tables (per unit)	Chairs (per unit)	Total for month
	£	£	£
Direct costs:			
Materials	40	25	
Labour	20	10	
Indirect costs/overheads:			
Glue (tables and chairs)			2,000
Rent (workshop/office)			7,500
Supervisors' salaries			20,000
Light and heat (workshop/office)			2,500
Administrator's wages			4,000
Cleaning (workshop)			2,000
Insurance (workshop/equipment)			1,000
Phone/sundries			1,000
Insurance (office equipment)			1,000

In Table 14.5 the direct costs per unit have been allocated to each product. All the other costs have been shown as monthly amounts for later apportionment to the appropriate cost centres.

Woodhouse now needs to deal with these overheads to determine how much each table and chair costs to make and thus how much profit each makes. Remember that it is not possible to work out one 'true' and definitive cost per chair and table, because there is more than one way of sharing overheads between departments and more than one way of absorbing the departmental overheads into the chair and table cost units.

Obviously, Woodhouse needs to find an appropriate way of absorbing the overhead costs into each chair and table. It might decide that the overhead costs should be apportioned evenly across the chairs and tables, but this might be inappropriate if more time is spent making tables than chairs. Then the company could have a system that ensured tables receive a higher charge for overheads than chairs. Different rationales used in attributing overheads can result in different reported costs being determined.

In Table 14.6 you can see one way in which overhead costs could be allocated or apportioned. Note that:

- the rent is apportioned on the basis of area, the workshop occupying 80% of the space and the office 20%, a ratio of 4:1
- lighting and heating is apportioned, as with rent, on the basis of area
- the administrator's wages, insurance on office equipment and phone/sundries do not need to be apportioned as they are all administration costs and are thus allocated directly to the office cost centre
- the glue, supervision, cleaning and insurance on workshop equipment are clearly related to the workshop and so do not need to be apportioned – they have been allocated.

Table 14.6 Apportioning and allocating overheads

	Basis	**Workshop**	**Office**	**Total**
		£	**£**	**£**
Glue	Allocated	2,000	–	2,000
Rent	Apportioned area 4:1	6,000	1,500	7,500
Supervisors' salaries	Allocated	20,000	–	20,000
Light and heat	Apportioned area 4:1	2,000	500	2,500
Administrator's wages	Allocated	–	4,000	4,000
Cleaning	Allocated	2,000	–	2,000
Insurance (workshop)	Allocated	1,000	–	1,000
Phone/sundries	Allocated	–	1,000	1,000
Insurance (office)	Allocated	–	1,000	1,000
		33,000	8,000	41,000

Now we can work out how a production overhead charge is calculated and applied to the tables and chairs as an overhead absorption/recovery rate per unit. There are a number of different ways of absorbing overheads, but we will concentrate on the rate per unit approach for now. It is worth noting, however, that applying different ways of absorbing overheads produce different reports of costs and thus different reported profits per chair or table.

A simple basis for calculating the overheads per unit would be to divide the production overheads from the workshop cost centre by the total number of units of production, as follows:

$$\frac{£33,000}{2,000 \text{ units of production}} = £16.50 \text{ per unit}$$

We can now add £16.50 to each chair and table to reflect the production overheads. The direct production costs have already been established and together with the charge for workshop costs provide the total production cost. We can see this in Table 14.7.

Table 14.7 Total production costs

	Tables			Chairs		
	Unit costs	Units	Total costs	Unit costs	Units	Total costs
	£		£	£		£
Materials:						
Table tops	20.00	1,000	20,000	–	–	–
Sets of four legs	20.00	1,000	20,000	–	–	–
Chair kits	–	–	–	25.00	1,000	25,000
Direct labour	20.00	1,000	20,000	10.00	1,000	10,000
Overheads	16.50	1,000	16,500	16.50	1,000	16,500
Total cost	76.50	–	76,500	51.50	–	51,500

Now this presents us with only the production cost per unit. If we want to establish the full cost per unit we need to calculate and add in a cost per unit for the office costs. From Table 14.3 we know that the office costs total £8,000; we also know that the numbers of chairs and tables to be produced total 2,000. So the office cost per unit is:

$$\frac{£8,000}{2,000 \text{ units of production}} = £4.00 \text{ per unit}$$

Adding this figure to our production cost per unit we can work out the total cost and then the profit, as in Table 14.8. The profit is calculated by deducting the total cost from the sales revenue. The sales price per table is £100 and per chair is £50.

Table 14.8 Total costs and profits

	Tables			Chairs			Company total
	Per unit	Units	Total	Per unit	Units	Total	
	£		£	£		£	£
Production costs	76.50	1,000	76,500	51.50	1,000	51,500	128,000
Office costs	4.00	1,000	4,000	4.00	1,000	4,000	8,000
Total costs	80.50		80,500	55.50		55,500	136,000
Sales price	100.00	1,000	100,000	50.00	1,000	50,000	150,000
Profit (loss)	19.50		19,500	(5.50)		(5,500)	14,000

In this example we have apportioned the overhead costs, absorbed them into the cost of each chair and table and worked out the profit or loss per unit as if there were no difference between the overhead costs relating to chairs and to tables. In apportioning we might have tried to reflect more closely the reality of the situation. We could have apportioned the overheads not just in relation to the number of units made, but by production time per table or chair, or by direct labour cost per unit, or by reference to anything else we felt was appropriate to reflect the usage of our resources in making tables and chairs.

This is an important point. Table 14.8 shows that tables are producing an apparently healthy monthly profit of £19,500 while chairs are making a loss of £5,500. Assuming that increasing the price of chairs is not an option because of competitors' prices, Woodhouse might be tempted to drop chair production, or at least spend valuable time trying to find out why it is losing money on it. This begs the question as to how overheads have been absorbed. Should the chairs have received a lower production overhead charge per unit and the tables a higher one? After all, the implication of the direct labour costs (£20 per table as opposed to £10 per chair) is that the tables take twice as long to make. If we were to charge overheads on that basis we might find that the relative amounts of reported profits/losses differ. Also, if we were to stop making either chairs or tables the remaining product would have to bear the whole burden of overhead costs.

Example 14.2 shows how important it is to think about the way in which the costs of outputs are worked out, and the danger of trying to make decisions using cost information in an uninformed way!

This applies just as much in public and not-for-profit services. Depending on how costs are apportioned, some services can appear more (or less) cost-effective than others. Significant decisions are taken on the basis of how the information appears, as illustrated in Example 14.3.

Example 14.3 Orchard House

Orchard House provided specialist accommodation, education and assessment services for young men who could not live at home. It ran a secure accommodation block for young offenders sentenced by the courts for whom prison was not appropriate and an open accommodation block for young men who were in the care of social services while suitable foster (temporary) families were identified. Orchard House received various capital and other grants from the government. Also, different departments of central and local government were recharged by Orchard House according to the services provided to them. The government needed more secure accommodation and Orchard House had to decide whether to build a third accommodation block or close its open accommodation service and turn it into a secure one.

The trustees were about to decide to do the latter because cost information appeared to show that Orchard House was losing money on its open accommodation service. This information apportioned general overhead costs on an equal basis, on the grounds that each block occupied a similar area and had a similar number of residents. Before the decision was finalised, figures were presented that showed the biggest overhead was the salaries of the general managers and educational psychologists. A study of their diaries revealed that two-thirds of their time was spent in dealing with issues and problems relating to the secure accommodation and its residents. Recalculating the information made it clear that the open accommodation more than covered its costs. Orchard House decided to seek capital funding for a third accommodation block.

A variety of different bases of apportioning costs are used in real life, often alongside each other within the same organisation. Accountants can sometimes choose a method that seems neat and logical to them, but as a manager, you may know whether the method is fair or absurd. Absorption costing is not a wrong approach just because there are different ways of apportioning indirect costs, but it does need to be used with care.

Absorption costing, if applied thoughtfully, may provide a convenient framework for calculating a full cost. This may be a helpful simplification of an extraordinarily complex real situation. Absorption costing provides a framework for ensuring all costs are covered appropriately, but it can be arbitrary, misleading and prone to problems when estimated costs differ from those actually incurred; however, more advanced cost determination methods have become available under the general description of activity based costing. The development of these methods has been assisted by the increased availability and capability of computer-based models.

Activity based costing

The principle underlying activity based costing is as follows: overhead costs are caused by various service and support activities that enable production to take place. A particular product's consumption of these activities does not necessarily depend on the amount of it produced (i.e. its volume). Accurate product costing requires ascertaining the cost of activities and then charging products according to their consumption of these activities. Although originally developed as a tool for ascertaining product (or service) costs, activity based costing has been increasingly employed to assist managers in assessing the profitability of different customers or business/market segments.

Activity based costing (ABC) is a different approach to the challenges of charging overhead costs to products and services. It attempts to charge overheads to costs on the basis of activity relationships. Costing systems tend to assume a simple relationship between resources used, costs and the outputs produced. ABC recognises that between cost inputs and the product or service outputs there is a series of activities or processes, and these produce costs. If the activities that give rise to costs – the cost drivers – can be identified, and if the amount of activity can be clearly related to the output products/services by way of activity drivers, the subsequent charge for overheads will be more soundly based, easily explained and controlled. Moreover, the analysis of activities allows them to be categorised into those that add value and are to be encouraged and those that do not add value and should be eliminated or reduced. Thus ABC is a more sophisticated form of absorption costing. There are financial and administrative implications in implementing such a costing method.

Example 14.4 An application of ABC

A factory produced fibre-tip pens on two machines. Its set-up and production cost details were as follows:

Table 14.9 Production data

	Machine A	Machine B
Production	1,000,000 pens	1,000,000 pens
Direct materials cost	£0.10 per pen	£0.10 per pen

There were fixed overheads of £1,000,000 for the factory as a whole.

Using the traditional absorption approach, the overhead absorption rate was £0.50 per pen (£1,000,000 ÷ total production of 2,000,000 pens).

However, Machine A's entire output was red pens, whereas Machine B's output comprised 200,000 green pens, 300,000 blue pens and 500,000 black pens. While the basic production process was common to both machines, the supporting activities differed. For example, there were more machine start-ups and stops for Machine B, taking time and thus costing money. There were more materials handling movements in and out of the warehouse relating to Machine B, again costing money. Rather than use the £0.50 per pen rate calculated earlier, it was more appropriate to charge warehousing costs to production costs by establishing and applying the number of materials-handling movements. With all the extra activity associated with Machine B's output, the overhead cost should have been higher than for Machine A's production. Under traditional absorption costing, high-volume runs (Machine A) were over-costed and low-volume runs (Machine B) under-costed, when the reverse should have applied. The company determined what percentages of the activity of a particular overhead cost centre were used by each of the two machines. It established a more reliable basis for charging overhead costs. To do this it needed information about activities.

Activity analysis

To undertake activity-based costing it is vital for managers to map their activities clearly. Accordingly, many organisations considering implementing ABC do an activity analysis, and then link the activities with the costs arising from them. The significance of such an analysis is captured below. If you worked in the purchasing section of an organisation, a typical cost statement (say, on a budget sheet) might look like Table 14.10. It indicates how much the annual budget is for the section and its composition.

Table 14.10 Cost statement

	€	€
Staff costs:		
Fred	30,000	
Maria	20,000	
Igor	15,000	
		65,000
Non-staff costs:		
Office costs	20,000	
Consumables	5,000	
Central management charge	10,000	
		35,000
		100,000

You now know it costs €100,000 a year to run the section. That is useful information, but only in a limited way. It only tells us about the resources used and nothing about the activities that cause those resources to be consumed. Nor does it say what is obtained – the outputs and outcomes – for the money spent.

One useful addition would be the number of purchase requisitions/orders processed. These are outputs resulting from the inputs of staff costs. These, and the outcomes that are expected to result from these outputs, can be incorporated into an activity cost analysis – see Table 14.11.

Table 14.11 Cost of activities

Inputs

	€	€
Staff costs:		
Fred	30,000	
Maria	20,000	
Igor	15,000	
		65,000
Non-staff costs:		
Office costs	20,000	
Consumables	5,000	
Central management charge	10,000	
		35,000
		100,000

Outputs/Activities

	% of time spent	€
Finding new suppliers	10	10,000
Negotiating with existing suppliers	40	40,000
Processing orders and requisitions	50	50,000
		100,000

The outputs and outcomes reflect the breakdown of the activities undertaken by staff in exchange for the resources devoted to the section. There are three major activities. The percentage of time spent by staff on each activity is shown. This would be discovered by asking staff to monitor their activities over a period of time. You can thus see that the time spent on finding new suppliers costs €10,000, negotiating with existing suppliers €40,000, and processing orders and so on €50,000. This gives a better picture of what happens to the resources used in this operation. It enables the purchasing section to establish whether €10,000-worth of time spent on finding new suppliers adds value of at least €10,000 to the organisation.

Activity based management

Activity based management is an extension of the activity based costing approach that tries to use an improved understanding of what causes costs in order to help manage costs. If you can find different and better ways of carrying out your activities, you may be able to reduce the costs of the inputs, and thus the cost of the outputs. You can also try to relate the value of outcomes to the cost of inputs, essential in any organisation and sector. An organisation can consider the activities in its value chain and assess if they are value added activities or non-value added activities. In theory an organisation should seek to eliminate or at least minimise its non-value added activities while performing its value added activities as efficiently as possible.

This can be illustrated by extending the purchasing section scenario described in Example 14.4. Assume that Maria processes the orders and requisitions. A closer examination of her work reveals that she spends only 50% of her time on straightforward, uncomplicated processing. The other 50% is spent on correcting forms filled in incorrectly, returning forms to originators for changes, and telephoning and emailing originators to resolve queries. Thus, of the €50,000 spent on processing, only 50%, €25,000, is spent on outputs and thus outcomes. It costs the organisation €25,000 to carry out the unproductive activity of redoing other people's work. If the others involved managed to 'get it right first time', think how much resource could be saved and/or released for other activities.

Limitations of activity based costing

The technicalities associated with designing and operating an ABC system can be numerous and difficult. These include the difficulty in practice of adequately identifying all the cost drivers and the rates to apply to them. The technique is complex and may be difficult for some staff to fully understand.

It is often said that the advantages of ABC lie in its intentions and its philosophy, and the disadvantages in the practicalities of really analysing what people do and what activities are worth. At the very least, an awareness of the principles of ABC should enable you to ask intelligent questions about the way costs are classified in your organisation.

Chapter 15 Financial decision-making

Identifying relevant costs and making financial decisions

Financial information can play an important role when making decisions in an organisation. The costs and benefits of a particular decision can be compared in financial terms in order to assess the financial viability of the decision. Those costs that relate to a specific course of action are termed the relevant costs.

In a rational decision-making approach, if the benefits of a decision outweigh the costs, then it is financially worthwhile. In making the decision the manager should consider the financial aspects. However, often when faced with a decision not all the factors can be expressed in financial terms. The decision should also take into account factors such as the ethical. environmental and corporate social responsibility aspects of the decision. The associated risk and strategic suitability in relation to organisational objectives may also need to be taken into account. Therefore the financial aspects as illustrated here should be viewed as decision support assisting the decision-making process. The eventual decision should be based on managerial judgement after weighing up all the relevant factors and not simply those that can be expressed in financial terms.

We start by meeting the ideas of relevant and non-relevant costs, opportunity costs and sunk costs and see how they affect our view of what we now understand by the term 'cost' when faced by a decision. We will then consider some of the limitations of financial information as the basis of decision-making.

Relevant and non-relevant costs

In terms of a particular decision some costs are defined as relevant or not relevant. The definition is dependent on the individual decision's ability to influence a particular cost. Costs that are going to be changed by a particular decision are considered relevant to it. If the decision at hand cannot influence a particular cost it is considered not relevant to that particular decision. It may be that a cost is relevant to one decision and not another, based on which decision is going to change the cost. We illustrate relevant costs in Example 15.1.

Example 15.1 Imelda's choice

Imelda is a junior marketing manager, dissatisfied at earning £50,000 a year in a large organisation. She is considering leaving and setting up as an independent market research consultant. She intends to use her home PC for her business. She currently pays £250 a year under a PC maintenance contract, and this would continue. Over the past three months she has paid £2,000 to a business advice bureau to undertake a feasibility survey for her. The survey report indicates that over the next three years the consultancy could earn about £200,000 in fees, incurring about £40,000 in direct expenses. The report also concludes that she would need to invest about £60,000 capital into the consultancy. Imelda has £60,000 earning 10% interest per annum in a special bank investment account. With reference to the calculations below consider whether or not it would be worthwhile for Imelda to proceed.

The obvious items are the £40,000 direct expenses and the likely fee income of £200,000. If that was all, she would have an initial profit of £160,000. Under the traditional cost/profit statement approach this profit would be further reduced by other expenses, producing the following (Table 15.1) for a three-year period:

Table 15.1 Imelda's choice (1)

	£	£
Income		200,000
less direct expenses	40,000	
PC contract (£250 x 3 years)	750	
Feasibility survey	2,000	
Total expenses		42,750
Reported profit		157,250

The consultancy business, if the forecasts are accurate, would be a profitable one, But is this the figure on which she should base her decision? For decision-making, as opposed to financial reporting, what Imelda needs is a relevant cost statement. This approach views costs from a different perspective: it considers all the cash flows affected by the decision, but *only* those affected by the decision. There is the interest on the £60,000 investment and her annual salary to take into account. If she embarked on the project she would lose the interest of £18,000 (£60,000 x 10% p.a. x 3 years). (This calculation assumes simple rather than compound interest, which would add the interest earned back into the capital to itself earn more interest.)

She would also forgo her salary, amounting to at least £150,000 (assuming no pay rises!) over three years. Such amounts 'forgone' should be taken into account as costs of going ahead with the decision. They are called opportunity costs and must be considered relevant to her decision. What about the £2,000 on the feasibility study? It has already been spent even if the project does not go ahead and so can be disregarded, since it does not depend on the decision to be taken. It is classed as a sunk cost – one that cannot be retrieved – and is therefore non-relevant. Another non-relevant cost is the PC maintenance charge, because she is already paying it anyway. The calculation below takes all this into account and shows that in cash terms she would be £8,000 worse off over the three years, so she should not proceed!

Table 15.2 Imelda's choice (2)

	£
Fees (additional cash inflows)	200,000
Less direct expenses (cash outflows)	(40,000)
	160,000
Less opportunity costs:	
Interest forgone (potential cash inflow forgone)	(18,000)
Salary forgone (potential cash inflow forgone)	(150,000)
Increase/(decrease) in incremental cash terms	(8,000)

Of course, Imelda may wish to reassess the accuracy of her forecasts. In addition, she may wish to take account of being her own boss and place a value on that. And what about the prospects and risks after three years?

You will note that the £60,000 capital is not included in Table 15.1 or Table 15.2. There are two reasons for this. First, each statement is looking at operational outcomes, not investment. Second, the investment of £60,000 is the same in both cases.

In making a decision, alternative courses of action must be compared with one another: the challenge is to decide which costs are relevant and which are not. Remember, a relevant cost is one that will be incurred only if the course of action in question is undertaken – in other words, it can be avoided by taking another course of action. Income lost as a result of the decision also counts as a cost, and opportunity costs – in terms of lost benefits from opportunities forgone by a particular action – are also relevant.

Non-relevant costs can be divided into two categories:

- costs that have already been incurred, known as sunk costs (for example, the feasibility study in Example 15.1)
- costs that will occur in future, but which will be the same no matter which course of action is taken (for example, the PC contract in Example 15.1).

The concepts of sunk costs and non-relevant costs are another aspect of marginal costing considered in Chapter 13. Only costs affected by the decision – that is, marginal costs of the decision – should be taken into account in making the decision. A relevant cost or revenue is one which, as a result of going ahead with a proposal, would represent:

- an additional cash inflow
- an additional cash outflow
- an existing cash inflow lost
- an existing cash outflow avoided.

This is a useful checklist when preparing relevant cost statements. If you look back over the monetary figures in Imelda's case to see whether they fit under any of these four headings, you will find that the only figures that do so are the ones appearing in the calculation that showed the £8,000 decrease in cash terms.

We now have a second scenario and an activity for you to work through before you try to apply these concepts to your own work. These activities are important to tackle fully in order to understand and apply these concepts.

Example 15.2 The Dream Machine

The Dream Machine is an entertainment business providing virtual reality experiences. A potential client has approached The Dream Machine, looking to place 17 people for a week's training event using the virtual reality facilities. The event would run for seven consecutive days. The client is prepared to pay €1,000 per participant. The Dream Machine's managers have calculated the following:

- The number of days' work by full-time, permanent staff on this project is estimated to occupy about 25% of the month's work of all company staff. Dream Machine's monthly payroll costs are €40,000. No work will be needed on the event beyond this month.

- Additional staff will be required. They will be employed on a temporary basis for the week and will earn a total of €5,000.

- Specific software costing €1,000 for the week will be required. The software will not be used for anything else. The Dream Machine will pay a special insurance premium of €1,000 for the week.

- The computer equipment used during the week will be used exclusively for the event. It was purchased three years ago at an original cost of €52,000 and has a remaining useful life of seven years, being depreciated on a straight-line basis (i.e. one-tenth of its cost is assumed to be 'used up' each year). At any point in time the equipment, being of a specialised nature, has a zero resale value: no-one else would pay anything for it.

- The Dream Machine absorbs its fixed overhead costs into its various activities. For this event, the managers have costed overheads at the rate of €10 per participant.

Compare for The Dream Machine:

- profit and loss account
- a relevant cost-based statement to support your view of whether The Dream Machine should proceed with the contract.

profit and loss account
Note that the profit and loss account will be introduced in greater detail later in the book. You do not need more detailed knowledge of the profit and loss account to understand this example.

Table 15.3 Profit/cost statement for The Dream Machine project

	€	€
Income		17,000
Less		
Existing staff	10,000	
Additional staff	5,000	
Special software	1,000	
Insurance	1,000	
Equipment depreciation (€52,000 ÷ 10 years ÷ 52 weeks)	100	
Overheads – 17 x €10	170	
		17,270
Net reported profit/(loss)		−270

Table 15.4 Relevant costs for the one-week event

	€
Income	17,000
Temporary staff	5,000
Software	1,000
Insurance	1,000
Total relevant costs	7,000
Excess of relevant revenues over relevant costs	10,000

This is how we determined which costs were relevant or not:

- Income for event. The sales price of €17,000 is a positive relevant revenue: it will only arise if the decision to proceed is taken. However, managers should question if the asking price of €1,000 per delegate really is enough for an event of this kind given the resources required.

- Existing staff and temporary additional staff. Future cash outflows will increase by €5,000 by employing temporary staff; it is thus relevant. The €10,000 existing staff cost is not relevant, assuming that it will be spent whether the event takes place or not.

- Special software and insurance costs. Both costs of €1,000 represent additional cash outflows and are thus relevant.

- Equipment. The original cost and the written-down value are sunk costs and therefore not relevant to the decision, nor is the depreciation charge (since it is not a cash flow).

- Overheads. There is no reference to any increases or savings. The overheads are still incurred by the company but are only being reallocated.

The organisation will be better off in the short term by €10,000 in cash terms if the contract is undertaken. On this basis, the contract should go ahead. However, other factors may affect the decision, such as the opportunity costs of other potential work the company could get. Also, the fact that it takes all our staff a whole week's effort for a relatively small return. Could they negotiate a more realistic price than €1,000 per delegate?

Limitations to financial evaluation based on relevant costs

The financial evaluation of a decision's acceptability may only give us a partial indication of which course of action to take. Not all aspects can be expressed in financial terms and therefore the financial aspect should be seen as decision support. Other factors in no particular order may include the following.

Corporate social responsibility

Managers should consider the organisation's responsibilities and commitment to all its stakeholders. The degree of corporate social responsibility shown by an organisation is the extent to which it is willing to be socially responsible beyond its legal obligations. Being seen to be socially responsible generates goodwill among customers and other stakeholders and such goodwill is often crucial for the long-term prospects of an organisation. While this is difficult to quantify in monetary terms, being seen as a socially responsible company can have very real financial benefits in the long term, apart from often being the right thing to do.

Sustainability/environmental considerations

In making a decision it may be appropriate to consider its sustainability/ environmental impact. In addition to cost involved in running an organisation in a sustainable way. There may be financial benefits from an 'environmentally friendly approach' in terms of aspects such as additional sales and cost saving related to using resources less wastefully. However, many aspects that may need be considered by a manager cannot be readily expressed in financial terms.

Time span

Decisions that are going to have long-term ramifications should use a more sophisticated approach to weighing the costs and benefits which takes into account the timings involved.

Organisational objectives

The financial contribution from a decision is expressed in terms of its contribution to profitability – not all organisations have profit as their *raison d'être*.

Risk

The risk associated with a decision should be considered. As the future is not known most decisions involve some degree of risk and uncertainty. Relevant cost calculations are only as accurate as our ability to forecast future outcomes.

Strategic fit

Consideration needs to be made as to how well a particular course of action fits the strategic direction of the organisation.

Ethical considerations

The ethical stance of the manager and the employing organisation can influence whether a decision is acceptable based on more than just financial terms.

Legal obligations

There may be legal or regulatory considerations that act to constrain decisions.

Management and technical ability

Does the organisation have the ability to successfully implement the decision?

Different types of decision using relevant costs

There are a number of different decision-making contexts under which relevant cost calculations may provide useful information to support decisions made by managers. Such decisions as: to consider the closure of part of an organisation, how to make best use of scarce resources and should an organisation outsource some of its operations? The relevant costs and benefits calculated may assist managers make such decisions; however, managers should also consider the wider non-financial factors as well.

Assessing the viability of an existing operation or activity

In the previous section we considered a decision about whether to do something new. In the case of an existing activity you may have to consider whether it should be discontinued. Again, we focus on the contribution made by the activity in question towards the general overheads of an organisation.

Example 15.3 Woodhouse Carpentry

Woodhouse Carpentry produces tables, beds and chairs. It has prepared the operating statement in Table 15.5.

Table 15.5 Woodhouse Carpentry (1)

	Tables	Chairs	Beds	Total
	£'000	£'000	£'000	£'000
Sales	500	300	200	1,000
Variable costs	200	180	120	500
Contribution	300	120	80	500
Fixed costs:				
Salaries	60	40	50	150
Advertising and marketing	12	8	10	30
General administration	68	37	25	130
Rent, light and heat	30	25	15	70
Total	170	110	100	380
Net profit/(loss)	130	10	(20)	120

Table 15.5 might suggest that Woodhouse should stop making beds. Would you agree with such a viewpoint?

The best answer is that it depends on which of the fixed costs are clearly associated with each activity area and which are shared. It is likely that some fixed costs could be avoided by stopping bed production. If the total of fixed costs saved is greater than the contribution of £80,000 that would be lost by this course of action, then the company should cease this activity. Otherwise it should not.

We now build on this idea, using the additional information below.

- All bed production-related salaries (£50,000) will be eliminated if the line is dropped, as will all bed production-related advertising and marketing costs.

- The total of general administrative costs, currently £130,000, will only be reduced by £5,000 if bed production is discontinued. As most general administration costs were merely allocated, they would now have to be borne by the remaining products.

- Rent, light and heat will be reduced by only £5,000 if bed production is dropped. Rent is on a long-term basis and is payable on the property as a whole; the saving is on lighting and heating costs.

The calculation relating to continuing bed production becomes, therefore:

Table 15.6 Woodhouse Carpentry (2)

	£	£
Contribution currently generated		80,000
Costs saved:		
Salaries	50,000	
Advertising and marketing	10,000	
General administration	5,000	
Rent, light and heat	5,000	
		70,000
If bed production were closed down, the business would be worse off by		10,000

It is assumed in the Woodhouse example that the financial contribution is central to the decision on viability. There are clearly other, non-financial, factors involved in any decision to curtail activities. For example, dropping one product or service line may have an effect elsewhere; customers may transfer their allegiance to other suppliers that can provide a wider range of products or services; the effect on internal staff relations may be a significant factor in the decision. Closing may also not be the only option available to us if it is possible to improve returns from parts of the business by, for example, new product development, automation or marketing. This is explored in Example 15.4.

Example 15.4 Mattem Bookshop

Mattem Bookshop has had disappointing results for some time now from its Travel section, which sells maps, guides and holiday books. The Mattem management team wishes to assess the section's viability.

The operating statements for the firm's three departments are as follows in Table 15.7.

Table 15.7 Mattem Bookshop (1)

	Fiction	Non-fiction	Travel	Total
	$	$	$	$
Sales	250,000	150,000	100,000	500,000
Cost of sales (variable)	150,000	80,000	70,000	300,000
Gross profit	100,000	70,000	30,000	200,000
Overhead costs:				
Salaries	30,000	30,000	20,000	80,000
Rent	15,000	6,000	9,000	30,000
Heat/light	10,000	4,000	6,000	20,000
Depreciation	3,000	1,000	1,000	5,000
Insurance	3,000	1,000	1,000	5,000
General expenses	15,000	9,000	6,000	30,000
Total overheads	76,000	51,000	43,000	170,000
Net profit/(loss)	24,000	19,000	(13,000)	30,000

Other information:

- if the section closed, 50% of the salaries relating to Travel could be eliminated
- the rent is payable on the entire building; there will be no rent savings if the Travel section is closed down
- if Travel is closed the heating and lighting costs will reduce by $5,000
- the bookshelves and equipment used in Travel could be transferred and used elsewhere in the store; thus there would be no reduction in depreciation
- insurance would still cost $1,000 even if the Travel section were closed down
- only a 10% reduction in the total of $30,000 costs for general expenses (purchasing, warehousing, accounting, office services) would be made if Travel closed
- there is the possibility of sub-letting the space of the Travel section at an annual rent of $20,000 (the new tenant would pay any heating and lighting costs).

In order to assess what Mattem's bookshop should do we can start by offsetting the savings resulting from closure, and the potential for new income, against the current contribution, something along the lines shown in Table 15.8.

Table 15.8 Mattem Bookshop (2)

	$	$
Lost contribution from closure (gross profit)		−30,000
Costs saved:		
Salaries	10,000	
Heat and light	5,000	
General expenses	3,000	
Total expenses saved		18,000
Lost contribution		−12,000
Income from sub-letting		20,000
Overall net gain from closing section		8,000

On this basis, Mattem Bookshop would benefit from closing the Travel section. Of course, there will be further information the management team should gather and consider before making a decision. The team might like to consider the indirect impact of not having a Travel section. Some existing Travel section customers may also be buying books from other sections. The team might investigate a variety of statistical data, such as the value of purchase per customer, the number of visitors who purchase and the number of visitors who browse.

Utilising scarce resources

Every organisation is in a situation where some of its resources are limited and it may not be able to undertake all the activities it would like to. Important managerial decisions have to be made about the use of resources to ensure that they are put to the best use. The key factor in such decisions is the scarcity of the particular resource concerned. This applies across the private, public and not-for-profit sectors.

Resources may be limited: there may be a limit to skilled staff, a limit to space, a limit to available cash. The decision as to which service to provide must take any such resource constraints into account. The underlying principle in such decisions is that when any resource is scarce, managers should maximise the contribution from using that scarce resource.

Example 15.5 Limited staff

A not-for-profit organisation provided care-related services for elderly people under a contract with a local government department. In Centre A, more intensive care was needed, so twice as many hours of staff time were needed for every elderly person looked after as at another centre, Centre B. However, variable costs in caring for elderly people (food, transport, etc.) were higher in Centre B. The care organisation had great difficulty in recruiting and retaining skilled staff to work in the centres. Therefore, even though the 'contribution' towards the organisation's fixed costs was greater in Centre A, the scarcity of staff resources meant that it wanted to develop Centre B's capacity rather than Centre A's.

Outsourcing decisions

Another decision managers often face is the choice between an in-house activity and an external contract. Should a service be bought in or provided in-house? Should a component be manufactured internally or purchased from an external supplier? As with any other decision there will be non-financial factors to consider, but the financial figures are likely to be an important aspect of any decision. Example 15.6 illustrates this.

Example 15.6 To contract in or out?

Overshire Council (a local government authority) had its own printing section, staffed by local authority employees on temporary contracts, printing Council leaflets, notices, posters and stationery. Normally the section printed 10,000 items in any one accounting period. These had been costed on a 'per item print run' basis as shown in Table 15.9.

Table 15.9 Contracting in or out

	£
Variable costs (paper and ink)	8.00
Depreciation of print machine	3.00
Administration cost charge	6.00
Salary costs	3.00
Total	20.00

The Council, keen to obtain better value for money, sought estimates from an independent print business that could provide the same print service but at a cost of £15 per item print run, an apparent saving of £5. The Council was of the opinion that the printing equipment could not really be sold, but print staff could be released from their contracts to obtain work elsewhere. No administration costs would be saved if the service went outside.

What do you think the Council should do about its print service? At first glance it looks as though the Council would save £5 per unit by buying in. We need, however, to return to the ideas of relevant and non-relevant costs. In this case, the depreciation of £3 can be treated as a sunk cost because the plant had been purchased and would continue to exist (unless a resale value could be obtained, which the Council believed was not possible). The administration costs would remain even if the materials were bought from outside. The salary costs were avoidable, since it was possible for the employees' contracts not to be renewed. So only the variable costs (£8 per print run) and the salary costs (£3 per print run) would be avoided if the print service were bought in. In relevant costs terms, it would cost the Council £11 per item print run to continue printing in-house, £4 less than to buy the service in at £15.

However, we might also consider the opportunity cost of the print section. In our calculation the assumption has been made that, if print services were outsourced, the equipment that had been used previously would be unusable and would have no value. The Council funded a local consortium of voluntary and community organisations which needed items to be printed regularly. Although the Council could not sell the equipment to the consortium, if it gave it to them there could be (a) a political gain in helping voluntary and community organisations achieve their objectives and (b) a potential financial gain in not needing to subsidise the consortium's annual printing costs to the same extent in future. These factors would need to be brought into the decision.

In the private sector, such decisions are often referred to as 'make or buy' decisions. In addition to the actual costs involved, businesses need to weigh up any 'transactional' costs of dealing with different external suppliers, and any costs that are perceived to result from being distracted from the core services or products of the business. There are also other issues concerning the long-term ramifications of any decision, such as the loss of capability and flexibility, and the dependence on the supplier and a loss of employment for the organisation's staff.

Cost information in pricing decisions

Although some organisations do not have much freedom or flexibility in how they price their services because of regulatory or market constraints, many organisations do have to decide an appropriate price for their products or services. This applies to the internal pricing of services between departments within an organisation as well. Pricing decisions are important to an organisation's image, profitability and survival. If prices are too low, an organisation can struggle to survive; if they are too high, customers may not be willing to pay.

Cost is obviously a major factor in price determination, although it is by no means the only one. Cost tends to provide the starting point for pricing decisions. Even when prices are determined with reference to strategy rather than cost the viability of such strategies may need to be considered in relation to costs.

Sometimes organisations have little pricing discretion. Market competition or government funding decisions may set 'the price' and it is up to organisations to make their costs lower than the price. Whether there is much pricing discretion or not, most organisations charge prices with the intention of recovering costs. They may want just to ensure that all costs, direct and indirect, are covered, or they may want to cover them and make large profits as well. Whatever the objective, some knowledge of the underlying cost structure of the products or services provided is essential.

Cost-plus and rate of return pricing

A simple approach to pricing is cost-plus pricing, likely to be based on absorption costing. The total unit cost of a product or service at the organisation's normal capacity level is calculated and a percentage 'mark-up' added. The size of the mark-up is calculated on the basis of what seems a reasonable and sustainable profit margin. Thus a company might decide that a product costs £5 to produce, has a £5 share of indirect costs, and should have a 20% mark-up in order to generate profits: £5 + £5 + £2 = £12 selling price (£10 plus 20% mark-up).

Cost-plus pricing may not be considered to be a very satisfactory method of pricing from the buyer's point of view because it allows the selling organisation to recover all its costs whether or not its operations are efficient or cost-effective. Even so, it can be used in cases where there is no available market price and where the buyer feels obliged to acquire supplies from a preferred supplier, as is sometimes the case with government contracts for specialised or secret equipment or research.

A more sensitive variant of this is rate of return pricing, in which an organisation sets a desired 'rate of return' on its investment in a product or service and calculates the mark-up on cost to achieve this figure. The rate of return is a term which means the percentage surplus an investment makes. Interest earned from bank accounts is a percentage rate of return. If investments in new systems lead to an increase in profits worth 5% of the investment (or, in a not-for-profit organisation, to a saving in other costs worth 5% of the investment) this is called a 5% rate of return. The basic formula for calculating rate of return pricing is:

$$\text{Percentage mark-up} = \frac{\text{Resources employed} \times \text{required rate of return}}{\text{Unit of output cost} \times \text{sales volume}}$$

An illustration of this formula in practice is shown in Example 15.7.

Example 15.7 The Onyer Bike Company (1)

The Onyer Bike Company decided to introduce new production facilities for making a new bicycle, the Speedline, and invested £1,000,000 on new capital equipment and working capital. Sales of the Speedline were expected to reach 5,000 per year. The cost per unit of producing this bicycle was £120, using absorption costing. The company required a rate of return of 15% on its investment.

The percentage mark-up was calculated as:

$$\frac{\text{Resources employed} \times \text{required rate of return}}{\text{Unit of output cost} \times \text{sales volume}}$$

$$\frac{£1,000,000 \times 15\%}{£120 \times 5,000} \times 100 = 25\%$$

The selling price to the retail trade for the Speedline was calculated as shown in Table 15.10.

Table 15.10 Onyer Bike Company (1)

	£
Total cost of unit	120
Mark-up at 25%	30
	150

Alternatively, this can be presented as follows:

	£
Sales (5,000 units @ £150)	750,000
less	
Cost of goods (5,000 @ £120)	(600,000)
Net profit	150,000

The required percentage return on investment was 15%, and the profit of £150,000 is a return of 15% on the investment of £1,000,000.

The most significant assumption about the price calculation in the above example, which uses an absorption cost, is that it relates to a particular level of activity and sales. If activity and sales go up, the rate of return increases and so does the profit. Conversely, in a period of low activity, the rate of return and profit go down.

Rate of return pricing has the important advantage of aiming at a planned rate of return on capital employed. It is particularly appropriate when there is not a competitive market to dictate the prices that can be charged. Like any system of cost-plus pricing, however, it also has a number of disadvantages:

- it assumes that prices are simply a function of costs (i.e. that prices are based solely on costs)
- it does not take account of demand
- it is difficult to determine the total cost to apportion, and how to apportion it
- it may include past costs, or fixed costs, that are not relevant
- it does not provide information that aids decision-making in a rapidly changing market environment
- there is little incentive to be efficient in controlling costs.

Moreover, use of this system may lead to the rejection of profitable business. The total unit cost will tend to be regarded as the lowest possible selling price. An order from a customer at a price that is less than the total unit cost may be refused, even though this order may actually be profitable, as in Example 15.8.

Example 15.8 The Onyer Bike Company (2)

The company has been invited to supply a special export order of 200 units of another model, the Speedwheel, at £120 each, when there were already orders for 800 a year of this model, selling to retailers at £170 each. Overheads had already been fully recovered at 800 units. Domestic retailers would not want the extra 200 bikes that could be made. No extra indirect overheads would be incurred. Before receiving the enquiry the company used absorption costing to arrive at the cost of each of the 800 bicycles being produced, as follows:

direct cost per unit £80

overheads per unit £60

total cost per unit £140

The company was tempted to reject this order. After all, why sell bicycles for £120 when they cost £140 to make?

However, obtaining the business for the 200 extra bicycles meant that there was no need to include any element in the selling price for the overheads, because these had already been recovered by the existing sales of the other 800 bicycles. Looked at from a *contribution costing* point of view, the calculation was:

Table 15.11 Onyer Bike Company (2)

	£ per unit	£ per 200
Selling price	120	24,000
Variable costs	80	16,000
Contribution	40	8,000

So the company could actually make additional contribution to profitability by accepting the special order.

The contribution costing approach to pricing enables managers to ask: 'What will happen to our profits if we increase or decrease the prices of particular products?' The approach can thus be used to examine the way in which:

- costs change as output changes
- changes in promotional costs and the level of sales affect profit
- raising or lowering a price affects sales and profit
- the sales mix relates to profit.

Marginal costing is sometimes useful for short-term pricing decisions and when spare capacity is available. It simplifies the decision-making process and is relevant in multi-product organisations where the absorption of fixed costs into individual product or service costs is regarded as arbitrary or unreliable.

Example 15.9 A scenic journey

Steam Stoker Railway has the capacity to provide 150,000 passenger journeys (PJs) a year on its scenic railway line, but is currently providing only 130,000, selling at £40 per journey. At 130,000 PJs a year the costs are as shown in Table 15.12.

Table 15.12 Steam Stoker Railway (1)

	£ per unit
Direct costs (all variable)	28
Fixed overheads	6
Total costs	34

Steam Stoker Railway is considering an offer for an additional 10,000 PJs at £33. Variable selling and administration costs on these passengers would be £2 per PJ. The Railway has rejected the order, calculating (using absorption costing) that they will make a loss of £3 per PJ (£33 − (£34 + £2)).

But have they made the right decision?

Using a contribution costing approach, the railway would receive a contribution of £3 per PJ, as shown in Table 15.13:

Table 15.13 Steam Stoker Railway (2)

	£ per PJ
Selling price	33
Variable costs:	
Direct	28
Selling and administration	2
Total variable costs	30
Contribution	3 x 10,000 PJs = £30,000

The special order for 10,000 PJs will increase profits by £30,000 and should not be rejected on the basis of its impact on those profits under absorption costing. As fixed costs are already covered and this proposal accrues no extra fixed costs, all its contribution will be profit.

Example 15.9 shows how marginal costing can be used to resolve decisions on pricing. It is dangerous to base price decisions on marginal cost, however, except in specific circumstances. Marginal costing should only be used for pricing purposes in exceptional cases to gain marginal business; there is a danger of setting a precedent that the customer will expect to be repeated and which other customers will expect to benefit from. If all products or services were priced at marginal cost rates, an organisation would make losses, as they would not cover their fixed costs and may soon go out of business. Marginal costing may be used by manufacturers to help justify the supply of cheap 'own brand' goods to a retailer, or by airlines or hotels to sell rooms/flights at reduced rates to try to fill spare capacity.

Other approaches to pricing

As well as cost considerations, prices may be set with reference to the market. There may be a link to the marketing strategy being followed by the firm, such as market penetration and market skimming. For example, a low-cost airline adopting a low-cost strategy would set its prices accordingly. It would then need to find ways to reduce its operating costs in order to make the low-cost strategy viable.

Target costing takes the opposite approach to cost-plus pricing, as it starts by determining the market price and then deducts a profit margin to get to the so-called target cost. This is compared to an estimated cost of producing the good or service. If this estimated cost is greater than the target cost, then ways need to be found to reduce costs such that the target cost and margin can be achieved.

Some organisations are not in a position to determine their prices. These may be determined by market rates for commodity items such as oil and agricultural produce. Other organisations may have their prices set or regulated by government or its agencies. These organisations will need to make sure they are efficient enough to operate with costs below these revenues.

Chapter 16 Financial statements – the income statement and balance sheet

Inputs, transformation and outputs

A common way of picturing an organisation is as a transformation process. The money pays for the resources – the inputs – that it uses. Through its managers, it is concerned with using these inputs for generating outputs. This is a useful framework for relating organisational processes to financial frameworks. Look at Table 16.1. It shows a range of organisations and examples of their outputs. You and your colleagues may or may not be directly concerned with generating such outputs. However, there will be some outputs, or results, from your work.

Table 16.1 A range of organisations and typical outputs

Retailers	Voluntary organisations	Public sector organisations	Manufacturing concerns	Service providers
Items sold	Counselling sessions run	Tenants housed	Engines made	Passengers flown
Customers served	Flood victims fed	College students enrolled	Furniture parts sold on	Buildings designed
Shelves filled	Outpatients transported	Visits made by midwives	Soup canned	Phone calls connected

Generating outputs requires inputs: resources such as time, equipment, offices, information technology and materials are consumed in the process. This transformation of inputs into outputs is at the heart of organisational and managerial activity. It is outlined in Figure 16.1.

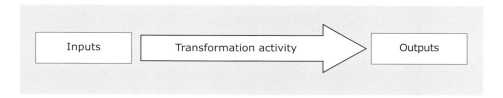

Figure 16.1 The basic transformation process

However, we expect many of the outputs will be variants of those listed in Table 16.1, and that many of the inputs will be variants of the following:

- people: paid and/or voluntary staff, and their time, know-how, skills and expertise
- materials: the various things that are used in the process of generating outputs; these can be raw materials that are processed into products, or consumables used in carrying out the transformation process

- equipment: the machinery, information technology, furniture, buildings, vehicles and other equipment that you need
- money.

Accountants spend a lot of time simply categorising inputs into different groups. There are conventions about what should be in each group and how they are presented in financial information, and procedures for ensuring accuracy and consistency in putting figures against each of the inputs and the groups they belong to. Most of these groupings of inputs have some compelling logic, but always remember that the resulting financial information reveals choices that have been made in order to try to present reality in a picture.

Some inputs, such as money and materials, are used up in the transformation process. These are tangible – we can count how much has been used and how much it cost. Others, such as people's knowledge and skills and systems, remain to work on the process again and again – these are intangible. Within the tangible inputs are the simple short-term ones – pieces of paper used, train and taxi fares paid, raw materials consumed in the transformation process. Then there are the more complicated long-term ones – the lorry, computer or building which are bought to be used repeatedly, but which gradually wear out or become obsolete.

In financial terms, the inputs that organisations need to generate outputs are called *assets*. As shown in Figure 16.2, they are grouped into:

- tangible assets
- intangible assets.

Figure 16.2 Groupings of inputs

Tangible assets are the resources you can see and touch. They can be divided into:

- day-to-day (short-lived) assets, such as the stocks of day-to-day materials that organisations use
- fixed (long-lived) assets, such as their land, buildings and computers.

The intangible assets are the ones you cannot see or touch, such as people's know-how, skills and expertise. It can be difficult to attach values to them, so many organisations avoid doing so. Other examples of intangible assets are reputation, brands, ideas, experience and relationships with suppliers, subcontractors and distributors.

In the light of Figure 16.2 we can adapt the picture of the transformation of inputs into outputs, as shown in Figure 16.3.

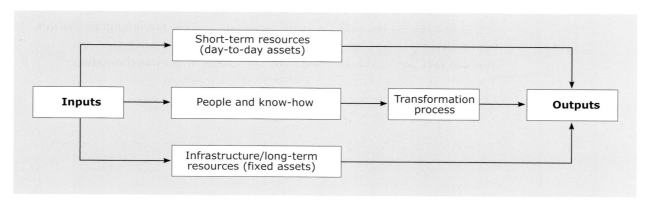

Figure 16.3 The transformation process with different types of input

This simple model applies to the work of most managers in any sector. However, when we discussed sources of organisational finance earlier, we found that the outputs of commercial and public and not-for-profit organisations serve very different purposes. In commercial organisations, outputs directly or indirectly generate sales revenue, which in turn provides profits for their owners (their shareholders, who often receive dividends from such profits) and the money to pay for more inputs to generate more outputs, sales revenue and profits. Thus a commercial organisation aims to make money both for those who have invested in its assets – its providers of capital – and for itself, so it can fund more of its future assets itself. Although commercial organisations also raise capital from other sources, you can view their inputs–outputs conversion process as a self-sustaining cycle, as in Figure 16.4(a). This cycle can also apply to those public and not-for-profit organisations that generate significant trading income. However, most public and not-for-profit organisations are budget-financed, that is financed by periodic injections of funds, usually from local or central government or other grant-awarding bodies. Parts of other organisations also generate no sales revenue and are financed by funds from elsewhere in the organisation; these can also be described as budget-financed. Their inputs–outputs conversion process can be viewed as a different cycle, as in Figure 16.4(b).

Note that these diagrams highlight some of the weaknesses of the inputs–outputs model: whereas the self-sustaining commercial organisation is attempting to increase the value of its capital, the budget-financed

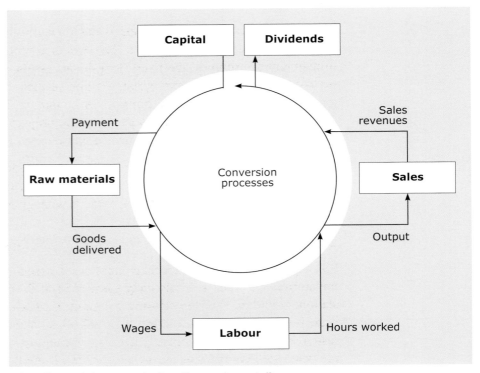

(a) Self-sustaining organisation (i.e. commercial)

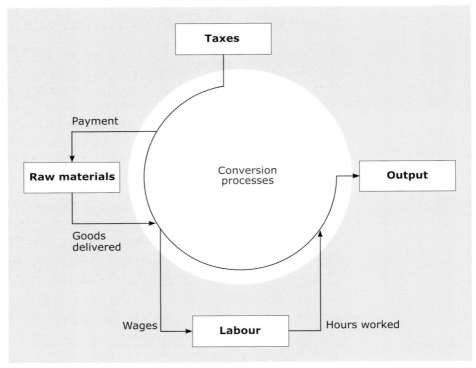

(b) Budget-financed organisation (e.g. public sector)

Figure 16.4 Resource flows in self-sustaining and budget-financed organisations

(Source: based on Rutherford, 1983, pp. 12–13.)

organisation may not be, often seeking to recover costs and break even. Thus, when we come to measure the financial results of the conversion process, reporting what has happened to capital will be important to commercial organisations and to those charities with significant capital investments, but budget-financed organisations will primarily be interested in their achievements and expenditure against budget.

Not all resources will be consumed at once. Day-to-day assets – the short-term resources – are likely to be consumed within a year. But the infrastructure resources, the fixed (long-lived) assets, will be consumed over, perhaps, many years, an appropriate portion of their costs being charged in any one year. After all, if the furniture or equipment in a building has a useful life of ten years, it seems sensible that only one-tenth of it is recognised as having been consumed in any one year.

One challenge is to understand the inputs–outputs transformation process where you work. Another is to understand the ways in which accountants attach money values to the various boxes in your process diagram.

Attaching monetary values to day-to-day assets

Placing a monetary value on those day-to-day assets consumed in the transformation process is relatively easy. If $100 is spent in a year on stationery and 50% of the stationery bought has been consumed during that year, it seems sensible to record that 50% of the amount paid for those resources has been consumed. Thus, in working out the cost of outputs in the year, $50 would be added to the short-term inputs costs. Given that there will be copies of the invoices for the stocks purchased, you will know with some degree of certainty that for stationery stocks consumed, $50 being counted towards the cost of the outputs is accurate.

Similarly, if you know exactly how much was paid for electricity or vehicle fuel during specific periods and what percentages were consumed during those periods, you can calculate the cost of electricity actually used in generating outputs. Such figures, when included in financial statements, will be broadly true, although in calculating what percentage of the electricity that was paid for in, say, year X was actually used, you may decide that a reasonable estimate based on past consumption patterns is as accurate as you can be.

However, you may not be able to be as certain when determining the cost of the long-term resources consumed. This may require a judgement, sometimes a best guess, resulting in some figures that will be 'fair' (based on a fair judgement) rather than 'true'. Thus all financial statements, be they internal or external, will comprise both true and fair figures.

Attaching monetary numbers to fixed (non-current) assets

For convenience, we will use the term 'fixed assets' to refer to all long-lived and infrastructure resources. When determining the cost of outputs, we must ensure that a certain portion of the fixed assets is recorded as having been consumed. We said earlier that if equipment has a useful life of ten years, it seems sensible that 10% of its cost is recognised as having been consumed in one year. Accountants call this charging of the cost of a long-lived asset depreciation. Thus if building and equipment resources cost £1,000,000, their 'consumed cost' in this period will be £100,000 (10% of £1,000,000).

However, this is only the case if it is fair to say that the resources will last ten years and that their value will be used up evenly over the ten years. If the equipment were vehicles with, say, a useful life of four years, it would seem fair to record that 25% of the vehicle cost (i.e. the vehicle resource) is consumed when calculating the cost of outputs in each of the four years. For some fixed assets, vehicles in particular, it may not be appropriate to apply this linear, 'equal portions' approach to determining the annual resource consumption charge. For them it may be appropriate to base the charge on a pattern that reflects much higher decreases in the earlier years of useful life, and lower decreases in later years: say 40% in the first year, 30% in the second, 20% in the third, and the balance of 10% in the fourth and final year.

Indeed, a number of other patterns of charging may be appropriate. If a vehicle with a four-year useful life cost €20,000, when determining the cost of outputs for Year 1 the vehicle resource consumed (the depreciation charge) could be recorded as:

If 25% is used

€20,000 × 25% = €5,000

Or if 40% is used

€20,000 × 40% = €8,000

Neither figure is necessarily wrong – they are just based on different assumptions, both of which could be said to be fair.

At times it might be inappropriate to depreciate some assets such as land and buildings. In these cases a fair value (or independent market value) may be appropriate.

The role of judgement in financial information

So, while the cost of day-to-day resources consumed can very often be determined with ease and reasonable accuracy, determining the cost of the fixed assets consumed requires further calculation and a degree of judgement. You are becoming acquainted with the notion that financial information is only as accurate as it needs to be, or as it is practical to be, for its purpose. Formal public financial statements have to conform to national and international accounting standards of what constitutes truth and fairness in the ways that accountants check, calculate and present figures, whether in private, public or voluntary sector organisations.

Although the figures that flow around within organisations come in all sorts of formats and degrees of accuracy, they obviously need to correlate with the figures in their published accounts. The internal figures that state how much money there is left in a particular budget at any one time are putting monetary values on the same inputs and outputs that the organisation's formal financial statements are concerned with. Both sets of figures require judgements and guesses to be made, informed by what seems a reasonable, fair and consistent way of attaching specific monetary values to the inputs and outputs in their transformation processes. Many of the methods that accountants use to attach monetary values in formal accounting statements apply to the figures you may see in internal reports and data.

So while the figures in some financial information are completely accurate, others are fair calculations, as Example 16.1 illustrates.

Example 16.1 Lunch at the launch

A telecommunications company launched a new package targeted at small to medium-sized businesses offering particular combinations of fixed and mobile services, call time and support services that the company believed offered flexibility, simplicity and economy. The company held a lunch for people who had worked on the launch and for media contacts. A consultant who had worked on the design of publicity material for the new service package attended the lunch. She asked a company manager how much this launch had cost. In the noise of the occasion, the manager thought the consultant had said 'lunch' and he told her that the outside caterers charged £5,000. No more, no less.

When it transpired that the consultant was asking about the *launch*, the manager answered that if the company:

- did not count staff time spent thinking about, planning and discussing new service options before the year when the launch was actually decided on

- did not yet count the investments in new billing equipment and staff training that should really be spread over the next three years during which the company was planning to offer the service

- did not count half his team's costs over the last year, because they had also been working on other projects

... then it was probably in the order of £5m. But if we counted ...

Without our getting into the details of what should have been counted or not, you can see that if a method of attaching a monetary value is widely recognised, and can be checked, it can be said to be both true and fair. However, depending on the calculation, estimates of resources consumed are precisely that, only estimates. Adding the reasonably accurate cost of day-to-day resources consumed to the less accurate cost of fixed assets consumed gives a cost of outputs, but not the cost. This is important: accountants never establish the cost, only a cost, the result of judgement and assumptions. And they do this by making many assumptions about cost behaviour and the rate of consumption of fixed assets, expressed by particular conventions.

This will affect you if your performance is partly judged by the cost of outputs, or if you have to make decisions involving the cost of outputs. In a commercial activity, a consequence might be that after cost is compared with sales income, a manager is uncertain whether money has been made or lost. In not-for-profit organisations, managers may be uncertain whether or not costs are being controlled and budgets adhered to. For managers who are urged to manage their costs, understanding the general conventions underlying how values are attached to inputs, their transformation and outputs is both revealing and useful.

Attaching money values

With this important proviso – that all financial pictures are based on the methods used to present reasonably true and fair depictions of reality – we now return to trying to attach some monetary values to the picture of the processes you are involved in. The challenge is to know what inputs and outputs to include and then to assign appropriate values to them. Figure 16.5 shows where we have reached in this, and adds some important features. Because it is difficult to attach monetary values to people and know-how, all we can do is put in how much it costs to employ them. We thus include this in the short-term inputs costs. Note that we have added some information from preceding figures about where, in different sectors, the money for inputs comes from. Note, too, the 'non-traded' item (for example a public service such as education), which refers to outputs that are not sold for cash, but the cost of which, especially in the public sector, needs to be known to assess value for money and future spending priorities, and to provide accountability for the expenditure of public resources.

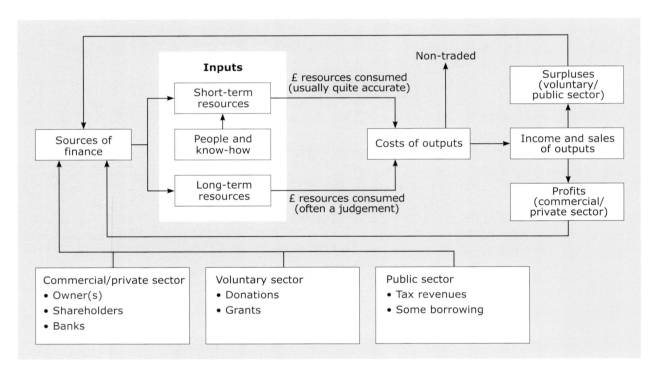

Figure 16.5 Expanding the inputs to outputs model

If everything were paid for in cash, you could assign the relevant cash values to each stage of the process. If you are really lucky, the cash flow may occur when the activity or transaction does. Unfortunately, in organisational life not all transactions and activities are undertaken on a cash basis, and very few are paid for at the same time that they are consumed. There are often time delays, for instance when cash is spent on a resource well before it is consumed (as in the case of fixed assets). Or sometimes an activity or transaction occurs at one time, but the associated cash flow takes place later. The stationery we discussed earlier could be ordered one week, received the next, half used (or consumed) the following week and paid for the following week; the remaining half could be used the week after that. It could be consumed and paid for in countless other ways.

Because of these delays, methods of attaching monetary values to inputs and outputs have been developed to complement the more straightforward cash approach. Example 16.2 illustrates this:

Example 16.2

Imagine you are a trader. On Monday you buy a table for €50 cash at an auction. On Friday you sell it for €100 to a customer who takes it away then. You give your customer an invoice for €100 which they agree to pay you in one month's time. What do you think will, on Friday, be:

- the immediate effect on your cash?

- the profit or surplus calculated using accounting methods?

The impact on your cash can be calculated relatively easily:

Impact on cash	€
Cash in (receipts)	–
Cash out	–50
Cash decrease as a result of the activities	–50

In order to assess the profit/surplus we should include the sale 'on account'. The rationale for this is that the values of activities and transactions should be shown on a financial statement whether or not the associated cash flow takes place at the same time, took place before or will not take place for some time. It looks like this:

Profit/surplus calculation	€
Value of sale (i.e. the output)	100
Cost value of item sold (i.e. the input)	–50
Profit or surplus	50

Of course, this profit assumes that the customer will pay eventually!

This kind of value statement is produced in all kinds of organisation, following the same principles. It is known as:

- in most commercial business, the profit or income statement (the profit and loss or P&L account)

- in many voluntary sector organisations, the statement of financial activities or income and expenditure account

- in many public sector organisations, the income and expenditure account or revenue account.

In this kind of value statement, the cost of any outputs is matched against any income – value received or to be received – for those specific outputs. This statement thus reflects what is known as the matching principle. This is another convention that we will refer to a great deal in this book. What is really important is that you recognise at this early stage that it is entirely possible for an organisation to report profits or surpluses yet have no cash – or to report healthy cash balances but be making losses. Here we do not know how profitable the trader's business is. The trader may have made or lost money on other transactions that week, or in preceding weeks. Nevertheless, by matching specific outputs to inputs in specific periods, we can begin to construct meaningful value statements.

In the not-for-profit sector, income and costs are matched in the same way in the income and expenditure account. Income is the funds provided to an organisation in the period, which could be the budget or charges made for the organisation's outputs. This is different from the inputs–outputs model of the commercial sector, because outputs in the not-for-profit sector are often provided free of charge.

This matching principle approach attempts to measure the resources consumed in a period irrespective of the cash flow during that period; it is known as accrual accounting. Although it is a financial framework developed for commercial organisations, its use is increasing in central government and public sector accounting. It is sometimes known as resource accounting. It is worth noting here, in the context of financial stakeholders, that not-for-profit organisations, by definition, do not exist for the prime purpose of making money for shareholders. Consequently, in public and not-for-profit organisations there is more emphasis on year-by-year income and expenditure rather than on the amount by which their value has grown. This has important implications for the kind of financial information managers in these organisations are likely to need and to have provided to them.

Financial accounting

It is usual for most substantial organisations, whatever their type, to prepare and publish external financial statements. Often this is done because the law and external investors require them, but the detail and rules that govern any particular organisation are likely to be complex and vary between countries and for different types of organisation. Although by implication these statements are produced to be a matter of public record, they also have a number of internal uses. Some statements are prepared entirely for internal use, including budget, cost and project statements. These statements are usually referred to as management accounts. As we have previously pointed out, the principles and concepts that underpin these accounts are similar to those used in drawing up the formal financial accounts that are seen by external stakeholders such as the tax authorities, creditors and investors.

The financial statements do not, of course, tell the whole story about an organisation's performance. In particular, they do not tell stakeholders about the environmental impact or ethical behaviour of the organisation. The financial statements are only part of the organisation's annual report which is prepared for various stakeholders. Increasingly, the annual report includes narrative reporting on corporate social responsibility (CSR). Such narrative reporting discusses the social, environmental and ethical impact of the organisation's activities. Many organisations publish separate CSR reports, either as a section of their annual report or within a section of their website – try accessing one for an organisation of your choice to see what it reveals! Companies are legally obliged (with certain exemptions for small companies) to provide, within their annual report, a business review, incorporating various key performance indicators (KPIs), which increasingly include non-financial performance measures relating to environmental and employee matters. Examples include waste disposal, CO_2 emissions, employee health and safety, staff satisfaction (and retention) levels, and so on. In this week's material, you will focus primarily on the financial aspects of organisational performance, in order to make understanding of the topics easier. You should remember, however, that the statements that report on financial performance are only a part of the much larger annual report.

Accountants employ a number of accounting principles and conventions when depicting an organisation from a financial perspective. This usually results in 'income', as defined by accountants, being different from cash received and 'expenditure', as defined by accountants, being different from cash paid out during a particular period. Consequently, 'profit' (i.e. income minus expenditure), as defined by accountants, will not usually be the same as the net cash inflow during a particular period of time. This week, therefore, you will also look at the nature of 'profit' (or 'surplus of income over expenditure' in the case of not-for-profit organisations) and how it is measured.

Financial statements

There are three main external financial statements that most organisations prepare to value and account for activities and transactions:

- the balance sheet (or financial position statement)
- the profit and loss account (or income statement, income and expenditure statement or statement of financial activities)
- the cash flow statement.

The balance sheet specifies the amounts of finance from each source coming into an organisation and identifies what assets (long- and short-term) they are financing. The profit and loss account is the way in which accountants try to calculate how much wealth has been created in a particular period by deducting expenses from revenue. Both these statements are prepared according to the matching principle, which applies choice and judgement to the valuation of the activities and assets, as shown in Figure 16.6.

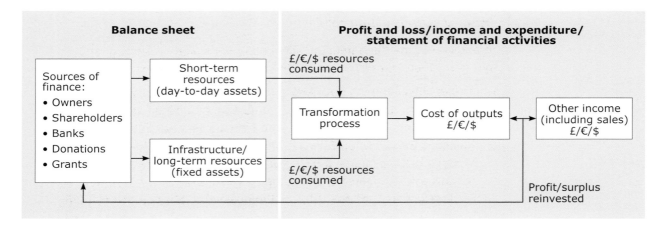

Figure 16.6 The inputs-outputs process in two financial statements

The third statement – the cash flow statement – is less concerned with valuing the activities and assets, and more with totalling the cash that has come in and gone out in the whole process.

A regulatory framework

The construction of all three of the formal statements we have introduced you to is based on accounting concepts that attempt to provide consistency and accuracy. One of the most widely used set of accounting concepts was developed by the International Accounting Standards Board (IASB) in its 'Framework for the Preparation and Presentation of Financial Statements' (finalised by the International Accounting Standards committee in 1989 and adopted by the IASB in 2001). The two fundamental accounting concepts in the IASB framework are set out in Box 16.1. Note also that this framework is intended to ensure best practice and also to ensure consistency among companies across the world to facilitate comparison of financial statements of different organisations. The latter is very important in an increasingly interdependent world. In global capital markets, for example, investors will want to compare companies in different countries and a common approach to profit measurement and asset valuation is necessary for such a comparison to be meaningful.

Box 16.1 Accounting concepts

Fundamental accounting concepts

- Accruals concept/matching principle: revenues and costs are accrued, that is, they are recognised when they are earned rather than when money is received or paid. In addition, such revenues and costs are matched with one another and dealt with in the periods to which they relate. Depreciation also illustrates this concept.

- Going concern: this convention makes the assumption that an organisation will continue operating, that is, it is a going concern. This enables assets to be valued at what they are worth, if an organisation continues to use them, which is usually more than their sale value if it closed down the day after the date of the balance sheet.

Other accounting concepts

In addition to the 'fundamental' accounting principles: 'matching' and 'going concern', there are many others including the following.

- The entity concept: a business is treated as a separate 'person' or 'entity' from the owner/s. This has a number of implications, in particular that the capital provided by the owner/s is a liability of the business to the owner. Similarly, any profit earned by the business belongs to the owner/s, thus increasing the amount the business owes the owner/s. Conversely, any funds (or other assets) removed from the business by the owner/s reduces the business' liability to the owner/s.

- The prudence concept: preparers of accounts should avoid overstating income or asset values under conditions of uncertainty. An example of the application of this principle is that stocks are valued at the lower of cost and net realisable value, rather than at the normal selling price.

- The revenue recognition concept: revenue should be recognised as earned when the legal obligation for the customer to pay is created (normally when the customer takes possession of the goods or a service is actually performed). Therefore, as long as there is a high degree of probability that the customer will pay for the goods (or services), it is not necessary to wait until the cash is actually received before the sale is recognised in the financial statements.

The accrual/matching principle in practice: depreciation

Depreciation is the charging of parts of the cost of non-current (also called fixed) assets as expenses against the profit statements of the years during which an organisation benefits from the use of the assets. As each year goes by, the value of its non-current (fixed assets) in the formal accounts is decreased and the amount by which it is decreased is charged against profits as an expense. This is another aspect of the matching principle. By charging depreciation, the organisation is effectively matching its true costs against its income (revenues) in each year so as to give a 'true and fair' view of its profit or surplus. In the UK's public sector, depreciation is usually charged to departments and activities in the form of a 'capital charge', which includes an allowance for depreciation over an appropriate number of years.

A number of methods can be used to depreciate fixed assets, producing different results. Earlier in this chapter we suggested that a car costing €20,000 could be depreciated over four years using the straight line method, by which its value will be 'used up' in equal proportions each year:

€20,000 × 25% = €5,000 first year depreciation charge against profits.

Or we could apply the reducing or declining balance method, which reflects much higher decreases in the earlier years of an asset's useful life. For the car we assumed 40% in the first year, 30% in the second, 20% in the third, and the balance of 10% in the fourth and final year:

€20,000 × 40% = €8,000 first year depreciation charge against profits.

The choice made depends on an organisation's depreciation policy. Four factors should be considered when developing an appropriate policy for valuing assets:

- Acquisition cost. The acquisition cost should include not only the invoice price but also any additional costs of acquiring and locating the asset. These may include delivery charges, non-recoverable taxes and installation costs. Subsequent repair and maintenance charges are usually charged directly to the profit statement at the time they are incurred.

- Estimated useful life. It is important to understand what is meant by the term 'useful life'. It means more than an economic life: how long is it more cost-effective for an organisation to use an asset than to obtain a more up-to-date one to replace it? Many assets can be depreciated over four years, yet still be in perfectly good working order at the end of that period and usable for years to come. Thus their technical lives can be longer than their economic lives, especially in the case of advanced technology. A depreciation policy should take account of both economic life and technological obsolescence.

- Estimated residual or scrap value. Remember that our original definition stated that the cost of an asset should be depreciated. Consider what the term 'cost' means. In economic terms, if past experience shows that a non-current (fixed) asset could be sold for a residual or scrap value at the end of its useful life, then the true cost to the organisation must be: original acquisition cost less anticipated residual or scrap value. The resulting figure will be that on which annual depreciation charges are calculated, sometimes called the depreciable base. The depreciation process is effectively combining the historic cost of an asset with estimates about its uncertain future value. The resulting depreciation charges are likely to be subjective and can only ever be estimates.

- Pattern of expected benefits. An asset such as a desk is likely to be used to the same degree during each year of its useful life. The pattern of expected benefits in this case will be even, and the straight line depreciation method may be considered appropriate. We have already suggested that some assets are suited to the reducing balance method. Others decrease in value according to how heavily or lightly they are used. They could be depreciated against the level of activity, thus ensuring that costs are matched to resulting benefits. Some organisations invent their own depreciation approaches as appropriate.

- Fair value. An alternative approach to valuing at historic cost or net book value (after depreciation) is to value non-current assets, such as plant property and equipment, in relation to a current market value. How much it could be sold for in an arm's length transaction? A reliable valuation is required from, for example, an independent surveyor. Organisations may be keen to use fair value where they feel their non-current assets had appreciated in value.

The IASB has also defined the characteristics that make information in financial statements useful. These are set out in Box 16.2.

Box 16.2 Desirable characteristics of financial statements

- Understandability. Information should be understandable. It should be presented in a way that is readily understandable by users who have a reasonable knowledge of business and economic activities and accounting.

- Relevance. Information in financial statements should be relevant. It is relevant when it influences the economic decisions of users.

- Reliability. Information in financial statements should be reliable. It is reliable if it is free from material error and bias and can be depended on by users to represent events and transactions accurately.

- Comparability. Users must be able to compare the financial statements of an organisation over time so that they can identify trends in its financial position and performance.

International Financial Reporting Standards

The stated goal of the IASB is to develop a 'single set of high quality, understandable and enforceable global accounting standards' or International Financial Reporting Standards (IFRSs) which are based on the concepts and characteristics defined in Boxes 16.1 and 16.2. Countries that adopt IFRSs can specify whether they want them to apply to public companies whose shares are listed on a stock exchange, or all companies or all business and non-profit organisations. The EU is requiring IFRSs for consolidated accounts (the 'adding' together of all the company accounts within a group of companies that together form one body) of public companies, but member states can permit or require the use of IFRSs for other organisations. Nearly a hundred countries, including all 25 EU nations, have adopted these international standards. Other countries, including the US and China, have indicated an interest in bringing their own regulations in line with IFRSs.

Benefits of International Financial Reporting Standards

As the world's economies have become more interdependent in terms of trade and investment, so the arguments for international standards of accounting have become stronger. It is now widely understood that economic growth is stimulated by organisations being able to compare different profit-making opportunities in different countries. Global accounting standards make this possible. Public sector and non-profit organisations who work internationally can also benefit from global, transparent accounting standards. The accounting concepts and characteristics (set out in Boxes 16.1 and 16.2) which underpin IFRSs are equally relevant to profit and non-profit organisations.

Political interference in accounting standards

It is important to realise that regulations such as IFRSs are applied more rigidly in some countries than in others. Additionally, individual governments have their own legally enforceable regulations which companies must follow in their financial reporting. An example of political interference is the decision of the EU to reserve the right not to endorse IFRS if they so wish. Political interference in Europe and elsewhere has meant that worldwide adoption of IFRSs is piecemeal. If you want to find out more about a specific country's formal framework you should seek information from the financial staff in your own organisation.

Income statements

The income statement of an organisation summarises its revenues and expenses over a period to see if the organisation has made a profit/surplus or a loss/deficit. It differs from a balance sheet, which looks at the accumulated value of an organisation at one particular date as it considers the revenue that it generates and the expenses it consumes over a period of activity. This period is normally a year in formal financial statements, but – again – the principle of identifying and matching revenue to expenses is a universal one that can be applied across sectors, and to projects as well as to organisations. The conventions about how accountants construct such statements vary from sector to sector and from country to country, but the underlying principles are similar. Likewise, we are using the term 'profit and loss statement' as a convenient short-hand title for all statements that attempt to match revenue or income to expenses or costs, although different terms are used in different sectors and in different countries.

- Commercial companies need to know whether their sales revenue (the proceeds from outputs) exceeds their expenses incurred in generating the sales; they can then work out how much they can reinvest in their businesses. The income statement of commercial organisations is frequently referred to as their profit and loss account.

- Public and not-for-profit organisations need to know whether they are delivering their services for less than, as much as or more than the income they receive from taxation, annual grants, contracts or donations. The calculation would determine if the organisation made a surplus or a deficit over the period in the accounts. Some smaller not-for-profit organisations still use a simple form of cash accounting (rather than accruals accounting) which simply records cash in and cash out within a particular period. Such organisations prepare a receipts and payments account rather than an income and expenditure account – the form of income statement prepared by not-for-profit organisations using accruals accounting.

Example 16.3 Terrestrial Trading (TT)

To explore the construction of profit and loss statements and their connections to balance sheets and later to formal cash flow statements, we shall consider a fictitious animal feed processing company, Terrestrial Trading (TT).

Table 16.2 is a basic set of data about the finances and operations of TT in a particular year (Year 1), which we will use first to construct its profit and loss statement. We will need to refer to this table at various stages during this book – you may wish to bookmark the page.

Table 16.2 Terrestrial Trading Company: Year 1 data

Line	Data
A	Sales totalled £60,000, being 50% for cash and 50% to account customers (debtors) on credit
B	Materials for stock costing £25,000 were purchased on account
C	The stock of materials held at the end of the year had cost £10,000
D	Sundry operating expenses totalled £10,000, of which £1,000 remained unpaid at the year end
E	Depreciation on fixed (non-current) assets amounted to £5,000
F	Loan interest of £1,000 was paid
G	Debtors paid £25,000 in cash
H	Trade creditors were paid £20,000 in cash
I	Fixed assets (non-current) costing £20,000 were purchased for cash
J	The owners contributed £25,000 in cash as capital to establish the business
K	A long-term bank loan for £10,000 was obtained, repayable within five years with an interest rate of 10% a year

Remember, the profit and loss statement is prepared using the matching principle: it states what revenue has been earned in the year and what expenses have been incurred, each of which may be more or less than the actual cash flowing in and out of the organisation during the year. Table 16.3 is a basic listing of TT's revenue and expenses. Note how and where the information in Table 16.2 appears in it.

Table 16.3 Terrestrial Trading Company's revenue and expenses

	£000	£000	Table 16.2 line reference
Revenue			
Cash sales	30		Line A
Account sales	<u>30</u>		Line A
		60	
Expenses			
Cost of stock sold	15		Line B minus C
Operating expenses	10		Line D
Depreciation	5		Line E
Bank loan interest	<u>1</u>		Line F
		<u>31</u>	
Profit		<u>29</u>	

This is all well and good. We can, however, now move from such a purely linear list of expenses to one that categorises them to enhance the information utility of the profit and loss statement. The enhanced statement can be laid out as in Table 16.4.

Table 16.4 Terrestrial Trading Company's profit and loss statement for Year 1

	£000	£000
Sales		
For cash	30	
On account	<u>30</u>	
		60
Less		
Cost of stock sold		<u>(15)</u>
Gross profit		45
Less		
Operating expenses	10	
Depreciation	<u>5</u>	
		<u>(15)</u>
Operating profit		30
Less		
Bank loan interest		(1)
Net reported profit		<u>29</u>

Note the new terms, or categories, for profit. The first section determines the gross profit – also referred to as the gross margin. Gross profit here is the difference between the cost of the raw materials that the company buys in and what it receives for selling them to its customers. The cost of the materials is £15,000 because TT spent £25,000 on materials but had £10,000-worth still in stock at the end of the year. It is important to calculate this figure correctly – you cannot know the cost of items used up in a year's sales unless you know how much you start with and finish with in stock:

	£
Opening stock before day 1	0
Plus stock bought in year	25,000
Less stock unused at end of year	(10,000)
Cost of sales	15,000

From its gross profit of £45,000, TT has to cover all its other expenses and make a net profit. The price it pays for the materials is 25% (£15000/ £60000) of the price it receives when it sells on the processed finished foodstuffs. Thus we can say that TT has a gross profit margin of 75 per cent: for every £1 it receives for sales, 25p is the cost of sales and 75p is available to contribute towards its expenses and profit. If the price it buys or sells at changes, this affects the gross profit margin. Gross profit margins are particularly important for manufacturing, processing and retailing businesses. However, it is a useful concept to apply to any service, because it encourages managers to look at the difference between the revenue that is earned from outputs and the money that is spent specifically in order to generate the outputs. In the simple case of TT as shown above, we count only the materials used in calculating the gross margin. One final point about the gross profit: the more sales TT makes, the more materials it consumes. In other words, the cost of the sales varies according to the volume of the sales. This is normally a characteristic of the expenses counted when establishing the gross margin, unlike the next category of expenses, which we count to calculate the operating profit.

The operating profit is the surplus TT makes on its day-to-day operations. It takes into account both the expenses it incurs when making the sales – the expenses we discussed above – and the more general operating expenses needed to run the business. The operating expenses (for instance salaries, electricity, cleaning, insurance, short-term overdraft interest) are required for the day-to-day business to operate. Many assets would depreciate in value over the year. So taking these two expenses away from the gross profit leaves an operating profit of £30,000, which reflects TT's surplus on its business operations. Again, this concept of an operating profit or surplus has utility beyond formal profit and loss statements: it enables managers of discrete organisations, sections and projects to calculate their surplus or deficit on operations (service or manufacturing) across a range of sectors and contexts. However, in TT's case it is not yet the final profit figure.

The long-term bank loan interest (£1,000) is kept apart from the operating expenses and the depreciation charge, because it is not classed as an operational expense; rather, it is a cost of financing the business and is thus somewhat detached from day-to-day operations. The loan interest is deducted from the operating profit to give the net reported profit of £29,000. This is the sum that can be used to make a distribution to the owners (i.e. as dividends to shareholders), to pay the tax on profits, to repay loan capital or to retain to reinvest in the business – or, as is common, some of all four.

The layout shown in this profit statement seems straightforward and logical. Unfortunately, very few profit and loss statements (and very few internal revenue and expenses statements) are presented quite so straightforwardly. As a manager you need to be able to see where different layouts, categories and vocabularies are used to present information of the same type as TT's. Tables 16.5, 16.6 and 16.7 are adaptations of the annual profit and loss statements (or equivalents) of three organisations: a European publishing business, an international not-for-profit development charity and a New Zealand university. They include terms and headings different from those we have introduced so far. Note that as consolidated or summary statements, they often show only the totals, not the calculations used to reach the totals. All adopt the normal practice of showing the previous year's accounts to the right of the most recent year's figures. They are fairly typical of the layouts used by a range of organisations. Note the common elements in terms of showing revenues and expenses but also how the different organisational contexts are reflected in the contents of the statements. There is also a difference in the terminology of surplus/deficit or profit/loss.

Table 16.5 Summary consolidated profit and loss account of a European publisher

Year ended 31 December	20XX	20XX–1
	€m	€m
Turnover in joint ventures	2,577	2,375
Share of joint venture operating profit before amortisation and exceptional items	603	605
Amortisation and exceptional items	(466)	(306)
Operating profit	137	299
Non-operating exceptional income	6	508
Net interest	(63)	(30)
Profit before taxation	80	777
Tax on profit	(128)	(203)
(Loss)/profit attributable to ordinary shareholders	(48)	574
Dividends	(179)	(263)
Retained (loss)/profit taken to reserves	(227)	311

Table 16.6 Consolidated statement of financial activities of an international not-for-profit development charity

Year ended 31 December	20XX	20XX–1
	£000	£000
Incoming resources		
Child and community sponsorships	27,828	25,097
Other donations	5,989	4,644
Contributions from official bodies	5,570	7,018
Net income from trading operations	165	263
Miscellaneous income	1,588	1,820
	41,140	38,842
Contributions from European partners	3,808	3,531
Total incoming resources	44,948	42,373
Resources expended		
Direct charitable expenditure		
Project costs		
Grants to other organisations	8,226	7,615
Development and emergency expenditure	14,930	15,186
Influence, education and research	3,836	2,969
Support costs	7,393	7,383
	34,385	33,153
Other expenditure		
Fundraising	8,433	7,012
Administration	1,001	1,194
	9,434	8,206
Total resources expended	43,819	41,359
Net incoming resources	1,129	1,014
Fund balances brought forward at 1 January	20,598	
Fund balances carried forward at 31 December	21,727	20,598

Table 16.7 Statement of financial performance of a New Zealand university

Year ended 31 December	20XX	20XX–1
	NZ $000	NZ $000
Revenues		
General operating revenue		
Government grants	154,671	151,710
Tuition fees	55,918	48,527
Interest and dividends	2,896	3,380
Other income	88	488
	213,573	204,105
Revenue attributable to significant activities		
Trading income	1,640	4,149
Research sponsorship	24,975	23,401
Service income	38,451	36,330
Special funds	5,261	5,171
	70,327	69,051
Total operating revenue	283,900	273,156
Expenses		
Academic salaries	98,701	93,746
General salaries	63,892	63,248
Operating costs	100,477	102,618
Depreciation	18,688	18,708
Total operating expenses	281,758	278,320
Net surplus/(deficit) for year	2,142	(5,164)

The balance sheet

The balance sheet is a picture, a snapshot if you like, at a particular moment in time, of the resources that are available for future use and of the funding that has made those resources available. As we know from our previous considerations of the inputs–outputs process, resources are consumed as inputs in the generation of outputs. Those that are not used remain on the balance sheet until such time as they are used.

Look at the left-hand side of Table 16.7. Note how the sources of finance and the resources funded by these sources have been grouped together. These two elements of the inputs–outputs process represent the balance sheet. This financial statement matches (or balances) where the funding has come from with the resources that have been bought with the funding and/or are available to be used.

The relevant section in Table 16.7 has been reproduced in greater detail in Table 16.8, with some simple hypothetical figures added. Note that we have put the sources of finance on the left, to complete the process illustrated in Table 16.7. In practice, most balance sheets list the assets first, as you will discover later in this session.

Table 16.8 A basic balance sheet layout

Sources of finance 31 December 20XX	£000	Assets 31 December 20XX	£000
From owners (e.g. shareholders' investments, grants from government)	300	Long-term (non-current or fixed) assets (e.g. buildings and equipment)	450
Profits/surpluses generated from previous years' activities	100	Day-to-day (current) assets (e.g. stocks of materials, cash in the bank)	150
From lenders (e.g. long-term bank or other loans)	150		
Current liabilities (such as creditors)	50		
Total	600		600

This simple balance sheet is telling you that on 31 December 20XX the organisation is worth £600,000. Of this, £300,000 has come from those who own the organisation. A further £150,000 comes from the lenders who have lent to the organisation; such long-term loans can come in many forms in different types of organisation, but they should be distinguished from the day-to-day overdraft borrowing that may be needed to keep an organisation's operations 'liquid'. A further £50,000 com from money owed to creditors (current liabilities). Finally, £100,000 has been generated from the organisation's surpluses up to 31 December and reinvested in the organisation. These accumulated surpluses retained in an organisation are often called its reserves. They are not the cash reserves of everyday language. The term simply describes how much of the total assets of an organisation have been financed by the surpluses generated by the organisation.

All three sources of funds represent the worth on 31 December 20XX only. Over the years, millions more may have been invested or lent, but what the organisation has paid back is obviously no longer a source of finance for it on 31 December 20XX. Similarly, and importantly, millions more may have been generated in surpluses. However, some of that may then have been lost in bad deficit years, or a portion of it paid out as tax on profits, or some of it distributed as dividends to shareholders rather than reinvested in the organisation. The balance sheet shows only the cumulative net surplus available as a source of finance to the organisation on 31 December 20XX.

In the right-hand column of Table 16.8, this simple balance sheet is telling you that of this organisational worth of £600,000, £450,000 can be found in the value of its non-current (often called fixed or long-term) assets at 31 December 20XX, and £150,000 in the value of its current (day-to-day) assets. Again, what matters is the value on that date, the 'net book value'. Thus it values fixed (non-current) assets after depreciation for age and usage has been accounted for.

We have shown how a balance sheet matches sources of finance to the resources funded by the sources, at a particular point in time. It is customary to prepare one balance sheet at the start of a financial period and another at the end. If the net worth of an organisation increases or decreases during that period, the difference will be explained by what the profit and loss and cash flow statements tell us about operations and finances during the year. This is why it is important to understand the connections between the three statements.

Example 16.4 Terrestrial Trading

Using the data in Table 16.9, we can generate the balance sheets at the start and end of the first year of Terrestrial Trading's operations. These are shown in Tables 16.10, and 16.11. Follow the changes to each item in these carefully. Please note that for the purpose of simplicity we will assume that the transactions detailed in Table 16.9, items B (purchase of £25,000 stock of materials), I (purchase of £20,000 of fixed assets), J (investment of £25,000 owners' capital) and K (receipt of long-term bank loan of £10,000) all occurred on day 1 of the first year. The opening balance sheet thus summarises the sources and resources as at the close of business on day 1; the values would all have been zero at the start of the day.

Table 16.9 Terrestrial Trading Company: Year 1 data

A	Sales totalled £60,000, being 50% for cash and 50% to account customers (debtors) on credit
B	Materials for stock costing £25,000 were purchased on account
C	The stock of materials held at the end of the year had cost £10,000
D	Sundry operating expenses totalled £10,000, of which £1,000 remained unpaid at the year end
E	Depreciation on fixed (non-current) assets amounted to £5,000
F	Loan interest of £1,000 was paid
G	Debtors paid £25,000 in cash
H	Trade creditors were paid £20,000 in cash
I	Fixed (non-current) assets costing £20,000 were purchased for cash
J	The owners contributed £25,000 in cash as capital to establish the business
K	A long-term bank loan for £10,000 was obtained, repayable within five years with an interest rate of 10% a year

Table 16.10 Terrestrial Trading Company: basic balance sheet as at end of day 1, at the start of Year 1

Sources	£	Resources	£
Owners' capital	25,000	Fixed assets	20,000
Loan	10,000	Stock	25,000
Creditors	25,000	Cash*	15,000
	60,000		60,000

* The cash balance of £15,000 reflects cash from owners (£25,000) and the bank (£10,000) less the cash paid (£20,000) for the purchase of fixed assets.

Table 16.11 Terrestrial Trading Company: basic balance sheet as at <u>end</u> of Year 1

Sources	£	Resources	£
Owners' capital	25,000	Fixed assets[1]	15,000
Retained profits[2]	29,000	Stock	10,000
Bank loan	10,000	Debtors[3]	5,000
Creditors:		Cash[4]	40,000
Materials[5]	5,000		
Sundries[6]	1,000		
	70,000		70,000

Notes to Table 16.11

1 Fixed assets purchased for £20,000 less £5,000 of depreciation in the year: the net book value is now £15,000.

2 See the profit and loss statement in Table 16.4. It presumes the reported profit is not taxed and the owners took no dividends.

3 Account sales of £30,000 less £25,000 already received, leaving £5,000 owed by debtors.

4 Cash balance implied by the transaction detailed in Table 16.9 – and as would be shown in a cash flow statement, as you will see in Week 17.

5 Materials of £25,000 purchased on account for stock less £20,000 already paid, leaving £5,000 owing to creditors.

6 Sundry operating costs of £10,000, of which only £9,000 has been paid.

It has been convenient for the purposes of this book to view the balance sheet in a format that shows the sources of finance on the left and the resources they finance on the right. As we shall see shortly, it is a more common practice to use a vertical format: to start with the resources – or assets – at the top and to title the sources of finance as *liabilities*. Liabilities is the accounting term for amounts owed to those financing an organisation – the sources of funding. Amounts owed to its creditors, while being liabilities, are also sources of funding. Until their bills are paid the creditors are effectively funding the organisation's activities. The debtors are treated as an asset, because they represent a sum of money that an organisation has earned and that technically belongs to it: the sum of money has just not been paid over yet.

By showing where funding comes from and where it goes, this simple balance sheet summarises TT's financial position: what it owes – the funding – and what it owns – the unused resources. For this reason the balance sheet is sometimes referred to as a position statement (particularly in the USA, New Zealand and Australia): it reflects the financial position (at least as recorded in the accounting records) of an organisation at a particular time. The scales shown in Figure 16.7 capture the balancing dimension, and you can see why it is called a balance sheet: the ins and outs balance. The assets are a physical representation of the funding, and thus should balance.

Figure 16.7 The balance sheet scales

Why do we need balance sheets?

We now have a grip on the nature of the balance sheet and what it sets out to do. In addition to listing the sources of funding and the resources acquired (or liabilities and assets, as we now know them), the information shown on a balance sheet has a number of practical uses:

- Management information and control: if no account of the ins and outs is kept, no one knows what is going on; frauds could be committed, or people could work efficiently in pursuit of the wrong targets. This purpose goes beyond formal organisational balance sheets in accounting statements. Matching the monies that have gone into a project to the value of all the resources currently tied up in that project can serve a useful project management function across many different organisations and sectors.

- Information to outside parties: taxation authorities are interested in the values of assets and financial activities; investors, lenders, suppliers and other future creditors may want to see how much a business is worth and how much cash it has, and so may competitors or companies thinking of acquiring another company.

- Stewardship responsibilities: managers have a legal obligation to keep records – to provide an account of what they are doing. The shareholders or governments or trustees who 'own' an organisation are rarely the people who manage it. By placing an obligation on those who manage an organisation to produce statements that follow appropriate accounting conventions and are verified by accountants acting as *auditors*, the owners can know what is happening to 'their' organisation.

Assets and liabilities: long-term and current

Throughout this book we have made a distinction between long-term sources of finance and assets and the day-to-day financing of organisations' operations. We now develop our basic balance sheet to reflect the distinction more clearly.

Assets such as equipment, cars and machines that will be used as resources over a number of years are usually grouped together and called fixed or non-current assets. Other assets such as stock (also known as inventory), debtors and cash, which change almost daily, are grouped under the heading current assets. The dividing line between the long- and short-term items is usually taken as 12 months.

Liabilities can also be grouped into categories. As we have mentioned, money owed to owners (in a commercial company, shareholdings plus the accumulated retained profits) is both a source of finance and a liability, because ultimately it is their money. You will often see the balance sheet heading 'capital and reserves' or 'shareholders' funds', to cover this. Liabilities are also grouped on the basis of being longer-term and shorter-term. Where a bank loan is owed and is repayable over more than one year, it can be classified as a long-term liability, often referred to as 'creditors falling due after more than one year'. Other debts and liabilities are owed by organisations in the shorter term. Money owed to suppliers and short-term overdrafts owed to a bank are usually called current liabilities, often referred to as 'creditors falling due within one year'. The balance sheet thus shows a list of values relating to the liabilities and assets of an organisation at a particular date.

Example 16.5 Terrestrial Trading

We can present TT's balance sheet as Table 16.12 to reflect this distinction between long-term and current values.

Table 16.12 Terrestrial Trading Company: rearranged balance sheet at <u>end</u> of Year 1

	£	£		£	£
Capital and reserves			**Fixed assets at net book value**		15,000
Owners' capital	25,000				
Retained profits	29,000	54,000			
Long-term liabilities			**Current assets**		
			Stock	10,000	
Bank loan		10,000	Debtors	5,000	
			Cash	40,000	55,000
Current liabilities					
Creditors:					
Materials	5,000				
Sundries	1,000	6,000			
		70,000			70,000

The figures are still the same, but the categorisations are different. In practice, most organisations offset their current liabilities against their current assets to arrive at a net current assets figure. This usefully highlights the value of the working capital flowing around in an organisation. Thus the balance sheet in Table 16.12 becomes the one shown in Table 16.13.

Table 16.13 Terrestrial Trading Company: <u>end</u> of Year 1 balance sheet with working capital shown

	£	£		£	£	£
Capital and reserves			**Fixed assets at net book value**			15,000
Owners' capital	25,000					
Retained profits	29,000	54,000				
			Current assets			
			Stock	10,000		
			Debtors	5,000		
			Cash	40,000	55,000	
Creditors: amounts falling due after one year			**Less current liabilities**			
Bank loan		10,000	Creditors:			
			Materials	5,000		
			Sundries	1,000	6,000	
			Working capital/net current assets			49,000
		64,000				64,000

The balance sheet still balances and contains all the same figures as before. Think of a simple equation: whether you add 3 to the left-hand side or take 3 away from the right-hand side, the result will be the same.

Note that where a horizontal format is used for a balance sheet in published financial statements, assets are usually shown on the left and sources of finance and other liabilities on the right.

We are now ready to look at the summary balance sheets of our three sample organisations (Tables 16.14, 16.15 and 16.16).

These use a range of different ways to express the equation between assets (resources) and liabilities (sources of finance). You are not expected to know all the headings and conventions behind these layouts, but you should be able to pick out the main ideas and totals from our preceding discussion.

Table 16.14 Summary consolidated balance sheet of a European publisher

As at 31 December	20XX	20XX–1
	€m	€m
Financial fixed assets	1,559	1,661
Accounts receivable	61	58
Short-term investments	19	17
Current assets	80	75
Current liabilities	(102)	(177)
Net working capital	(22)	(102)
Long-term liabilities	(8)	(11)
Provisions	(36)	(36)
Net assets	1,493	1,512
Share capital issued	43	32
Paid-in surplus	385	388
Legal reserves	847	949
Other reserves	218	143
Shareholders' funds	1,493	1,512

Table 16.15 Balance sheet of an international not-for-profit development charity

As at 31 December	20XX	20XX–1
	£000	£000
Tangible fixed assets	3,396	3,144
Fixed asset investments	73	–
Current assets		
Stock	16	5
Debtors	4,449	3,812
Short-term bank deposits	12,850	13,000
Cash at bank	3,532	4,326
	20,847	21,143
Creditors		
Amounts falling due within one year	(2,589)	(3,689)
Net current assets	18,258	17,454
Net assets	21,727	20,598
Funds		
Restricted funds	16,060	15,640
Designated funds:		
Fixed assets	1,457	1,262
Emergency	200	150
General fund	4,010	3,546
	5,667	4,958
	21,727	20,598

Table 16.16 Statement of financial position of a New Zealand university

As at 31 December	20XX	20XX–1
	NZ$000	NZ$000
University equity		
General equity	580,535	580,063
Revaluation reserves	35,781	35,781
Trust and special funds	11,488	9,768
Total equity	627,754	625,612
Assets		
Current assets:		
Cash and bank	208	1,452
Short-term investments – unrestricted	8,597	2,550
Short-term investments – restricted	4,600	3,700
Accounts receivable and prepayments	14,410	14,413
Inventories	1,482	1,988
	29,297	24,103
Non-current assets:		
Long-term investments – restricted	7,276	6,523
Loans	406	410
Intangible assets	71	95
Fixed assets	635,907	629,393
	643,660	636,421
Total assets	672,957	660,524
Liabilities		
Current liabilities:		
Bank overdraft	–	–
Accounts payable	26,142	17,199
Employee entitlements	9,538	5,615
	35,680	22,814
Non-current liabilities:		
Employee entitlements	9,523	12,098
Total liabilities	45,203	34,912
Net assets	627,754	625,612

Rather than learn all the various ways in which accountants set out balance sheets in different sectors and countries, learn what to look for: the sources of finance and where that finance is at the moment the balance sheet refers to. Or look with a specific question in mind: whether stock has gone up or down, whether there is a large proportion of long-term loan financing rather than financing from self-generated profits/surpluses, and so forth.

Do balance sheets show the true value of organisations?

Organisations can be busy places: monies are coming in and going out all the time; surpluses and deficits are being made on particular services and operations; equipment and materials are all over the place. The balance sheet provides a framework and a discipline that enables organisations to present pictures that are as realistic as feasible about the sum of this activity. Some of the values may be subjective, even artificial, but if the method for calculating the various figures on an organisation's balance sheet is as fair as possible, its total value on that document has some meaning and validity.

The values in a balance sheet are not a reliable guide to an organisation's market value: perhaps some of its debtors will not pay the full amounts of their debts. A balance sheet does not value staff, their knowledge, and their capacity to invent successful new services and products – some of the most valuable assets of an organisation – although some organisations attempt to put a value on 'goodwill'. As we noted when we discussed costs, accountants use balance sheets to provide a useful value (or net worth) of an organisation, but we cannot say it is the true or market value.

Reference

Rutherford, B.A. (1983) *Financial reporting in the public sector*, London, Butterworth.

Chapter 17 The cash flow statement, cash flow and working capital management

Cash flow

All organisations require money to pay for the resources they consume – some for day-to-day use, others for use over a longer period. Note that when accountants refer to 'cash' they mean money in general, such as funds in a bank current account, not just notes and coins. In a commercial enterprise, the owners want to get more cash out than they put in; they may also want to use some of this cash to help the business expand. Banks and other lenders will be expecting any loan to be repaid. Thus there needs to be a flow of cash through the organisation. If the business is generating more money from the sale of its outputs than it pays for its inputs (tracked following the matching principle), then it has an important and self-sustaining source of cash. However long it may take for an organisation to collect the cash from selling outputs, ultimately the cash coming in should be greater than the cash being spent on inputs. Public and not-for-profit organisations also need flows of cash that are greater than or equal to what they need to spend on inputs, both immediate (such as salaries) and long-term (such as new equipment). However, the income that comes from selling outputs is rarely a significant source of cash.

In this session we focus on cash flow. Profitable organisations often have plenty of cash. In the long term, organisations that are effective in generating a value for their outputs that exceeds the cost of their inputs (i.e. that are profitable) will normally generate the cash to survive on a day-to-day basis and to expand on a longer-term basis. However, this is not always the case. Organisations need cash to survive, whatever their underlying profitability or performance effectiveness. This session explores the flow of cash in organisations. This relates directly to your role as a manager in that it is you and your colleagues who make or influence decisions about spending cash, be it on minor stationery or consumables or on major long-term projects.

Cash flows and core activities

The cash flow approach differs from the matching principle approach. It is concerned with there being enough money coming in to pay for everything that is needed, not with matching specific revenue to specific expenditure in order to ascertain the underlying profitability or costs. Example 17.1 highlights that both are important in management.

Example 17.1 Who's paying?

The UK-based international airline British Airways (BA) put its new low-cost subsidiary Go up for sale, anticipating a substantial price for an airline that had never reported a profit and whose most recent figures showed an annual loss of £22m. This loss was calculated on the basis of matching the revenues received in the year with all the costs (inputs) that related to them. Yet the airline had never had a problem paying its salaries or other costs. Why?

As with many start-up companies, Go had secured enough cash from investors who believed that in the long run it would generate cash surpluses. BA was the main investor, or *financier*. In many start-up companies the financiers are individuals and institutions who risk their cash in the hope that eventually their investment will make them a profit. The cash coming into Go exceeded that going out because financiers were prepared to make up the difference between its sales revenues and its costs. However, the amount they needed to make up was less than it would have been if Go's customers had not made their cash contributions by buying tickets. Nearly all Go's customers bought their tickets well in advance of their journeys. Thus, money came into Go before it needed to pay its crews' salaries, landing fees and fuel costs associated with their journeys. If Go had had to pay for those inputs before it received the cash from customers, it would have needed even more cash from its financiers.

BA hoped to sell the airline for more than the total sum it had spent to start it up, thus showing a cash surplus from Go overall. Whoever bought the loss-making business would be basing their price on their faith (and the faith of their financiers) that before long cash surpluses would be generated.

What does this tell us about cash flow, at least in commercial organisations? It tells us that as well as working to ensure profitability, managers also need to plan to have enough cash coming in to meet all their organisation's requirements for inputs. Relying on the profits from selling outputs for cash is insufficient if:

- you need some time to build up a business before you can expect to start making profits from your outputs

- you need to spend a large initial sum on, for instance, new equipment, before that equipment will start to pay for itself

- you receive the money from selling outputs after you need to pay for inputs.

To describe the cash flow in commercial organisations, we consider the simple example of a retailer running a small shop. Figure 17.1 shows that its customers provide the business with cash, which it then gives to its suppliers for more stock (sometimes called inventory), which is then sold to the customers for more cash, and so on in a continuous cycle. However, even a simple retail business may sometimes spend more cash than it is receiving;

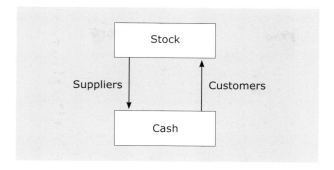

Figure 17.1 A simple illustration of cash flows

for instance, it may need to spend a lot of money on goods for the Christmas period long before the December shoppers pay for them.

In a business that has been established for a while, it is more common to buy stock on account or on credit (in accounting language, to make an 'account purchase'): that is, our retailer receives the goods now and pays for them later. It may also be that not all the stock is sold straight away. So at any point in time there may be an outstanding demand for payment from a supplier for stock which is still to be sold to customers and converted into cash. Account purchases have no immediate impact on cash: all they result in is a paper (or computer) debt to the supplier. Only the subsequent payment to the supplier gives rise to the outflow of cash. If stock remains unsold, this, too, will have an impact on cash flow, as no cash will be coming in. Of course, when the stock is sold not all the customers will pay straight away. It is normal to have some customers who do not pay immediately but run up accounts. So there may be debts to the business (what the customers owe it) as well as those the retailer owes to the suppliers.

Those who owe organisations money are usually referred to as its debtors, while those the organisation owes money to are usually called its creditors. All organisations – service or manufacturing, small or large, private, public or not-for-profit sector – have creditors; most have at least some debtors as well. Debtors are often referred to as receivables (or accounts receivable) and creditors as payables (or accounts payable).

For this sort of sale, it is not the sales but only the eventual payment of their accounts by debtors that gives rise to the receipt of cash. Figure 17.2 expands the basic model of Figure 17.1 to illustrate how stock, creditors and debtors fit in the cash flow cycle.

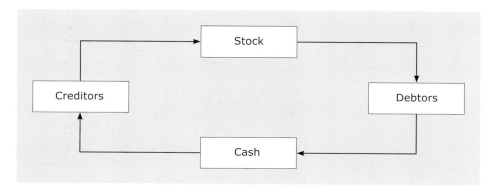

Figure 17.2 The flow of finance – the impact of debt, creditors and stock

Commercial organisations tend to have creditors, such as suppliers, to which they owe money (trade creditors), and a range of expenses to be paid, such as premises costs (rent, local taxes, heating and lighting, and so on). They may also owe tax to the government, either a tax on profits or purchase/service taxes such as value-added tax (VAT).

Public and not-for-profit organisations have the same kinds of creditor. Often a higher proportion of their expenditure is on staff and salaries than on supplies, so they may have fewer trade creditors relative to their total expenditure than commercial organisations. The tax they owe to the government may be made up largely of payroll taxes (such as income tax), which they deduct from the pay of their staff.

Debtors are likely to be rather different in the two types of organisation. Since not-for-profit organisations by definition do not primarily exist to sell products and services to the general public for commercial advantage, although some have important commercial trading operations but others receive their funds largely from taxation, grants or donations, in these cases there may be relatively few people owing money for products or services provided. On the other hand, grants or cash allocations from government may be committed but not yet paid. Although these kinds of payment are usually forthcoming eventually, until they are received, wages and salaries cannot be paid for long, and any delay can be serious.

Your organisation does not have to be a commercial concern to hold stocks. Think about schools, charities or the European Commission; stocks of stationery are required, costing a lot of money but not always consumed immediately. Similarly, healthcare organisations may hold stocks of drugs and other consumables. Local government organisations may have stocks of building supplies or road maintenance materials. All these will have an impact on the flow of cash.

There are, of course, many things other than stock that our retailer may spend cash on. The business has to pay its operating expenses, such as wages, rent and electricity. If it is a company with shareholders, it may want to give some of the cash it has earned from profitable trading to its shareholders, as a return on their investment, in the form of dividends. However, some of its profits will probably have to go to the government in taxes, which most governments levy on profits. These payments also draw on the organisation's pool of cash resources, as shown in Figure 17.3. Note that the figure assumes that some customers buy some things with cash that they pay straight away, and that the retailer similarly buys some of the stock as cash purchases.

You will note that the cash flowing in and out and through organisations is getting more complicated. The timing of the flows becomes critical. If our retailer pays creditors for stock before receiving the money from debtors who buy it, something will need to bridge the cash gap. Such issues can cause organisations to run out of cash. This can be a problem when a company grows rapidly. For example, taking on a big contract may be attractive but could place a burden on cash if the organisation is paying for materials, wages, etc. in advance of payment being received from the customer.

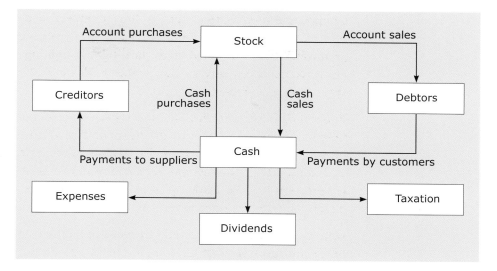

Figure 17.3 The flow of finance from core activities

There will be aspects of the timings of cash flow that relate specifically to your organisation and its context, but there are some general principles in relation to any increases and decreases of cash flow. For example, if the value of our retailer's debtors has increased, this may indicate that it is taking longer to collect money from its customers. However, if the volume of account sales has increased by more than the increase in debtors, it shows that cash is being collected more quickly. If the creditors' amount has increased, it is either because the retailer is buying more stock on account, or because it is taking longer to pay them.

Cash flows and non-core activities

It may be that, because of the irregularity of cash flows, our retail business sometimes has too little cash and at other times more than it needs. It may tend to run short just after paying monthly salaries. Thus it will be useful to have bank overdraft facilities available, the overdraft being increased or decreased quite frequently, depending on need.

Similarly, the retailer may deposit amounts of cash temporarily with banks or other financial institutions. Many organisations even earn interest by depositing sums overnight by electronic transfer at various banks or other financial institutions around the world.

So amounts may go in and out of short-term investments very frequently. These overdrafts and deposits are illustrated in Figure 17.4. Note that the arrows between 'deposits' and 'cash' and between 'overdrafts' and 'cash' are double-headed. This is because an overdraft facility enables cash to flow from the bank to the organisation when it needs it, but also from the organisation back to the bank when it is no longer needed. A reverse pattern applies to short-term deposits.

Of course, cash flow can be both unpredictable and irregular. As noted above, it is not just commercial organisations that suffer from fluctuations in cash flow. Regional and local government organisations may run short of cash if residents and businesses are late in paying or fail to pay various local taxes, levies and charges. At other times they may have large sums of money

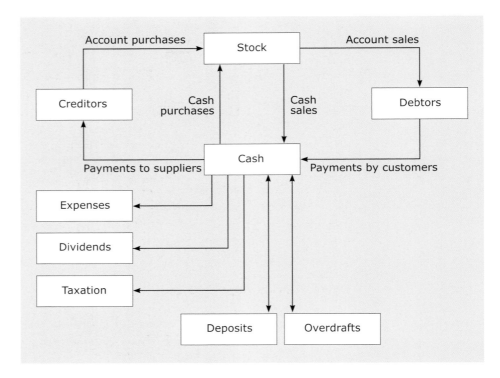

Figure 17.4 The flow of finance – a bigger picture

which they place on deposit with banks overnight. Voluntary organisations often have immense problems with unpredictable cash flows. At times, particularly during a recession, donations may decrease. At other times, such as following a major disaster or a well-organised appeal, there may be large sums of cash available for short periods of time. In all organisations there will be cash flows that are certain and others that are less predictable.

Finally, there are other sources of cash and expenditure to complete our picture of the flow of finance for our retailer (see Figure 17.5). It may wish to expand by opening a new branch and seek cash by issuing new shares to investors or obtaining long-term loans from its bank or other sources. There will then be expenditures to fit out and start the new branch (long-term assets) and eventually to pay off the loans. These cash flows are beyond the normal trading and short-term inflows and outflows we have been discussing so far.

This picture could apply to a private sector retailer established as a company with shareholdings. Whether the same boxes and flows, and their relative importance, apply in your organisation will depend on the nature of its work, and its size, sector and structure. However, it is certain that it will have a cash flow picture. For service organisations, the flow of money out for expenses is likely to be far greater than for stock. Not-for-profit organisations may have little or no cash going out in tax (at least as far as profit taxes are concerned – payroll taxes are really part of the cash spent on wages and salaries under 'expenses'). A state-funded school may get nearly all its income through block grants from a government department.

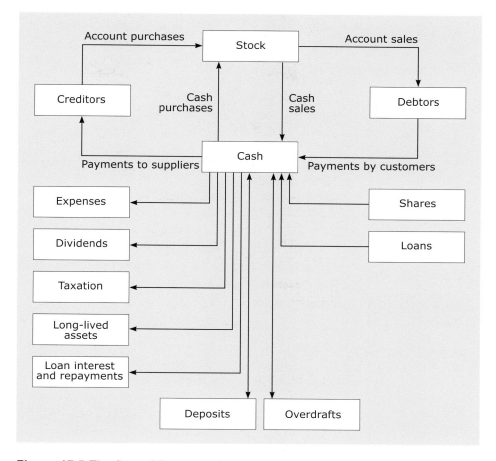

Figure 17.5 The flow of finance – the full picture

Liquidity

We have shown how having sufficient cash to pay wages or other bills, and to purchase resources, is of vital importance. A close examination of the sources and uses of cash is an essential part of the financial management of any organisation. If it lacks control, an organisation may be forced out of existence by those to whom it owes money, and who demand payment. If that happens, its managers could be affected in a very adverse way. Conversely, it is undesirable for an organisation to have too much cash sitting around and not being used to develop its services.

It may be that the organisation you work for has a very efficient and effective cash flow management. But the suppliers you do business with may not have. It would be unfortunate to sign a contract with a supplier and see it go out of business a few weeks later because of poor cash flow management. It may also be that your debtors have cash flow problems. Good business relationships are very important in managing cash.

The important term underlying all we have been discussing is liquidity. It reflects the speed at which an organisation can produce a cash flow so as to meet its current liabilities as they become due. The term solvency is used when an organisation can pay all its debts promptly (including any long-term liabilities) and generates enough cash to continue its operations; an insolvent organisation, technically speaking, is one that cannot pay its debts, although this does not preclude the possibility of its continuing or being rescued. Many organisations have reported sizeable profits or surpluses but had no cash to pay their debts.

An appropriate level of liquidity is thus crucial. Many organisations fail through lack of cash: running out of cash is a particular danger for young and fast-growing commercial firms and, increasingly, for not-for-profit organisations.

Cash flow statements

The cash flow statement effectively covers all elements of the cash flow process, reflecting how much cash was spent and how much cash was received. A cash flow statement is prepared by comparing the cash figure on the opening day of a specified period with that on the last day, and detailing all the pluses and minuses that will cause or have caused the cash balance to change. In theory it is quite easy to construct but, given the size of many organisations and the volume and complexity of their activities and transactions, in practice it can be quite difficult to produce statements that are useful to managers.

Financial reports drawn up using the matching principle are valuable in any type of organisation. They record the values of the resources consumed in undertaking activities and transactions during a particular period, which is useful information. Yet it is entirely possible for an organisation to report profits or surpluses but have no cash. Then the cash flow statement for an organisation takes on a new significance.

Example 17.2 Terrestrial Trading Company

Using the data in Table 17.1 we can prepare a simple cash flow statement for Terrestrial Trading. This is shown in Table 17.2.

Table 17.1 Terrestrial Trading Company: Year 1 data

A	Sales totalled £60,000, being 50% for cash and 50% to account customers (debtors) on credit
B	Materials for stock costing £25,000 were purchased on account
C	The stock of materials held at the end of the year had cost £10,000
D	Sundry operating expenses totalled £10,000, of which £1,000 remained unpaid at the year end
E	Depreciation on fixed assets amounted to £5,000
F	Loan interest of £1,000 was paid
G	Debtors paid £25,000 in cash
H	Trade creditors were paid £20,000 in cash
I	Fixed assets costing £20,000 were purchased for cash
J	The owners contributed £25,000 in cash as capital to establish the business
K	A long-term bank loan for £10,000 was obtained, repayable within five years with an interest rate of 10% a year

Table 17.2 Terrestrial Trading Company: a simple cash flow statement for Year 1

	£	£
Cash inflows during Year 1		
From owners, as capital	25,000	
From bank, as loan	10,000	
From cash customers	30,000	
From account customers	25,000	
		90,000
Cash outflows during Year 1		
Bank interest	1,000	
Purchases of fixed assets	20,000	
Payment for operating expenses	9,000	
Payment to creditors for stocks	20,000	
		(50,000)
Net cash flow during year		40,000
Opening cash balance		0
Closing cash balance		40,000

* See comment below

Table 17.3 Terrestrial Trading Company: cash flow statement for Year 1

	£	£
Cash flows arising from operations		
From cash customers	30,000	
From account customers	25,000	
Paid for operating expenses	(9,000)	
Paid for to creditors for stocks	(20,000)	
		26,000
Cash flows associated with funders		
From owners as capital	25,000	
From bank as loan	10,000	
Paid bank interest	(1,000)	
		34,000
Cash flows associated with fixed assets		
Purchase of fixed assets		(20,000)
Net cash flow during year		40,000
Opening cash balance		0
Closing cash balance		40,000

* As with the profit and loss statements, it is possible to enhance the usefulness of the information in this cash flow statement. Most organisations rearrange the layout by grouping the inflows and outflows

into areas of common interest. For example, inflows and outflows associated with funders are usually grouped together, as are those associated with the acquisition and disposal of fixed assets. Cash from customers and cash spent on day-to-day operational transactions and activities are grouped together to show cash flow arising (or not!) from day-to-day operations. Such sets of groupings are shown in Table 17.3.

Not all layouts are exactly the same as that in Table 17.3. In Tables 17.4, 17.5 and 17.6 we show the annual cash flow statements of our three example organisations. When looking at these statements note the commonalities in terms of each statement showing cash flows (actual receipts and payments). Also note how the specific flows of cash in each are a reflection of their organisational contexts.

Table 17.4 Summary combined cash flow statement of a European publisher

Year ended 31 December	20XX	20XX–1
	€m	€m
Net cash inflow from operating activities	1,155	1,011
Dividends received from joint ventures	6	16
Returns on investment and servicing of finance	(123)	(67)
Taxes	(150)	(214)
Capital expenditure	(185)	(208)
Acquisitions and disposals	(249)	(503)
Equity dividends paid to parent company shareholders	(515)	(540)
Cash outflow before changes in short-term investments and financing	(61)	(505)
Decrease in short-term investments	451	94
Financing	(300)	286
Increase/(decrease) in cash	90	(125)

Table 17.5 Consolidated cash flow statement of an international not-for-profit development charity

Year ended 31 December	20XX	20XX–1
	£000	£000
Net cash inflow from operating activities	424	1,797
Interest received	1,107	1,046
Purchase of tangible fixed assets	(2,647)	(1,945)
Purchase of investments	(73)	–
Proceeds from disposal of fixed assets	245	248
Cash (outflow)/inflow before management of liquid resources	(944)	1,146
Management of liquid resources:		
Decrease in short-term bank deposits	150	100
(Decrease)/increase in cash in period	(794)	1,246

Table 17.6 Statement of cash flows of a New Zealand university

Year ended 31 December	20XX	20XX–1
	NZ$000	NZ$000
Cash flows from operating activities		
Cash provided from:		
Government grants	154,204	153,454
Student allowances	39,626	36,917
Tuition fees	55,558	47,215
Dividends	240	179
Interest	3,809	4,066
Other operating receipts	72,893	65,793
	326,330	307,624
Cash applied to:		
Goods and services tax	(573)	(20)
Student allowances	38,804	36,465
Payments to employees	160,235	157,503
Interest	9	20
Other operating expenses	94,430	98,706
	292,905	292,674
Net cash flows from operating activities	33,425	14,950
Cash flows from investing activities		
Cash provided from:		
Fixed assets	85	535
Investments	754	0
	839	535
Cash applied to:		
Fixed assets and work in progress	27,058	32,733
Investments	1,503	(1,713)
	28,561	31,020
Net cash flows from investing activities	(27,722)	(30,485)
Net increase/(decrease) in cash held	5,703	(15,535)
Opening cash balance	7,702	23,237
Closing cash balance	13,405	7,702
This is shown in the statement of financial position as follows:		
Bank overdraft	–	–
Cash at bank	208	1,452
Short-term investments – unrestricted	8,597	2,550
Short-term investments – restricted	4,600	3,700
	13,405	7,702

Cash flow statements are far less subjective than the statements based on the matching principle (balance sheet and income statement). Cash flow statements record tangible inflows and outflows of cash, which can be tracked and monitored. That is, they are actual cash transactions (receipts and payments).

We now look at how cash flow statements are prepared and presented, taking the hypothetical organisation in Example 17.3 and working it through in the following table and activity. Follow this closely, as understanding how such information is put together is central to your ability to construct and comprehend simple financial spreadsheets.

Example 17.3 Terrestrial Trading Company

Terrestrial Trading Company prepares and sells specialist animal foods, buying vegetable by-products from agricultural businesses. After processing these by-products into animal feed, it sells them ready for use, partly on a cash-and-carry basis to customers who visit its premises, and partly on account to organisations: a mounted police unit and a local veterinary college are regular customers.

Having just completed its first year of trading, its managers are predicting what cash will come in and go out, and when, in Year 2 (January to December). They forecast the following:

- At the close of Year 1, the bank account and any cash on the premises will amount to a total cash balance of £40,000.

- In January, April, July and October, it will take delivery of raw materials, in batches of 10,000 units costing £1.00 per unit. Payment will be made in the month following the delivery. In Year 1 all the stocks were purchased for cash. Thus no sums are outstanding at the start of Year 2.

- Each unit of raw materials will be processed into units ready for sale at £5.00 each. Sales are likely to be divided evenly between cash sales and account (or credit) sales. Half the account sales will be paid for in the month following the sale, the balance during the next month.

- Sales are likely to be: January 1,000 units, February 2,000 units, March 3,000 units. In Year 1 all the sales were cash sales, and thus at the start of Year 2 no amounts were owed by account customers.

- Wages and salaries will amount to £2,000 per month, payable at the end of each month.

- Miscellaneous (or sundry) operating costs will amount to £500 per month. In Year 1 these were paid for in cash as they were incurred. In Year 2 revised purchase terms mean that all these bills will be payable in the following month.

- Processing equipment (fixed assets) costing £10,000 will be purchased and paid for on 1 January.

Based on the assumptions listed above, the cash flow forecast that the managers have prepared for the first three months is shown in Table 17.7. This shows where the inflows of cash are likely to come from and when they should arise, together with the projected timings and amounts of cash outflows.

Table 17.7 Terrestrial Trading Company cash flow statement: forecast for January, February and March, year 2

	Detail	January	February	March	3-month total
		£	£	£	£
	Receipts from sales				
1	Cash	2,500	5,000	7,500	15,000
2	(a) Debtors – Jan. Sales	–	1,250	1,250	2,500
		–	–	2,500	2,500
	(c) Debtors – Mar. sales	–	–	–	–
3	Total receipts	2,500	6,250	11,250	20,000
	Payments				
4	To stock suppliers	–	10,000	–	10,000
5	For wages and salaries	2,000	2,000	2,000	6,000
6	Sundries	–	500	500	1,000
7	Equipment	10,000	–	–	10,000
8	Total payments	12,000	12,500	2,500	27,000
9	Net inflow/(outflow)	(9,500)	(6,250)	8,750	(7,000)
10	Cash at start of period	40,000	30,500	24,250	40,000
11	Cash at end of period	30,500	24,250	33,000	33,000

The following notes explain the entries in the cash forecast. Refer to these explanations as you work through the logic of why and how the cash values shown have been placed where they are.

1 In Table 17.7, line 1 of the forecast cash flow statement shows the cash coming in from cash sales. Sales for January should be 1,000 units at £5.00 each = £5,000. But remember that only 50% of the sales will be for cash – the other 50% will be to account customers. Thus only £2,500 is received for cash sales. The money from the other 50% of sales, to account customers, comes in later and is explained in the note about line 2 below. Cash sales income in February and March is calculated similarly:

February: 2,000 units x £5.00 = £10,000, 50% of which is £5,000.
March: 3,000 x £5.00 = £15,000 x 50% = £7,500.

2 Line 2 shows the cash coming in from the debtors, those who buy on account. In (a) we see no entry in the column for January but we do see £1,250 (half of January's account sales of £2,500) entered in the February column and the balance of £1,250 in the March column. In (b) we see when the cash comes in for the half of February's sales that were account sales (£10,000 x 50% = £5,000). Debtors pay nothing in the month of sale, February, but 50% (£2,500) in March,

and if we were to show an April column, the other 50% (£2,500) would be there. In (c) we note that because none of the debtors who bought units on account will have paid yet, there is no cash shown as coming in. In each of the April and May columns £3,750 would appear. As we are showing the cash flow statement for the first three months only, we do not need to show these entries, but it is important to know that it will be coming in soon.

3   In line 3, the projected cash receipts are then totalled, followed by the payments made by Terrestrial Trading.

4   Line 4 shows the payment for the January delivery of raw materials. The 10,000 units purchased in January at £1.00 each will not be paid for until February. Thus the payment of £10,000 appears in the February column rather than the January column.

5   Line 5, for wages and salaries, shows these as constant at £2,000 per month. They are paid at the end of each month, thus each of the January, February and March columns has an entry of £2,000.

6   Line 6, sundry operating costs, will amount to £500 per month but will not be paid for until the month after. Thus there is no entry in the January column, but £500 in the February column (relating to January) and £500 in the March column (relating to February).

7   Line 7 covers the equipment costing £10,000, purchased and paid for in January. Thus the January column has an entry for £10,000 on this line.

8   Line 8 totals the payments.

9   Line 9 offsets the total receipts (line 3) against the total payments (line 8) to establish the net cash inflow or outflow per month. In January £2,500 comes in, but £12,000 goes out, resulting in a net cash outflow – hence the brackets around the figure – of (£9,500).

10 Line 10 shows the cash the company should have at the beginning of the month: the opening cash balance.

11 In line 11 the net cash inflow or outflow (line 9) is then added to or subtracted from the opening cash balance (line 10) to produce the projected closing cash balance at the end of the month (line 11). Think about your finances – the impact of receiving or paying out a large lump sum in a particular month depends on whether you started the month with a lot of money in the bank or a large overdraft. The final column on the right summarises the cash inflows and outflows for the three-month period.

By this process Terrestrial Trading is breaking down its annual figures into more manageable components, shorter periods, improving its opportunities for planning, monitoring and control. Some organisations use 12 monthly periods, others think 13 four-weekly periods more appropriate. Some organisations go for planning and reporting back on a weekly or even daily basis, if there is a risk of running out of the cash to pay salaries or other expenses or an opportunity to put large amounts of money into deposits to earn interest.

Managing the working capital cycle

Both the sources and uses of cash can be divided into two main categories: those of a long-term nature and those associated with day-to-day activities. Managers need to proactively manage the pattern of day-to-day cash flows. This is closely associated with managing the amount of working capital in an organisation. The amount of working capital in an organisation is defined as being current assets less current liabilities. Current assets include cash, stock and debtors (receivables). It is important for organisations to manage their working capital. Too much working capital is wasteful: an excess of resources tied up; this is called overcapitalisation. Too little working capital is called overtrading – this is risky as it may find it difficult to carry out business due to lack of stock or an inability to pay its debts as they fall due.

Example 17.4 Working Capital Cycle

Assume you are a retailer. Today (day 1) you buy one item of stock for resale. It costs you $100, payable immediately in cash. Assume your experience tells you that you are likely to hold it for 10 days before selling it. When you do sell it, it will be for $200. But the sale will be an account sale, not for cash. This is particularly unfortunate, as your debtors (the 'accounts receivable') normally take 40 days to pay, even though your invoices (documents stating how much is owed) always state that payment is due in 30 days – see Table 17.8.

Table 17.8 Retail trader data

Day	Activity/transaction
1	Stock bought for $100 cash
	(Stock held for 10 days)
10	Stock sold for $200; you give an invoice to the customer, who thus becomes a debtor
	(Debtors take 40 days to pay)
50	$200 received

As you can see, you part with the cash on day 1, but it is 50 days before it is returned (with the profit). The cycle is thus 50 days. For this length of time $100 is tied up in the cycle. Of course, this may not seem a great amount. Say, however, that you hold 500 of these items in stock at any one time. That means you have $50,000 (500 x $100) tied up in the cycle doing absolutely nothing.

Thus, there is a cash cycle. The return of the cash is delayed because of its investment in items that are needed for the everyday work of the business. The cash cycle is often referred to as the working capital cycle, because it is the money needed to finance the day-to-day working of an organisation, rather than the capital used to finance large, one-off, long-term assets.

Part of a manager's job is to make decisions about the use of resources. Cash is no different from other resources: it too needs managing. You can think of cash as the lubricant of an organisation, like oil in a car engine. The engine – the organisation – seizes up if it runs out of oil at any one point in its workings. However, you do not want to waste oil by putting in more than is needed. To manage cash well, time delays also need to be managed, to ensure that the time cash spends in the cycle is as short as possible. The amount of cash and working capital invested in the working capital cycle needs to be managed carefully. The aim is to have sufficient funds so as not to be overtrading while not being inefficient and having too much of your resources tied up in working capital (overcapitalisation).

Working capital is defined as being current assets less current liabilities. The make-up of which is detailed in Table 17.9 below.

Table 17.9 Difference between current assets and current liabilities

Current assets	Current liabilities
Cash/bank	Creditors and others payable within one year
Debtors	
Stocks	

Stocks can be for manufacturing, for delivering services, for resale or for office supplies: they are classified as current assets because they are there to facilitate day-to-day operations.

As a general rule, many organisations try to ensure that their total current assets usually exceed their current liabilities. Remember, this was not the case with the publishing company – such ratios need to be compared with those for other years or for similar organisations if they are to have real meaning. In theory, if its creditors ask for payment, an organisation should have enough current assets left to carry on operations after their bills have been settled. By expressing the relationship between current assets and current liabilities, we can produce what is usually termed the current ratio. Such a ratio reflects the working capital situation and shows whether or not there is an excess of current assets over current liabilities. If the ratio is too low, an organisation could have too few current assets to carry on its activities after meeting the claims of those who make up its current liabilities. If it is too high, the organisation could be wasting its resources, with too much spare cash, debtors at too high a level (with the danger of more bad debts and higher collection costs) and too high stocks (tying up capital and increasing storage costs and the risks of theft, deterioration and obsolescence).

Having enough current assets is one matter, but if they comprise mainly stocks with very little cash and/or very few debtors who are going to pay soon, it can be misleading to count stocks. This situation can be expressed by determining what is commonly called the quick ratio, which compares liquid current assets (normally cash and debtors) with current liabilities. The extent to which a business should be alarmed by a particular quick ratio depends on the context. For example, both a supermarket chain and a shipbuilder might have fairly high current ratios. However, while a supermarket might be able to survive with a quick ratio below 1:1, as it receives cash all day, every day, a shipbuilder needs a very high quick ratio to meet its bills, as it is likely to receive cash from its customers only periodically. In recent years, large supermarket groups have managed to lower their current ratios by significantly improving stock management systems.

Digging below the surface

It is important not to consider just the overall working capital and cash position but also to manage each aspect of the working capital cycle. The current and quick ratios provide, in a sense, the 'headline news'. We can dig deeper to find out which components of the working capital are being managed well. Three further calculations help us here. These are the debtors turnover, creditors turnover and stock turnover.

Debtors turnover

We can measure our efficiency in terms of moneys we are owed with reference to debtors turnover. Consider an organisation that over a year had £30,000 of sales on account and an average debtor balance of £5,000.

$$\text{Debtors turnover} = \frac{\text{annual account sales}}{\text{average debtors balance}} = \frac{£30,000}{£5,000}$$
$$= 6 \text{ times per annum}$$

Or an average time to receive payment from customers was 61 days.

This means that at any one time one-sixth of the year's sales have yet to be paid for. As one-sixth of a year is 61 days, we can say that it takes the company an average of 61 days to collect its money. Calculating this figure from the financial statements and comparing it with formal invoicing terms, targets, previous periods and other firms can be a hugely revealing exercise for managers.

Organisations should be concerned about the amount of resources tied up in debtors as it's wasteful and can lead to bad debts. It may be preferable to have customers pay cash; however it may not be competitive not to offer credit terms. While it is desirable to have debtors pay as quickly as possible, organisations need to remember the importance of customer relations before chasing their debts too aggressively. It may be worthwhile to offer a discount for early payment in order to encourage prompt payment.

Creditors turnover

Another efficiency ratio that can help us to understand our working capital position is creditors turnover. If during a year a company bought £25,000 of materials on account. During the year it owed an average of £5,000 to the materials suppliers.

$$\text{Creditors turnover} = \frac{\text{annual account purchases}}{\text{average creditors balance}} = \frac{£25,000}{£5,000}$$
$$= 5 \text{ times per annum}$$

Or an average time to pay creditors of 73 days.

This means that at any one time one-fifth of the company's purchases during the year have yet to be paid for. As one-fifth of a year is 73 days, we can say that it takes the company an average of 73 days to pay for its materials.

As before, calculating this figure from the financial statements and comparing it with formal invoicing terms, targets, previous periods and other firms can be very revealing. In addition, we can see that the company is paying its materials suppliers more slowly (every 73 days) than it takes to get cash from its debtors (61 days) – this is indicative of a healthy working capital cycle. Organisations that receive their cash before they have to pay for the things that they buy have inherently lower financing needs than those that do not.

In calculating creditors turnover we have focused on materials that come into stock. This is normal and enables us to make comparisons, as we did, with sales debtors. We could also have calculated a total creditors turnover by including the sundry items and how much was owed for them. In terms of working capital management it may be desirable not to pay our debts too quickly; however we must consider also the importance of managing our supply chain and business relationships. We may also choose to pay promptly in order to take advantage of any discounts for prompt payment that may be available. It is important to consider the financial health of your supplier. If you are a significant customer of theirs, your late payment can create liquidity problems for them. In such business relationships all parties should behave ethically for their mutual wellbeing.

Stock turnover

We can asses our inventory efficiency with reference to stock turnover. If during the year the cost of the stock sold was £15,000: the company bought £25,000 of materials on account and had an average £10,000 worth of stock during the year.

$$\text{Stock turnover} = \frac{\text{annual cost of stock sold (or used)}}{\text{average stock balance}} = \frac{£15,000}{£10,000}$$

$$= 1.5 \text{ times per annum}$$

Or an average time to sell its stock of 243 days.

This means that at any one time the company has 1/1.5 of its annual usage of material held in stock. We can say that at this rate it takes it an average of 243 days (365/1.5) to use its stock. Superficially this is high, although buying in smaller amounts may have lost it bulk purchase discounts. Again, context is important if the figure is to make sense. Holding too much stock is wasteful and can lead to shrinkage. However, it may also be important to consider how much stock is needed given our organisational context. Some organisations operate a just in time system to minimise their stock holdings, whereby they try to arrange deliveries just in time for their needs. This can lead to savings but there is also a risk of running out of stock if arrangements breakdown.

The comparisons and ratios that are important and available in organisations will vary hugely. We have only just touched on the range of uses to which data in formal and informal financial statements can be put. However, we hope we have identified some ideas and frameworks for doing so.

Chapter 18 Analysis and interpretation of financial statements

Percentages and ratios

The income statement and balance sheet are prepared for a purpose: to provide meaningful information to various stakeholders about the financial performance and financial position of the organisation. In many cases, the figures shown will only be meaningful in terms of their relationship with other figures. For example, consider an organisation that has achieved a net profit of £2,000,000. Is this good, bad or indifferent? Such a question can only be answered by, for example, comparing the profit figure with the capital employed in producing it. If capital employed was £1,000,000 the profit would represent a return of 200% – exceptional by the standards of most commercial organisations! On the other hand, if capital employed was £100,000,000, this would represent a return of 2% – unacceptable by the normal standards of commercial organisations. This example illustrates that the financial performance and financial position of an organisation can usually only be evaluated in a meaningful way by using various ratios that express the value of one variable in relation to another.

Percentages and ratios are important ways of analysing and interpreting financial results. No single figure has much significance unless it is compared with another. One way is to compare actual with budgeted figures to show variances. Other comparisons can be made with previous years or benchmarked against competitors or industry averages. These trends and comparisons between two figures are often facilitated by using percentages and ratios. Financial ratios conveniently assess performance and are commonly used in financial analysis.

Example 18.1 Percentages

Consider two organisations – if one charity had 100 new donors last month and another had 10, how meaningful is this information? The raw figures take on meaning when they are compared to other figures. If the first had 1,000 existing donors and the second had 10 at the start of the month, then we can say that the first charity increased its donors by 10% (100 ÷ 1000) and the second by 100% (10 ÷ 10). Already the figures begin to have much more meaning.

If the first charity lost 50 existing donors and the second only 1 during the month then the net increases can be calculated as follows:

First charity:

net change in donors = 100 − 50 = 50 and percentage change 50 ÷ 1000 = 5%

Second charity:

net change in donors 10 − 1 = 9 and percentage change 9 ÷ 10 = 90%

We can then say that in that month the ratio between new and lost fund providers was 2:1 (100:50) in the first business and 10:1 in the second. This ratio can then be compared with previous months, with other similar companies and with the targets that the firms may have set themselves.

Box 18.1 expands this principle to financial information.

Box 18.1 Ratios

When certain ratios are calculated the information contained in the financial statements of an organisation enables interested parties to gain a deeper insight into its finances. The ratios calculated usually require comparison with other ratios. Comparisons may take three forms, with:

- predetermined standards or targets (actual ratios with budget ratios, for example)
- the same ratio in a previous or different period (this year's ratios with last year's, for example)
- the same ratio in another comparable organisation (your ratios compared with a competitor's, for example).

For external comparison, the ratios for one organisation could be compared with those of other similar concerns. Comparison with an organisation that is known to be especially excellent in a particular activity is referred to as 'best practice benchmarking'. All organisations find ratios useful when assessing performance, although financial ratios are particularly relevant for private sector organisations participating in the capital markets, as you will see from the city pages of any newspaper.

Ratios are a primary means of analysing accounts for both internal and external purposes – they are useful tools both for managers and as a guide for investors, creditors and others. They provide a means of interpreting and comparing results and establishing performance objectives or yardsticks. They can be used with financial data or with non-financial data, as we will see later.

We are looking for patterns and comparisons that convert raw figures into more meaningful information for managers. Example 18.2 illustrates this further.

Example 18.2 The arts mean business

Torvig Arts Centre served a city with a resident population of approximately 100,000, boosted by a university of 10,000 students and approximately 200,000 tourist visitors each year. Torvig's programme included drama by touring theatre companies, specialist films, jazz and small-scale classical music performances and art and craft exhibitions. It also ran a café. The information in Tables 18.1 and 18.2 existed in various places on the desk of Torvig's manager as the budget and targets for the financial year 20X3 were about to be set.

Table 18.1 Information about Torvig Arts Centre (1)

	20X1	20X2
Total income	£860,000	£800,000
Direct costs of running the café	£45,000	£40,000
Ticket sales	£200,000	£200,000
Number of subscription-paying members	7,000	8,000

(Subscription members received various benefits – mailings, reduced admission prices, private viewings etc. – for their average £10 p.a. per person subscription. There were discounted rates for pensioners, students, unemployed people, etc.)

A survey of 200 people attending events during a typical month during 20X2 recorded that 80 of them were tourists, that these 80 spent a total of £400 in the café immediately before or after an event, compared with the total of £500 spent by the other 120 attendees.

Table 18.2 Information about Torvig Arts Centre (2)

	20X1	20X2
Number of business sponsors	90	80
Total income from business sponsors	£150,000	£160,000
Legacies, gifts, donations received	£54,000	£64,000
Takings from the café	£110,000	£120,000
Grants from local authorities and arts funding bodies	£260,000	£160,000
Other income (e.g. sales of catalogues)	£16,000	£16,000
Salary costs excluding café staff (paid casually)	£215,000	£200,000
Overheads and running costs	£570,000	£580,000

From the information in Tables 18.1 and 18.2, it is possible to construct a basic table of income and expenditure (see Table 18.3). Do this before comparing it with the one in the response.

Table 18.3 Torvig Arts Centre income and expenditure statement

	20X1		20X2	
	£'000		£'000	
Income				
Ticket sales	200		200	
Grants	260		160	
Sponsorship	150		160	
Café	110		120	
Membership subs	70		80	
Legacies and gifts	54		64	
Miscellaneous	16		16	
Total income		860		800
Expenditure				
Café direct costs	45		40	
Salaries	215		200	
Overheads and running costs	570		580	
Total expenditure		830		820
Surplus/(deficit)		30		(20)

Now consider the following examples, which illustrate the range of information that could be gained by analysing the above data.

Table 18.4 Torvig Arts Centre café profitability

	20X1	20X1	20X2	20X2
	£'000	%	£'000	%
Sales	110	100%	120	100%
Cost of sales	45	40.9%	40	33.3%
Gross Profit margin	65	59.1%	80	66.7%

1   Calculating the café's gross profit for the two years, in percentage terms, and note what that suggests to you. The gross profit is the income less the direct costs of generating that income. The gross profit margin increasing from just under 60% (65 ÷ 110) to nearly 67% (80 ÷ 120) as the café is generating more income at less cost. See Table 18.4.

2   Calculating the grant income for the two years as a percentage of total income, and then the percentage decreases in grant income and in total income in 20X2. Even though grant income decreased by nearly 40% (100 ÷ 260), the total income fell by only 7% (60 ÷ 860).

This was because Torvig managed to sustain or increase its income from all the other sources, to the extent that grant income represented only 20% (160 ÷ 800) of its total income in 20X2, compared with 30% (260 ÷ 860) in 20X1.

3   How much café income did Torvig obtain per tourist and per other member. Is the difference significant? Each tourist spent on average £5 in the café (£400 ÷ 80), yielding £3.33 in net income (remember the 67% gross profit margin), compared with each non-tourist audience member's £4.17 (£500 ÷ 120), yielding £2.78 in net income. This difference is significant in the context of Torvig's reduced grant income and of its need to target customer groups who will generate most additional net income.

4   What was the ratio of sponsors to sponsorship income in each of the two years? What do these figures reveal, but also conceal? Here the increase from an average of £1,667 to £2,000 per business sponsor (£150,000 ÷ 90 to £160,000 ÷ 80) suggests that the sponsors were each giving more. But the total number of sponsors had decreased, and the sponsorship increase could have been due to one or two exceptionally generous sponsors rather than to each of them giving more.

5   What ratio of ticket sales to salary costs might be an appropriate target for 20X3? Here the manager has a choice of (a) maintaining the 20X2 ratio of 1:1 (£200,000:£200,000), (b) assuming a continuing 7.5% increase in cost-effectiveness in 20X3 and thus set a target 1.075:1 (note that each £1 spent on salaries in 20X1 generated only 93p in ticket sales – to get to £1 in ticket sales per £1 salary costs in 20X2 was a 7.5% increase), (c) being conservative and returning to the 20X1 ratio because he believes 20X2 was an abnormal year or (d) coming up with a different figure based on knowledge or judgement about the factors affecting this relation between staff costs and ticket sales. All the options are valid, but using the ratio makes them calculated estimates rather than purely arbitrary guesses.

6   What percentage growth in the number of members was achieved from 20X1 to 20X2? What was the percentage growth in ticket sales income? Could these figures be connected? Are they relevant to setting targets for membership subscriptions and ticket sales income for 20X3? In 20X2 there was a growth of over 14% in the number of members (1000 ÷ 7000) but no increase in ticket sales income. This suggests that the discounted rates for members might have cost Torvig some ticket sales income from those of the 1,000 new members who would have paid the full rate to attend the events they now attended as members. If so, the manager needs to set targets for 20X3 ticket sales and membership subscription income which take into account the relation between them.

7   What percentage reduction in overhead costs in 20X2 would have enabled Torvig to break even? Why should the manager use the answer to that question with care when setting overhead expenditure targets in the budget for 20X3? It should be easy to calculate the 3.5% decrease in overheads (20 ÷ 580) needed to have broken

even. However, these cost reductions might have cost Torvig some of the increased income its efforts generated during the year in the café, and in respect of membership, sponsorship and legacies. The manager will need to set an expenditure budget for 20X3 that targets reductions on those costs which least affect net income in the short and longer terms.

These are but a few examples of the sort of analysis we could carry out on the information presented, and many more could be asked if we had more detailed information. Even these few questions should illustrate quite powerfully how simple percentages and ratios can express comparisons between different figures.

The ability to look at a set of figures and to read meaning into them grows with familiarity, practise and technical competence. Ultimately, however, the ability to express one total as a percentage or ratio of another one lies at the root of most quantitative interpretations by managers.

Financial performance ratios

Financial performance ratios can be used to assist in the analysis and interpretation of financial performance from financial statements. Many parties have an interest in using ratios to asses an organisation's performance. Those providing finance to an organisation are concerned with its creditworthiness, whether they provide long-term finance as owners, investors or bankers, or short-term finance as suppliers. Employees, customers and clients will wish to assure themselves that their organisation is viable. In not-for-profit organisations, donors, beneficiaries and volunteers all have some interest in their financial performance. Assessing performance in terms of financial performance ratios alone will only give you a partial view, as not every aspect of an organisation's performance can be adequately encapsulated in purely financial terms. However, whatever the type of organisation, in whatever sector, the relevant parties frequently use financial ratios to pass judgement on its managers' financial performance (limited though such a perspective may be).

Assessing financial performance

Perhaps the most important financial ratio to measure operating performance is the return on capital employed (ROCE), also termed the primary ratio. In profit-seeking organisations this ratio shows their ability to generate a return on their investment. In practice there are a number of ways to express this ratio, but perhaps the most commonly applied in commercial concerns is:

$$\text{ROCE} = \frac{\text{profit before interest and tax (operating profit)}}{\text{capital employed}}$$

This ratio relates operating profit (profit before interest and tax, i.e. the profit generated from day-to-day activities) to all the capital sums invested in an organisation, such capital sums comprising owners' investments (capital and reserves) and long-term liability loans (bank loans and other creditors due after one year). This ratio measures the profit (the return) earned on commercial activity by private sector businesses or surplus from any trading carried out by public or not-for-profit organisations.

Example 18.3 Terrestrial Trading

We shall now calculate the ROCE for the fictitious organisation Terrestrial Trading (TT). Its planned and actual financial statements are detailed in Tables 18.5 and 18.6. The actual net profit before interest and tax (also known as operating profit) was £30,000 at the end of the first year (Table 18.5). The total capital employed at the end of the first year totalled £64,000 (£54,000 shareholders' funds and £10,000 long-term liabilities) (Table 18.6). We thus obtain:

$$\text{ROCE} = \frac{\pounds 30,000}{\pounds 64,000} = 46.9\%$$

Table 18.5 Terrestrial Trading Company: profit statement at the end of first year

	Actual		Planned	
	£'000	£'000	£'000	£'000
Sales				
For cash	30		40	
On account	30		40	
		60		80
Less				
Cost of stock sold		15		30
Gross profit		45		50
Less				
Operating expenses	10		10	
Depreciation	5		5	
Total operating expenses		15		15
Operating profit		30		35
Less				
Bank loan interest		1		–
Net reported profit		29		35

Table 18.6 Terrestrial Trading Company: balance sheet at end of first year

	Actual		Planned	
	£'000	£'000	£'000	£'000
Fixed assets				
At cost	20		20	
Less				
Depreciation to date	5		5	
		15		15
Current assets				
Stocks	10		5	
Debtors	5		10	
Cash at bank and in hand	40		33	
	55		48	
Less				
Creditors falling due within one year				
Trade creditors	(5)		(2)	
Accruals	(1)		(1)	
	(6)		(3)	
Net current assets		49		45
		64		60
Less				
Creditors falling due after one year				
Bank loan		(10)		–
Net assets		54		60
Representing				
Capital and reserves				
Capital	25		25	
Retained profits	29		35	
Shareholders' funds		54		60

Analysing ROCE

The items that go to make up what we call capital employed are important because the expression has implications for what is meant by return. If you were an investor of capital sums in TT – either a loan provider or a shareholder – you would, quite reasonably, expect to receive a reward for providing the company with the funds that its managers invest in various assets. If you had provided loans, you would expect to receive an appropriate amount of interest as a reward. If you were a shareholder, although not guaranteed a reward, you would certainly expect to generate a return on your investment in the long run. The shareholders' return comprises dividends and capital growth, 'appreciation', from gains and the reinvestment of any profits not taken out in the form of dividends.

Both lenders and shareholders will be rewarded out of the net profit available before the deduction of any interest or dividend payment and, since interest is usually a tax deductible item, it is usual to calculate the return using profit before deducting interest and taxation. This means we use operating profit (profit before interest and tax) rather than net profit when calculating a ROCE figure.

While it is possible to use just the year-end capital employed figure, as we have done for TT, many organisations calculate the average capital employed during the year, for example by averaging the opening and closing capital employed figures. This more accurately reflects the spread of investment over a year, a spread which has led to the generation of profits throughout the same 12-month period. Nevertheless, for most purposes the year-end capital employed figure is sufficient for ratio comparison purposes.

Analysing the flow of finance

The ROCE figure is a fundamental measure and a useful starting point in any calculation of a series of ratios. There are two principal ways to improve the return on capital: by making a larger profit each time a product or service is sold, or by selling more goods or services with the same investment. These two aspects of ROCE are expressed by the secondary ratios, which we shall consider shortly.

We can envisage the process as the cyclical flow of events shown in Figure 18.1, calling it a business cycle.

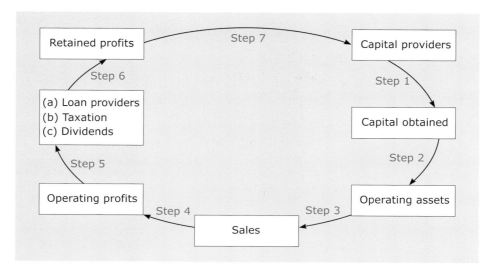

Figure 18.1 The business cycle

The figure depicts the following cycle of events in a commercial concern:

- Step 1: capital sums obtained from the two groups of providers, lenders and shareholders.
- Step 2: capital invested in sundry operating assets.

- Step 3: operating assets used to generate sales revenues by, for example, reselling goods, or manufacturing and selling products, or selling services.
- Step 4; operating cost expenditure controlled to a level lower than sales revenues.
- Step 5: sales matched with lower operating costs to produce an operating profit, the profit generated from day-to-day core activities.
- Step 6: operating profits distributed (or appropriated):
  - interest to loan providers, leaving net profit
  - taxation, leaving net profit after tax
  - dividends to shareholders.
- Step 7: balance from the year's operations added to retained profits (i.e. reserves) for reinvestment or future use.

If there is to be enough profit to:

- fund the payment of loan interest
- meet shareholders' earnings requirements
- provide for the reinvestment of profits after the payment of dividends to the shareholders

it is essential that an appropriate level of operating profit is generated. This is measured by ROCE.

If we calculate ROCE for a year and compare it with the budget (or the previous year, or competitors), and find it is better or worse, it is sensible to want to know why. We can establish this by focusing on the calculation of two further ratios; these are often termed secondary ratios.

The secondary ratios

These ratios focus on two major areas particularly concerned with the level of organisational operating performances as revealed by the ROCE ratio.

These two areas are:

- efficiency in the utilisation of the assets in which the capital obtained from the capital providers has been invested
- performance in relation to profit levels once sales have been generated, usually through cost control.

The performance of each area is measured by the 'asset utilisation ratio' and the 'return on sales ratio'.

The asset utilisation ratio (AUR)

This ratio is also called the asset turnover ratio or the capital turnover ratio. It reflects the level of intensity with which assets are employed. The higher the turnover, the harder the assets are being worked. If it is declining it is an area that needs attention and improvement. It provides information about Step 3 of Figure 18.1 above.

Looking again at TT's actual results for its first year (from Tables 18.1 and 18.2) we should find the following:

$$AUR = \frac{\text{sales}}{\text{operating assets (capital employed)}}$$

$$AUR = \frac{\text{sales of £60,000}}{\text{operating assets (capital employed) of £64,000}}$$

$$AUR = \frac{£60,000}{£64,000} = 94\% \text{ or } 0.94 \text{ times}$$

In other words, the company is generating 94 pence out of every £1 of assets.

If we found that similar organisations had an AUR of two times, or that the budgeted AUR was different from the actual, we should have highlighted areas for investigation. Having calculated this ratio, we can undertake a further asset analysis. For example, the asset utilisation efficiency level overall will be the result of high or low levels of the utilisation of the fixed assets portion and of the net current assets, or working capital, portion. Such an analysis would, for TT's first year of operations, comprise:

$$\text{fixed asset utilisation} = \frac{\text{sales of £60,000}}{\text{fixed assets of £15,000}} = 4:1 \text{ or } 400\%$$

$$\text{working capital utilisation} = \frac{\text{sales of £60,000}}{\text{working capital of £49,000}} = 1.22:1 \text{ or } 122\%$$

These can be subdivided further, as you will see when we look at the pyramid of ratios shortly.

The return on sales ratio (ROS)

This ratio measures the return of operating profit from sales. The difference between operating profit and sales is represented by various expenses, such as the cost of the stock sold and day-to-day operating costs. If the ratio increases over a period, this may be evidence of effective cost control; a decrease may indicate the need for investigation. The ratio analyses Steps 4 and 5 of Figure 18.1.

Using the figures for TT's first year of operations, the actual return on sales ratio is:

$$ROS = \frac{\text{profit before interest and tax (operating profit)}}{\text{sales}}$$

$$ROS = \frac{£30,000}{£60,000} = 50\%$$

The pyramid of ratios

When analysing business performance, managers can subdivide the primary and secondary ratios further. This helps them to evaluate each area of their organisation and show how much it contributes to the organisation's financial results. Let us return to the idea that the principal ratio of business performance is ROCE, the primary ratio.

ROCE can be broken down into:

ROCE = return on sales × asset utilisation

$$\text{Or} \quad \frac{\text{sales}}{\text{operating assets (capital employed)}} \times \frac{\text{profit before interest and tax (operating profit)}}{\text{sales}}$$

This shows that if ROCE is evaluated as unsatisfactory, there are two strategies possible to improve performance:

- improve the return on sales (ROS) by reducing costs (or increasing prices)
- improve the use of assets, and thus use of capital (AUR).

You then have the start of a pyramid scheme of related ratios, as shown in Figure 18.2.

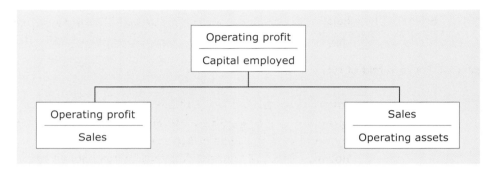

Figure 18.2 The primary and secondary ratios

These three ratios (ROCE, ROS, AUR) represent the top of the pyramid. A not untypical pyramid is shown in Figure 18.3. It will be appreciated that ROCE can be assessed on its own to allow you to form a judgement about whether the return is adequate, having regard to the risk involved. The adequacy of the secondary ratios can be judged only in conjunction with each other. A very low ROS may be quite acceptable if combined with a high AUR, in a wholesale business for example; whereas a shipbuilder is likely to have a very low AUR and must therefore seek a correspondingly high ROS. The secondary ratios will be considered in relative terms – relative to norms or to targets set by senior managers.

An analysis of each of these areas will provide a measure of past managerial achievement and may be used as a basis for future action. This aspect is often overlooked by the uninformed manager, who tends to use ratio analysis to look backwards rather than forwards. These ratios can be subdivided into many more at the discretion of the managers of an organisation.

For all managers in all organisations, the challenge of cost management is very important. Consider the main cost management ratios for you and your organisation. In the public and voluntary sectors they may be individual costs as a percentage of funding. In the private sector they will be variations on those in Figure 18.3.

Corporate social responsibility (including minimising carbon emissions and other damaging environmental impacts) and ethical behaviour are increasingly important. A major objective of commercial organisations is, nevertheless, profit. Consequently, the evaluation of their performance

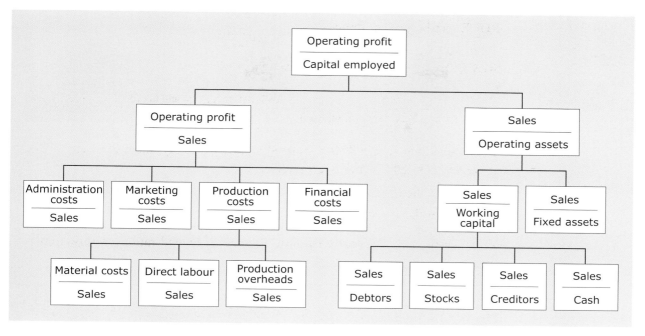

Figure 18.3 The pyramid of ratios

involves an analysis of profitability and the variables that influence profitability – asset utilisation and sales margin – as indicated by the pyramid of ratios. In not-for-profit organisations, such as charities, profit is not the objective, but the financial statements can still provide very useful information about how such an organisation is being managed and the extent to which it is achieving its objectives.

The business cycle and ratios in the public and not-for-profit sectors

If you are a manager in the public or not-for-profit sector, then the business cycle and the associated pyramid of ratios may be applied by you when you assess any commercial activities or trading subsidiaries. On the other hand, such activities will relate only to specific projects or programmes. The organisation as a whole cannot make the same use of ROCE, because its aim is not to earn profit (although some public sector activities are expected to generate an appropriate return on capital).

Figure 18.4 suggests a cycle of events and the accompanying flow of finance which may reflect the nature of operations in a not-for-profit organisation.

Even this may not mirror your organisation and you may be able to design a version of the figure more appropriate to you. The difficulty is that the flow of finance is not cyclical in a not-for-profit organisation, because the goods or services are likely to be delivered to beneficiaries free or below cost, while the funders (taxpayers and/or donors) expect no direct financial reward in return for their payments.

It will be important to compare the cost of services generated as a percentage of funds available accounting period on accounting period. If that figure is 100%, neither a surplus nor a loss is made – a reasonable aim in a not-for-profit organisation. If it is less than 100%, a surplus exists to be added to reserves. If it is more than 100% the deficit must be taken from

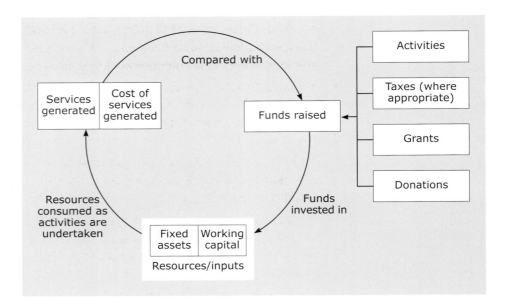

Figure 18.4 The business cycle for a not-for-profit organisation

previous reserves. In the UK, charities are not meant to hoard surpluses without good reason, and trustees may be required to declare their reserves policies in their annual reports.

The cycle may be broken down into whatever level of detail is required. For example, cost per activity may be established and benchmarked against other organisations. Certainly, it will be important to devise and apply appropriate cost management ratios for each activity area and for the organisation as a whole. Other financial ratios can be used which provide relevant information to specific organisational contexts. Ratios that a charity may use include the proportion of expenses spent on administration relative to the amount spent on charitable activities (see Box 18.2). A charity may also use a reserves: expenditure ratio (or working capital ratio) which provides an indication of how many years current activity (expenditure) could be maintained from reserves. In such not-for-profit organisations, financial ratios should be accompanied by key performance indicators (KPIs), many of which will be non-financial in nature.

Box 18.2 Examples of ratios for voluntary organisations

A number of financial performance indicators are widely used for evaluating voluntary organisations. These include the following:

- Programme expenses indicate the percentage of total expenditure for the year that is spent on the programmes or services the organisation exists to provide. (Average for all charities is 80%.)

- Administrative expenses indicate the percentage of total expenditure that is spent on staff salaries, and so on. (Average for all charities is 9.7%.)

- Fundraising expenses indicates the percentage of total expenditure that is spent on the actual process of raising funds. (Average for all charities is 7.4% or 17.6% for public broadcasting and media charities; these types of charities use expensive media such as television advertising to raise funds. Consequently, they tend to spend a much higher proportion of their income on fundraising.)

- Fundraising efficiency indicates the amount a charity spends on fundraising in order to raise every £1 of donations. (Average for all charities is £0.10 or £0.21 for public broadcasting and media charities.)

- Revenue growth indicates the year-on-year growth in total income – expressed as a percentage of the previous year. (Average for all charities is 9.6%.)

- Programme expense growth indicates the year-on-year growth in amount spent on the programmes or services that the organisation exists to provide – expressed as a percentage of the previous year. (Average for all charities is 10%.)

- Working capital ratio indicates how long (in years) a charity could sustain its level of spending without generating new revenue. It is obtained by dividing net current assets by total annual expenditure. (Average for all charities is 0.69.)

Source: http://www.charitynavigator.org/

Limitations of using ratios

When using ratios you should keep in mind the limitations of the financial statements: especially the important information they don't provide. In particular, accounting profit has been subject to much criticism from marketing managers (among others) because it reflects the costs of marketing activities but not necessarily the benefits. For example, so-called 'intangible assets', such as brands, may have been created or developed by a company itself rather than purchased externally. The regulatory framework governing the preparation of financial statements makes it very difficult for companies to bring such assets onto the balance sheet. Therefore accounting profit not only gives a misleading picture of a company's performance but can also act as a disincentive to invest in marketing or other activities that can improve the business performance in the medium to long term, as the costs will appear now but the benefits will not show before some unspecified date in the future!

In an attempt to deal with such problems, an alternative performance measure called Economic Value Added (EVA) has been introduced to aid users of financial statements in assessing company performance. Detailed consideration of this complex issue is beyond the scope of this particular course. Essentially, however, EVA is calculated by making a number of adjustments to accounting profit to remove the distortions created by including the costs but not the benefits of expenditures such as marketing and research and development.

Chapter 19 Performance management
Internal performance measurement

It is important for managers to be able to assess and manage the performance of their organisation. Internally, managers will have access to more detailed information (such as management accounting data) than may be available externally in the published financial statements. While financial information may be useful in assessing an organisation's performance, it will be insufficient to fully understand the performance and the context in which it took place. Non-financial and qualitative information will also be required.

The way that you and your organisation measure its performance will both determine and reflect its priorities and will illustrate its approach to its stakeholders. It is a basic principle of management that to control something you need to measure it: 'what gets measured gets attention'. By extension, what you choose to measure and how you measure it should be a reflection of your strategic direction and priorities.

When an organisation has social goals, measurement can be problematic. It may be easy to measure outputs such as the number of people attending a clinic or using a service. But are satisfactory outcomes being achieved? Is the quality of life of people with mental health problems being improved? Is global poverty being diminished, or are gender and race discrimination in a community being reduced?

It is not sufficient simply to measure that which is easily measurable – indeed, this can sometimes be damaging. The commonest effect is an over-emphasis on financial measures, leading to the complaint that 'the organisation is being run by accountants'. This emphasis on financial measures is the result of several factors:

- Financial measures are easily available.
- They can be more readily compared and evaluated than the 'soft' (non-quantifiable) information available from other functions. How do you evaluate improvements in an individual's self-perception, for example?
- For most organisations financial performance is fundamentally important.

Financial measures, however, should be only part of a range of measures used by managers.

The choice of measure is critical. You should normally use more than one measure, and as important as your choice of measures is your choice of performance standards. Performance measures are of value only if there is some yardstick against which to compare that performance. Specific performance measures may be developed for specific industries, for example retailers may use sales per square metre; restaurants may use meals served; airlines measure 'load factors' in terms of passengers numbers to seats ratio. Internal performance measures should have the following characteristics:

- acceptance
- ease of use

- common understanding
- a valid measure.

As a manager you need a set of agreed performance standards to serve as comparators for actual performance. There are a number of comparators that you can use, some internal to your organisation, and some external.

Past performance, as we have discussed under both budget setting and ratio analysis in this book, is commonly used as a standard against which to judge future performance. Improvement targets can then be set against these standards. While convenient and realistic, the use of past performance as a comparator is inwardly focused, and runs the risk of generating complacency. It tends to ignore both what others are achieving and what customers are demanding. Past performance can therefore be regarded as a necessary but not a sufficient comparator.

Budgets are, perhaps, the most widely used performance standard. However a budget is produced, it is likely to be an important internal control mechanism. Indeed, the achievement of budget figures may form the basis for managers' appraisal and reward. As with information about past performance, budget information is readily available and accessible, and the costs of collection and presentation are low. But there are two main problems. First, budgets are self-determined and therefore internally focused – they ignore competitors and customers. Secondly, they are based primarily on financial information, which is a narrow base on which to measure performance.

Of the external standards, competitors' performance is clearly important for organisations that operate in a competitive environment. For example, an organisation's market share performance will help it understand how it is doing in the marketplace. It must make sense for an organisation to adopt performance standards that at least match those of organisations providing comparable services. The main difficulty is the collection of appropriate information about these organisations. Whatever approach is used, there will be time and effort involved – the process will not be free. The sources of information may include some or all of the following:

- databases (libraries or online)
- interviews (secondary sources)
- 'mystery shopping' (enquiring as a potential user)
- primary market research
- an analysis of patterns of service provision
- 'soft' information (personal opinions from staff, and so on).

If you are determined enough, you will be able to collect a lot of data on other providers. You will have to collate it, and the resulting picture may have some gaps, but it should be sufficient to help you draw up some standards based on others' performances. The act of putting together such information will require you to look outside your own organisation, and will help you understand how others achieve their results.

Responsibility accounting

As organisations grow in size and complexity, it usually becomes necessary for senior managers to assign decision-making authority to lower levels within the organisation. This process is known as decentralisation. As a result of decentralisation, various separate areas of managerial responsibility are created. It will be necessary to ensure, however, that the manager/s of each separate responsibility area is/are acting in a manner consistent with the organisation as a whole achieving its objectives.

Responsibility accounting is concerned with establishing accountabilities which recognise the controllability principle. The controllability principle is that managers should be held responsible for those costs and revenues they are able to influence – and only those costs. In turn, managers expect to have a strong influence on the budgets for those items for which they are to be held accountable.

For responsibility accounting, managers' performance reports should be limited to those items that have been identified as controllable by those managers. There is a strong argument for excluding the apportionment of items such as head office costs, over which line managers have little or no direct influence, from their periodic statements of actual and budgeted performance. Many managers find it contentious and de-motivating to be assessed on items over which they have no control. It is quite common to see an item such as 'central management costs' appearing on a budget statement, even though the manager concerned has no control over them.

Responsibility centres

The ideas of responsibility accounting are linked to the organisational concept of responsibility centres. Common examples are listed below.

- Cost centre: the budget holder is responsible for using resources and performing activities efficiently, and for achieving outputs (often non-financial targets) effectively. Examples include an office manager or a payroll supervisor.

- Revenue centre: the budget holder is not primarily concerned with costs but is responsible for generating revenue, although they may also have their own cost budget to control. Examples include a fundraiser or a sales manager.

- Profit centre: the budget holder is responsible for both costs and revenues and for generating a particular level of profit and cash flow. An example is a project manager.

- Investment centre: the budget holder is responsible for costs, revenues, profits, cash flows and the returns on investments made by the investment centre. An example is a divisional manager.

It seems sensible to structure an organisation in such a way that it helps its managers to know exactly what they are responsible for. Of course, the responsibility accounting approach should not be applied rigidly or taken to extremes. You need to balance the interests of your responsibility centre with those of your organisation. When management reporting systems are designed and when interdepartmental charges are made, then it is important that the aims and work of all individual centres should be geared towards attaining the organisation's broad objectives. Such coordination, as we have already discovered, facilitates goal congruence where the parts of an organisation are working towards the overall goals of the organisation.

Difficulties with responsibility accounting

Although the idea of responsibility accounting is straightforward enough, its implementation is often difficult. Should managers be charged for office space, for example, when they have no control over the rental or other property costs? Even though it is outside his or her control, a manager who is charged for the use of office space will often be that much more anxious to move to a smaller office or to agree to sharing arrangements. Exactly where to draw the line between controllable and non-controllable costs is a matter for specific management judgement in each case.

The balanced scorecard

The balanced scorecard (BSC) is a multiple performance measurement system which includes both financial and non-financial aspects of performance. The balanced scorecard was developed in the USA by Robert Kaplan and David Norton in the early 1990s. It was a response to the criticism of traditional management accounting that it was too financially oriented and backward-looking. The balanced scorecard tries to bring in other non-financial measures of areas critical to the success of an organisation, and to use these measures to drive the performance of the organisation towards its longer-term goals.

A balanced scorecard need not be just at the organisational level but can also be cascaded down to separate parts of the organisation. For example an individual balanced scorecard would be very different for sales, human resource, production, and research and development departments as they would each have their own specific goals and measures towards achieving their part of organisational success.

There is a management adage that 'what you measure is what gets managed'. This reflects the well-attested fact that if only financial performance measures are used – profitability, cost, and so on – managers will focus their efforts on the variables that influence (usually short term) financial performance. This will often result in longer-term harm to the organisation. For example, an overemphasis on controlling the cost of inputs is likely to result in poor-quality outputs. Similarly, overemphasis on short-term profitability is likely to result in neglect of those activities essential for long-term success – research and development, employee training, strategic marketing, and so on. Note that the Balanced Scorecard does not prescribe specific performance indicators; rather it is a framework for thinking systematically about what should be measured to ensure that a particular organisation's strategy is successfully implemented and its objectives achieved. You should note, however, the inherent problems of such a multi-measure approach: correctly identifying the critical success factors, the availability of appropriate performance indicators (especially for non-financial variables e.g. employee motivation) and the problems of ranking and conflict that arise when multiple measures are used to evaluate performance.

The four perspectives of the balanced scorecard

The four critical areas of success that Kaplan and Norton (1996) identified were:

1 customer perspective
2 internal processes perspective
3 innovation and learning perspective
4 financial perspective.

The balanced scorecard is depicted in Figure 19.1.

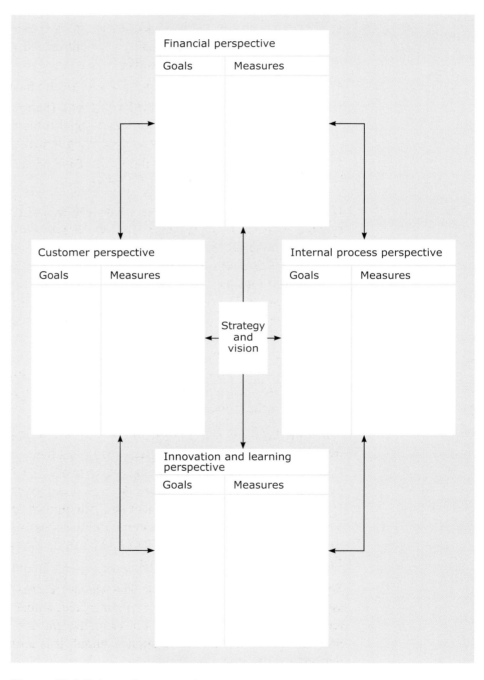

Figure 19.1 Balanced scorecard

- The customer perspective asks the question 'How do customers see us?' It converts the general objective of customer service into specific measures that matter to the customer.

- The internal processes perspective considers what the organisation must excel at. It identifies critical internal processes that enable the organisation to satisfy customers' needs. What are the core competencies and critical technologies needed to ensure market leadership?

- The innovation and learning perspective examines whether the organisation can continue to improve and create value. It sets measures for the ability to launch new products, create more value for customers and improve operating efficiencies.

- The financial perspective asks how we look to our shareholders. This recognises that improved quality etc. will only benefit the company when translated into improved results.

- It is possible to amend the perspectives of the balanced scorecard.

- Some organisations have added a fifth box (perspective) to specifically measure the organisation's corporate social responsibility and include measures relating to aspects such as environmental impact.

- Note in Figure 19.1 how at the heart of the balanced scorecard is the strategy and goals of the organisation.

If an organisation chooses to use a balanced scorecard it needs to design specific scorecards for its needs. The measures need to be chosen with reference to the context and objectives of each individual organisation. In each perspective measures are developed which can be seen as key performance indicators relating to those critical success factors which the organisation need to be perform well in order to achieve its goals. Therefore, for example the balanced scorecard of a charity would be very different from a professional service company, in terms of the objectives critical success factors and performance indicators. It is possible to use multiple balanced scorecards within an organisation, for example one for each department – each of these should be different to reflect the contribution each department should be making towards the overall goals.

When the balanced scorecard works well, it establishes goals linked to the overall strategy of the organisation, but leaves the necessary actions to achieve those goals to the manager's discretion. The focus of the performance measurement system becomes strategy and not control. However, it needs the involvement and commitment of senior management and the number of measures included in the scorecard must be limited to focus attention on the critical factors. A limit of four measures at most for each perspective is recommended.

Some organisations overlay their balanced scorecards with a traffic light system. Each measure is given a colour of red, amber or green to show if the required standard is being met. For example, green = ok, amber = possible problem, red = immediate attention required. It is a quick way for management to prioritise its actions.

Limitations

Even though there is an implicit aim in a balanced scorecard to achieve a balance between measures, a manager may place more emphasis on the financial aspects of performance than other perspectives. It is important to have appropriate reward systems to reduce the risk of this.

Trying to identify critical success factors and metrics that encapsulate them can be hard to operationalise in complex organisational contexts. Some aspects of performance are easier to measure than others but a good balanced scorecard should measure what is important to measure rather than just what is easy to measure including non-financial and qualitative aspects of performance.

The four Es: economy, efficiency, effectiveness and equity

While financial ratios certainly have their uses, unfortunately, they also have their limitations. They provide only a partial view and may give inadequate information to managers about the outputs and outcomes they obtained. How do you measure your establishment of the appropriate priorities and making of the right decisions? In this section we discuss some of the basic principles of measuring organisational performance and accountability. In all sectors the need to demonstrate accountability to its stakeholders encourages a company's managers to assess its performance. There is a need in the public and not-for-profit sectors to demonstrate good stewardship by means other than profit and to show that resources have been used in a responsible manner. Accountability raises questions such as 'In whose interests does – or should – this organisation operate?' and 'Whose organisation is this anyway?' The various stakeholders may well provide different answers to these questions.

In commercial organisations, an overall measure of performance (in terms of transforming inputs into outputs) is readily available: the profit earned during the period concerned. This figure compares the cost of the resource inputs with the valuation that consumers place on the outputs (i.e. revenue = the price they are prepared to pay, multiplied by the number of units they are prepared to purchase). In most cases, this is not available in the not-for-profit sector. In many central and local government activities, a monetary value cannot be placed on the outputs. It is then very difficult to assess whether too much, too little or just the right amount is being spent on these activities. One approach to performance measurement that has been adopted for the public sector is the value for money framework, based on the 'four Es': economy, efficiency, effectiveness and equity (See Box 19.1).

Box 19.1 The four Es

One framework for assessing this is the so-called four Es. In this framework, performance indicators are grouped under four headings:

- economy: concerned with ensuring that resources are obtained at the lowest possible cost, consistent with a specified quality and quantity

- efficiency: concerned with providing a specified volume and quality of service with the lowest level of resources capable of meeting that specification

- effectiveness: concerned with providing the right services to enable the implementation of policies and achievement of objectives

- equity: concerned with ensuring behaviour in providing services is ethical: for example ensuring equal opportunities and access to services provided.

This framework may be (and often is) applied also to responsibility centres, for which no monetary values can be assigned to outputs, within commercial organisations – for example research and development, marketing, human resources and IT services. The critical success factors and key performance indicators approach that you were introduced to in studying the balanced scorecard can also be used within the four Es framework, where it is not possible to assign monetary values to the outputs of an organisation such as a local government authority, or a department within a commercial organisation such as marketing.

Economy is the simplest measure. How cheaply can inputs be purchased? The most economical organisation is the one that can obtain its inputs at the lowest cost. However, this is unlikely to be the only measure considered, and there may even be strategic or competitive reasons not to purchase inputs at the lowest cost. It is important to consider, therefore, the appropriateness of the inputs purchased – for example, it would not be good economy to purchase materials of inadequate quality merely because they were cheapest.

Efficiency refers to the relation between inputs and outputs, usually expressed as a ratio. This can be seen as a measure of productivity. An organisation becomes more efficient if it produces more than it used to with the same resources, or can reduce its use of resources without a proportionate drop in its output. In a competitive or market-driven environment, there is constant pressure to improve efficiency, to reduce prices and/or increase margins. In non-competitive environments – monopolies and most public services – there are different and sometimes less urgent pressures to increase efficiency. The approach taken in non-competitive sectors is traditionally cost-based: resources are cut while demand remains high, so efficiencies have to be found.

Effectiveness is a measure of outputs and outcomes. How well do the final outcomes and impact of an organisation meet its objectives? It is important to understand the organisation's objectives in order to assess effectiveness. Effectiveness is more difficult to measure than efficiency, particularly in not-for-profit organisations, but is arguably even more important.

Equity is a particularly important concept in public services. The ethos of public service organisations, and often their statutory obligations, require them to treat all their customers and users fairly. This is an important distinction between public and private services, and complicates the application of commercial criteria to public services. An example in the UK is the obligation on the public postal service to provide a similar mail service to *all* the inhabitants, however remote they may be, whereas a commercial operator can select the more lucrative business.

It should be noted that it is possible to achieve some of the four Es without achieving others. For example, an organisation might be economic and efficient but not effective, as it may still not achieve its desired objectives. It is also possible to be efficient without being economic, as an organisation may be using its resources well but wasteful in their procurement. The concept of value for money (VFM) is used to refer to when an organisation is achieving all of the first three Es (economy, efficiency and effectiveness) simultaneously. That is, an organisation can be said to be offering value for money if it's achieving its goals in an efficient and economic manner. This concept arose from the public sector when governments wished to assess whether departments were offering value for money to the taxpayer. It has since been applied outside the public sector.

These four Es provide a useful framework for categorising the different components of performance. However, it is not a straightforward matter to translate them into easily understood and agreed measures that enable managers to know how well they and their organisations are doing, particularly when conflicting stakeholder interests are involved. Taxpayers', customers' or service users' requirements must be an important – perhaps the most important – set of measures for any organisation. Satisfying their customers' needs is clearly the major task for all organisations. Information on taxpayer, customer or service user satisfaction is likely to be relevant to measures of effectiveness. Measures of effectiveness focus on how well you are meeting the needs of your customers or service users. They therefore require you to collect external data – which may be difficult. You might collect information on market share or on customer satisfaction, although organisations often use more internal measures.

In commercial organisations, customers most clearly express an opinion on the quality of a product or service by their purchasing behaviour. In the time-honoured traditions of the market-place, dissatisfied customers vote with their feet – or wallets. From the supplier's point of view, this is less than ideal as a means of gathering information. It is reactive, and the delay in obtaining information means that your response is delayed. It is a very expensive way of gaining information from your customer. Perhaps, more importantly, it does not tell you why your customers are dissatisfied, and therefore does not help you to change or improve your service. For these reasons, purchasing behaviour should be regarded as a communication channel of last resort. Most organisations therefore try to measure customer satisfaction through surveys, analyses of complaints, and so on.

In public and not-for-profit organisations measuring effectiveness can be more problematic. Are there tensions between service users? Which one is the main customer? A service user may have no choice but to use your service, or a funder and a service user may have different ideas about what should be provided. Second, there is often a difficulty about professional judgement – giving the service users what they say they want or deciding what they need. Third, the measurement of satisfaction: in caring organisations in particular, vulnerable people may be wary of complaining in an evaluation. Finally, measurements that may be useful for an organisation in monitoring its own performance may have little relevance for its users. It is of little interest to someone whose disabled child has waited more than a year for a vital service to be told that 95% of the demands for the service are satisfied within three months.

References

Robert, K.S., David, P.N. (1992) 'The Balanced Scorecard – Measures that Drive Performance', *Harvard Business Review*, 1992

Kaplan, R. and Norton, D. (1996) 'The Balanced Scorecard: Translating Strategy into Action', Harvard Business School Press.

Tools and techniques

Introduction

This section of the book deals with tools and techniques for generating, gathering, using and presenting information and for problem-solving and decision-making in a management context.

Information is required to make plans, to solve problems and to make decisions on which actions are based. This ensures that the decisions made and the actions carried out are informed. Informed actions are more likely to be effective than those based on an opinion that may be biased. Sometimes information is readily available but needs to be put into a form that is easily communicated in order to support a case or argument. At other times, data will need to be gathered systematically for a particular purpose. Then, the data collected will need to be analysed and interpreted to turn the 'raw' numbers or words into information – a transformation process.

Graphs, charts, matrices, tables and diagrams are like pictures; they can 'speak a thousand words'. They are useful for expressing ideas and communicating them quickly to others. They are also visual thinking tools, however, and are useful when you are trying to figure out, for example, how a system works, where your part of the organisation fits into that system, or the root causes of a difficulty in order for you to try to resolve it rather than simply deal with the symptoms, which are the surface manifestations of it.

Not all tools and techniques introduced in this section of the book are visual: some are processes such as problem-solving and decision-making that are useful to follow; others are checklists, and some are simply helpful tips. Each tool, technique or tip is presented with information about the situations in which its use may be appropriate, but feel free to experiment. Equally, if a tool or technique doesn't work for you, try another one!

This section of the book introduces four groups of devices. The first deals with graphs, charts and matrices. The second covers the kinds of diagrams that are useful for identifying, investigating and solving problems, and for mapping the 'boundaries' of a problem. The third covers problem-solving and decision-making and methods for generating ideas and the fourth, checklists.

(Note that the word 'data' is plural – the singular of data is 'datum' – so you will come across phrases such as 'these data ...' or 'data are ...'.)

Graphs, charts and matrices
Line graphs

A line graph is a method of showing a relationship between two variables such as the output of an organisation and the associated costs. There are some special terms that you need to understand in order to create and interpret line graphs. These terms include the axes, the origin, the intercept and the slope (or gradient).

Table 1 contains data about the output of an organisation and the associated total costs. The relationship between the output and the total costs of producing the output is as expected: that is, the costs rise as the output rises.

Table 1 Output and total costs

Output	Total costs (£)
0	10
10	30
20	50
30	70
40	90

These data can also be displayed in a line graph, as shown in Figure 1.

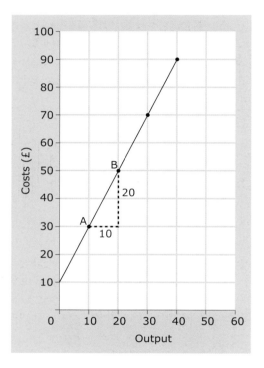

Figure 1 Output and total costs – a line graph

The horizontal and vertical axes

The total costs depend on the output, so the output is the 'independent variable' and the total costs are the 'dependent variable'. When there is a dependence of this kind, the independent variable is plotted on the horizontal axis, which is also called the x axis. In the graph, output has been plotted on the horizontal axis. The dependent variable is plotted on the vertical axis, also called the y axis. The total costs have been plotted on the vertical axis.

The origin

The origin is the point on the graph where the x axis value (the output) and the y axis value (the total costs) are both zero.

The intercept

When a line cuts an axis, the line is said 'to intercept the axis at' (the particular point). In this example, the line cuts the vertical y axis at £10, so 'the line intercepts the y axis at £10'. It can also be said that 'the intercept with the y axis is £10'.

The slope

The slope (or gradient) of the line describes its steepness. The steepness is measured by considering two points on the graph, A and B. The vertical distance between the two points is 20; the horizontal distance between them is 10. The steepness of the line is the ratio of these two distances:

vertical distance ÷ horizontal distance = 20 ÷ 10 = 2

In the example the slope is 2. This tells us that for every change of one unit in the value of x, there will be a change of two units in the value of y.

When you know the intercept and the slope, then you have a complete picture of the line. The particular graph in the example can be described mathematically as follows:

$y = 2x + 10$

In this equation the slope of the line is 2, and the intercept on the y axis is 10. The equation shows that the total cost (y) of an output can be found by multiplying the output (x) by 2, and then adding 10.

Time series line graphs

In time series line graphs, data are plotted or organised along a time dimension. Time series graphs are used for displaying data that show cyclical fluctuations or changes, such as growth over time. Suppose that you wanted to present the data shown in Table 2 as a graph.

Table 2 Number of staff in an organisation

Year	1	2	3	4	5	6
Total	10	25	40	55	60	65

As a rule, the variable plotted on the horizontal (x) axis is the interval of time: for example, years, months or minutes. This rule leads to the use of 'time series' to describe this kind of chart. The other variable, in this instance 'Number of staff', is plotted on the vertical (y) axis. The points are then joined up to form a continuous line, which shows how staff numbers have changed in the organisation over the years.

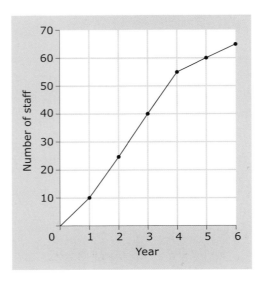

Figure 2 Number of staff – a time series line graph (large scale)

Selecting the scales

The scales that are used determine the look of the graph. For example, if the horizontal distance between 'Year 1' and 'Year 6' shown in Figure 2 were doubled, the line would be stretched to double its present length. If the horizontal distance were halved, then the length of the line would be halved. Each of the graphs would be mathematically correct.

Now suppose that you had to draw a line graph of the staff in a second organisation using the data shown in Table 3. Figures 3a and 3b show two ways of presenting the data.

Table 3 Number of staff in an organisation

Year	1	2	3	4	5	6
Total	200	220	240	255	270	260

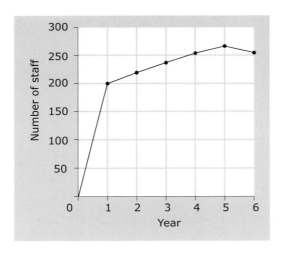

Figure 3a Number of staff – a time series line graph (small scale, compressed)

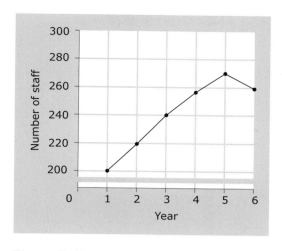

Figure 3b Number of staff – a time series line graph (small scale)

Although both of the line graphs are mathematically correct, they look different. The effect, in Figure 3a, of beginning from zero has been to compress the data shown on the y axis (from 200 to 260) and so make it harder to understand the graph. In Figure 3b the vertical scale begins at 200 and the scale has been extended so that the information presented in the graph is much clearer.

The presentation of data – the 'picture' of the data that is presented in a graph – varies according to the scales selected. Choose scales that are appropriate. As you examine a graph, pay particular attention to the scales.

Pie charts

A pie chart is a way of presenting proportional data in the form of a circle – the 'pie'. Each 'slice' shows its proportion to the whole. The whole itself must be finite and known: for example, the total number of staff in an organisation or the total Information Technology (IT) maintenance budget.

Suppose that the staff of an organisation is comprised as shown in Table 4.

Table 4 The composition of staff in an organisation

	Number	%
Senior managers	20	10
Other managers	30	15
Administrative	70	35
Clerical	80	40
Total	200	100

You could show this composition in a pie chart like the one in Figure 4.

The area of a segment (or 'slice') of the pie chart corresponds to the proportion that the category occupies in the whole. For instance, the segment marked 'Other managers' occupies 15 per cent of the whole pie.

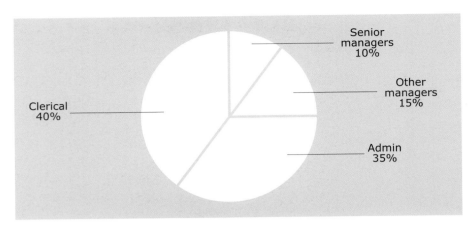

Figure 4 The composition of staff – a pie chart

You can use a pie chart when you want to show the components of a whole. It is possible to use a pie chart to illustrate the composition of the staff in an organisation because the data describe the whole organisation. Notice that the percentages add up to 100.

You could also use pie charts to show the composition of staff in an organisation in two (or more) years. Data are shown in Table 5, and data for each year are shown in two pie charts, Figures 5a and 5b.

Table 5 The composition of staff in an organisation

| | (a) Year 1 | | (b) Year 2 | |
	Number	%	Number	%
Senior managers	20	10	35	14
Other managers	30	15	25	10
Administrative	70	35	60	24
Clerical	80	40	130	52
Total	200	100	250	100

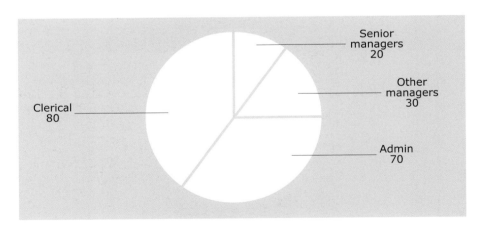

Figure 5a Composition of staff in Year 1 – a pie chart

The Year 1 pie chart (Figure 5a) is the same as Figure 4 because the data are the same. The proportion of senior managers is 10 per cent. Their number increases in Year 2, so in Figure 5b, which represents that year, they account for 14 per cent of the staff compared with 10 per cent in Year 1. The 'Senior managers' segment is proportionately larger. The 'Other managers' and

'Admin' segments are smaller compared with Year 1, and the 'Clerical' segment is larger.

Senior managers 35

Other managers 25

Clerical 130

Admin 60

Figure 5b Composition of staff in Year 2 – a pie chart

Bar charts

A bar chart is another way of presenting data. It is designed to show frequency distribution: for example, the number of staff in each of four categories in an organisation. You could present the data given in Table 6 in a bar chart as shown in Figure 6.

Table 6 The composition of staff in an organisation

Senior managers	20
Other managers	30
Administrative	70
Clerical	80
Total	200

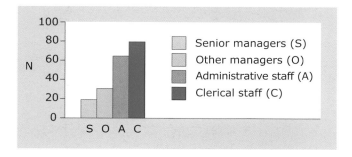

Figure 6 Composition of staff – a bar chart

You can see how the bar chart has been created. The four categories are marked on the horizontal axis, so the chart is built on that axis.

An appropriate number scale is marked on the vertical axis. A vertical bar is drawn for each of the categories. The height of each bar represents the number of staff in that category. The width of each bar is the same. In the resulting chart we can see that the bar representing 'Senior managers' measures 20 on the vertical scale; that representing 'Other managers' measures 30; that representing 'Administrative' measures 70; and that representing 'Clerical' measures 80.

Of course, you can show more than one set of data on a bar chart. Suppose that you wanted to present the data shown in Table 7.

Table 7 The composition of staff in an organisation

	Year 1	Year 2
Senior managers	20	35
Other managers	30	25
Administrative	70	60
Clerical	80	130
Total	200	250

Then the bar chart could be shown as Figure 7a or as Figure 7b.

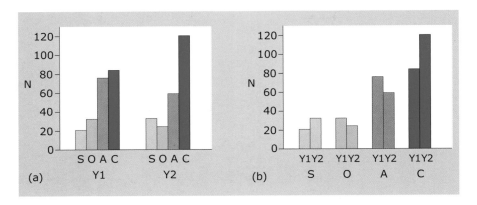

Figures 7a and 7b Composition of staff in Years 1 and 2 – two bar charts

Notice the difference between the two bar charts. In Figure 7a the dominant relationship, the one that will catch the reader's eye, is the one between the four categories in each of the two years. The emphasis remains on the composition of the whole staff in each of the years. In Figure 7b the dominant relationships are between each of the four categories. If you wanted to emphasise how the numbers in the four categories had changed during the two years, you would choose the type of representation shown in Figure 7b.

Matrices

A matrix is an arrangement of 'cells' in rows and columns. A spreadsheet is a simple example of a matrix. Each cell is described by its position in a row and in a column; the row is given first and then the column, so 'cell 6B' on your spreadsheet is the one that occupies row 6 and column B. The size of a matrix is described by the number of rows and the number of columns. A 'two-by-two' matrix has two rows and two columns. A 'three-by-two' matrix has three rows and two columns.

Using matrices

A matrix can be a useful way of organising your thinking about a topic. Suppose that you were asked: 'How will you know when you have written a good assignment?' Suppose as well that you thought 'usefulness' and 'mark' were the two measures by which you would judge an assignment. You could use a two-by-two matrix like the one shown in Figure 8.

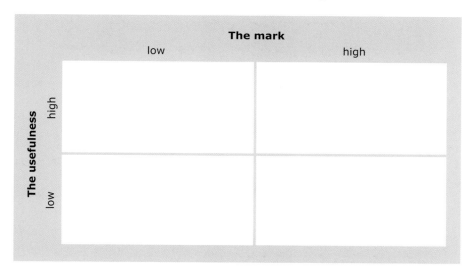

Figure 8 A matrix for judging an assignment

The labels on the two axes of the matrix (the rows and the columns) are your two criteria, 'usefulness' and 'mark'. Each of the criteria can be divided into 'low' and 'high' so that you now have four cells, each of which describes a particular combination of 'usefulness' and 'mark'. The four combinations represented by the matrix are: low usefulness/low mark, low usefulness/high mark, high usefulness/low mark and high usefulness/high mark. You would know that you had written a good assignment if it could be placed in the high usefulness/high mark cell of the matrix.

This two-by-two matrix describes the possibilities in a simple way ('high/low') and so enables you to think about them. The criteria ('usefulness' and 'mark') are the boundaries. Whenever you can confine the criteria (the boundaries) to just two, you can construct a two-dimensional matrix. You could also expand 'high/low' into three or more categories, or you could number your axes, for example, from 1 to 9, if you wanted to create a larger matrix than the two-by-two matrix in the example.

Evaluation matrices

When there are several courses of action, then one way of thinking clearly about the advantages and drawbacks of the different courses is to compile an evaluation matrix.

> ## Box 1 Six steps to creating an evaluation matrix
>
> 1   List the various options.
>
> 2   Identify the criteria by which you will judge the options.
>
> 3   Give an importance weighting to each of the criteria. (The preferred option will be the one that has the highest weighted score.)
>
> 4   Give each option a raw score from 1 to 5 under each criterion. Write the raw scores in each 'raw score' column.
>
> 5   Multiply each raw score by the weight of each criterion in turn. This gives a weighted score for the option under each criterion. In the example below, the walking holiday is given a raw score of 1 for 'Happy children'. That raw score is then multiplied by the weight of the criterion 'Happy children' (5), to give a weighted score of 5 in that column.
>
> 6   Add the weighted scores across the row for each option. The option with the highest weighted score is the winner. If two options tie, then the choice must be made either (i) randomly between the tied options, or (ii) in some other way (perhaps by a review of the matrix).

Suppose that a couple who have children are thinking about the next family holiday. They list five options, including staying at home. They also list four criteria and they give each an importance weighting on a scale of 1 to 5, where 5 is the most important and 1 is the least important. The evaluation matrix would look like Table 8.

Table 8 An evaluation matrix

| Options | Criteria and their relative weighting | | | | | | | | Totals | |
| | Happy children Weighting= 5 | | Low cost Weighting= 3 | | Happy adults Weighting= 2 | | Easy travel Weighting= 1 | | | |
	Raw score	Weighted (x5)	Raw score	Weighted (x3)	Raw score	Weighted (x2)	Raw score	Weighted (x1)	Raw score	Weighted
Walking holiday	1	5	3	9	4	8	4	4	12	26
Cruise	2	10	1	3	2	4	3	3	8	20
Beach holiday	4	20	1	3	3	6	2	2	10	31
Stay at home	1	5	5	15	2	4	5	5	13	29
Holiday camp	5	25	1	3	1	2	2	2	9	32

Using the matrix

The results of the evaluation reflect the scores that are awarded to each option and the weightings that are attached to the different criteria. A change in one or the other (or in both) will lead to a change in the results. Accordingly, when you construct a matrix of this kind be sure to think hard about the scores and weightings. A matrix like this can be used in many ways: for example, when interviewing applicants as part of a selection process.

Diagrammatic representations
Force-field diagrams

A force-field diagram shows the opposing pressures (or forces) that are bearing on a situation. Within the context of planning and managing change, the diagram shows the forces which are supportive of change (the driving forces) and the forces which are likely to be unhelpful or resistant (the restraining forces).

The diagram

Suppose that a manager is planning or exploring the possibility of a change (in working practices, for example). The manager can represent the current situation as a horizontal line. The driving forces, those forces or reasons that are supportive of a change, can be represented as downward-pointing arrows that are seeking to push the line. The restraining forces, those forces or reasons that are likely to resist the change, can then be represented by upward-pointing arrows that are supporting the line (the current situation) and are seeking to keep it where it is.

A general force-field diagram is shown in Figure 9.

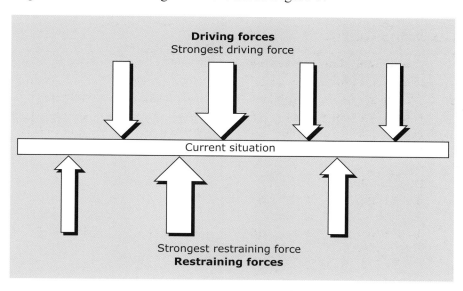

Figure 9 A general force-field diagram

The thickness of an arrow can be used to show the strength of a force. The length of an arrow can be used to show how difficult it would be to modify the force. However, these conventions are not hard and fast. You can adopt them or you can use your own convention. It is usual to explain your conventions in a note below your diagram.

How a force-field diagram can help:

- The diagram is a useful expositional or presentational device. When you are presenting an analysis or proposal, the diagram will enable you to describe (and distinguish between) the reasons for a change. It will enable you to do the same for the reasons why a change may be resisted.
- The diagram will be an explicit prompt for exploring the restraining forces. The more a manager finds out about these, and the earlier, the better placed the manager will be to find a way to deal with them. The idea of the restraining forces reminds a manager to look for and identify them.

Input–output diagrams

An input–output diagram shows the inputs to a system or to an operation and the outputs from it.

A first diagram

For example, think about the inputs to the running of a commuter rail operation and the outputs from it. The diagram might look like the one in Figure 10.

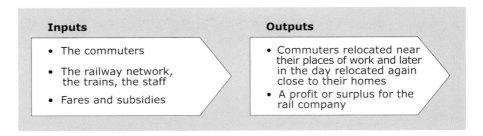

Figure 10 Inputs to and outputs from a commuter rail operation

The advantages of portraying inputs and outputs in this way are as follows:

- The portrayal will show the inputs and the outputs in a way that emphasises the flow of inputs into the operation and the subsequent flow of outputs from it. The use of the arrows will establish this sense of movement.
- At the same time, the diagram will provide the benefits of the two matching lists, the inputs and the outputs, allowing you to gain a sense of the transformation of the inputs into outputs.

A second diagram

This first representation can be developed in the way shown in Figure 11.

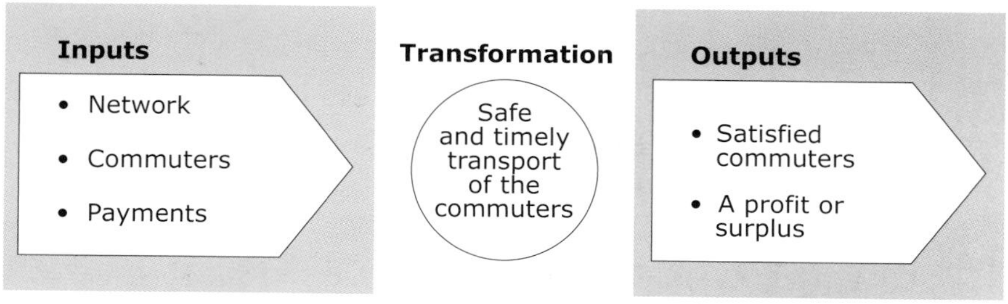

Figure 11 Inputs, transformation, outputs

Figure 11 includes a general representation of the process that transforms the inputs into outputs. In the example, the transformation is the movement of the passengers – the customers – from their home railway stations to the stations close to their work. The diagram can help your thinking in two ways:

- It emphasises the need for a transforming process – something must be done with the inputs in order to achieve the outputs.

- The transformation process is the reason for the existence of the organisation – it is the value that the organisation adds to the inputs.

You can apply an input–output diagram to an organisation or to a part of an organisation. You can apply it to your own work or to your activities outside work.

When you identify the inputs and the outputs, identify those that are sufficient for your purposes. Sometimes it will be appropriate to identify a relatively long list of both; at other times it will be sufficient to identify just the major inputs and outputs.

Influence diagrams

An influence diagram shows the influences, from within the organisation or from outside it, which bear on a person or unit.

The model

Figure 12 shows some of the influences which bear on an organisation. Of course, these influences are felt not by 'an organisation', but by people within the organisation. It is sensible, therefore, to talk about the influences on the management or on the manager within the organisation. Thus, Figure 12 shows the firm as the main system, while the manager and the other staff are shown as two subsystems within the main one.

The diagram provides the opportunity to identify the external systems or bodies which influence the manager's thinking. Some of the external systems are to do with the organisation's business. They include the competitors, customers and legal rules within which the firm must operate. If the firm is a subsidiary, then the parent organisation will be a powerful influence. But other influential systems lie outside what is probably understood as the business. For example, it is sensible to include the manager's family (as an influence to represent the whole of the manager's private life). It will be equally sensible to include the manager's goals.

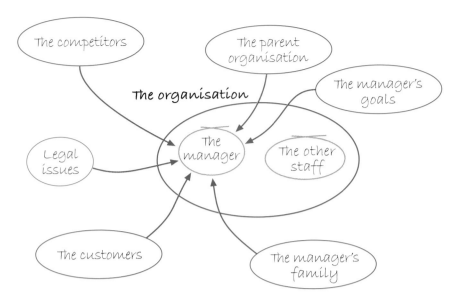

Figure 12 Influences on the manager of a firm – influence diagram

These two latter influences, the manager's family and the manager's goals, express the strength of this way of portraying the influences on a person's (in this instance, a manager's) behaviour. The range of the analysis is entirely up to the analyst – the person who draws the diagram – to decide. In the example, any system or body can be represented on the diagram if it exerts an influence on the person whose behaviour is being examined. Perhaps one member of the manager's family is particularly influential; in that instance, that one person can be represented, along with or to the exclusion of the rest of the family. In the same way, the manager's goals could be amended to show a particular goal to which the manager was strongly committed. An influence diagram can also be used to explore and identify the extent to which the powerful people within the organisation (the senior managers) are sensitive to the forces outside the organisation which are bearing on the organisation.

Systems thinking

'The whole is more than the sum of its parts' is a good place to start thinking about systems. A car is more than its individual components, a football team is more than a collection of individual players, and a family is more than a group of people who share the same name.

Each of these examples – the car, the football team and the family – can be seen as systems. Individual parts of a system are connected together in some way for a purpose.

An example of such a system is a local hospital catering system, which has the purpose of providing food for patients and staff as part of the hospital system for helping the sick and injured. But the idea of systems goes beyond collections of tangible components such as people, equipment and buildings that form part of various systems. Systems also include intangible items, such as ideas, values, beliefs and norms. These intangible things are factors in a system.

We can see that families have beliefs and behaviours that guide how they interact with each other and with those outside the family. Football teams and their football clubs have strong bonds of beliefs, loyalties and aspirations, and they show these in how they behave when they appear in their club colours. Their systems have tangible elements, such as the playing field, the seating areas, the players, officials and supporters, but also intangible elements, like their hopes and fears, their history and songs, and their reputation.

We also think about a boundary around each system. This defines those things that are part of the system and those that are outside it. Each element of the system is connected to every other, affects how the system behaves, and is affected by it. All members in a family system are connected with the other members of the system (both the people and the intangible values and beliefs) and are affected by them, and affect them too. The camera that takes the family photographs can see the tangible parts but cannot see the intangible parts of the system. In the family photograph we can see grandparents, parents and children. We can see within the larger family system a number of smaller systems: subsystems within systems.

Five key ideas about systems

Systems thinking will enable you to analyse complex issues in an illuminating way. It takes a whole (or holistic) view of a situation.

When you think of a system, bear in mind the following five ideas:

1 *Everything in a system is connected.* The elements of a system are interconnected. The members of a department or a voluntary group constitute a system. There are connections between the members. A system can comprise people, material objects, and even such intangible elements as ideas or common sets of beliefs. The idea of a system emphasises the interconnections between the elements.

2 *A system does something.* A system is defined by what it produces. Every system has an output of some kind. Once again, the outputs may be tangible or intangible. When you think of a hospital as a system, then the outputs will include measurable improvements in health as well as immeasurable outputs in the improvements in people's feelings about themselves. The only valid components of a particular system are those that contribute to the specified output.

3 *Systems have a boundary and an environment.* The system boundary encloses those elements that make up the system. Think of the hospital example again. The boundary of the system will separate the elements that make up the system and interact with each other from the elements that are outside the boundary. The elements that are outside the boundary constitute the environment in which the system operates. Elements in the environment affect the system but are not affected by it.

4 *The system is defined by your interest.* What goes into and what remains outside a system is decided by your interest. For example, in the local hospital, the system that provides care for accident victims may include counselling support if you feel it is important. Your system may differ from someone else's if they feel counselling is not essential. The way

that you express the local hospital as a system will reflect different understandings and different points of view.

5   *A system can have one or more subsystems within it.* Your local hospital, for instance, could include a catering subsystem (a tangible subsystem), as well as a subsystem which encompasses the values and standards that inform the medical practice in the hospital (an intangible subsystem).

A systems map

Mapping a system is like mapping a town. First we define the boundary and draw it on paper. The boundary separates those places inside the town from those outside. We do the same with the system. We show the system boundary with rounded corners to emphasise the imprecise nature of the boundary that separates those things that are interacting inside the system from those outside in the environment that have an effect on it.

We become selective when we draw a map. We consider the purpose of the map and choose a suitable scale. We include on the map only those things that are useful to our purpose.

Figure 13 shows the system boundary and the smaller subsystems inside the boundary. We include all those things that help our use of the map. A system is defined by what it does and shows only those components (those subsystems) that contribute to this output. The environment of the system lies outside the system boundary. In the environment of our system, we include all those things that are outside the system but have an effect on it.

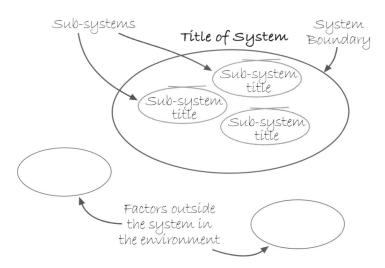

Figure 13 A typical systems map

In reality, the systems you consider at work may reside within your team and the near environment of the system will be the organisation you work for. Your system may be influenced by the structures and organisational cultures that surround you. Further away there may be important environmental factors such as national economic conditions or the legal and political framework.

Systems diagrams can become impossibly complicated if you try to include too many elements. Show only the most influential ones.

Box 2 Important points about systems maps

1 A system map shows the boundary of the system and the different subsystems inside the boundary. It may also show important influences outside the boundary, that is, in the external environment.

2 A map is a map. It does not have arrows showing relationships or influences between the subsystems.

3 The scale and the detail depend on the purpose of the system map. Keep the map as simple as possible to aid clarity.

4 Ensure the map is clearly labelled. All boundaries and subsystems need to be clearly identified.

When changing a system, we have to draw the existing real-life system and the new system we would wish it to be. To transform the existing system into the new one requires systems interventions.

Fishbone diagram

There are times when management problems seem too complicated and 'messy' to analyse. A fishbone diagram can be used by both individuals and groups to help to clarify the causes of a difficult problem and capture its complexity. The diagram will help provide a comprehensive and balanced picture and show the relative importance and interrelationships between different parts of the problem.

Box 3 Developing a fishbone diagram

1 On a wide sheet of paper, draw a long arrow horizontally across the middle of the page pointing to the right, and label the arrowhead with the title of the issue to be explained. This is the backbone of the fish.

2 Draw spurs coming off the backbone at about 45 degrees, one for every likely cause of the problem; label each at its outer end. Add sub-spurs to represent subsidiary causes. Highlight any causes that appear more than once – they may be significant.

3 Consider each spur and sub-spur, taking the simplest first, partly for clarity but also because a good, simple explanation may make more complex explanations unnecessary.

4 Circle anything that seems to be a key cause so that you can concentrate on it later. Finally, redraw the fishbone diagram so that the relative importance of the different parts of the problem is reflected by its position along the backbone. Draw the most important at the head end.

Figure 14 shows the possible causes of failure to meet project deadlines.

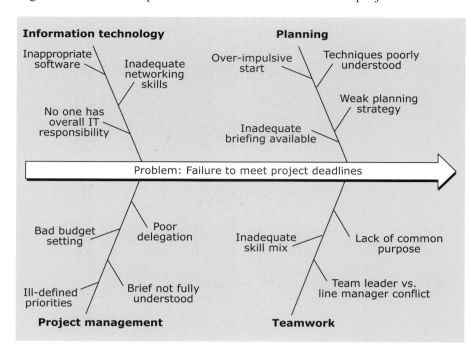

Figure 14 Failure to meet project deadlines – a fishbone diagram

We can see there are four main causes. These are the lack of teamwork, project management, information technology and planning. Each of these has been developed to show greater detail.

It is often helpful to develop the fishbone diagram with a group, as the analysis and consensus may provide a basis for group action and learning.

Mind mapping

The term mind mapping was devised by Tony Buzan for the representation of such things as ideas, notes and information, in radial tree diagrams – sometimes also called spider diagrams. These are now very widely used – try searching the web for 'Buzan', 'mind map' or 'concept map'.

Figure 15 shows an example taken from a real problem-solving session (Buzan, 1982).

Box 4 How to draw a mind map

1 Put your paper (ideally a large sheet) in landscape format and write a brief title for the overall topic in the middle of the page.

2 For each major sub-topic or cluster of material, start a new major branch from the central topic, and label it.

3 For each sub-subtopic or sub-cluster, form a subsidiary branch to the appropriate main branch. Do this too for ever finer sub-branches.

Tips

- You may want to put an item in more than one place. You can copy it into each place or draw in a cross-link.

- Show relationships between items on different branches by, for example, coding them using a particular colour or type of writing.

- Identify particular branches or items with drawings or other pictorial devices to bring the map to life.

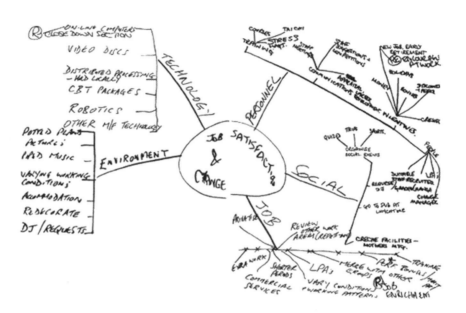

Figure 15 An example of a mind map from a problem-solving session

There are several mind mapping software packages available. They make it very much easier to edit and rearrange the map; they can sometimes hold notes and documents associated with labels (so that they can act as filing systems); and some can switch between map and text outline formats. However, computer-based maps have the disadvantages of the small screen, and are less adaptable than hand-drawn versions (for example, you can't usually make cross-links).

Multiple-cause diagrams

As a general rule, an event or outcome will have more than one cause. A multiple-cause diagram will enable you to show the causes and the ways in which they are connected. Suppose, for example, that you were asked to explain why a work group was under-performing. You could use a multiple-cause diagram both to help you to construct the explanation and to present it.

Figure 16 presents a picture of the problem. The eye can move from one element to another and can see the connections between the elements. From that point of view, a multiple-cause diagram is rather like a road map. If you can look at the diagram and say 'I can read that diagram, I can see how it explains the under-performance of the work group', then the diagram will have been effective as a means of exposition. If the diagram has been effective, then a similar one may be equally effective in explaining an event or outcome.

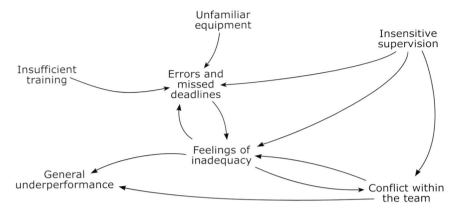

Figure 16 Why a work group is under-performing – a multiple-cause diagram

Using a multiple-cause diagram will help you to think about a problem, to explain the problem to other people, and to decide what to do about it. It will expose the connections between the events (including the loops – the occasions when one event leads to another which, in turn, reinforces the first). It will show you the possible routes into the problem. It will remind you of the complexity of the problem and it will help you to guard against taking an inappropriately narrow view of it.

As you construct and revise a multiple-cause diagram you will be reaching your own view of the problem. If someone else studied the problem they would probably draw a diagram that differed from your own. Different views, or different understandings, of the nature of a problem mean that there will be different ways of handling the problem.

Drawing a multiple-cause diagram

We can draw a multiple-cause diagram to explore and to communicate the complexity of a system, and to recognise that the effect of a particular system is normally the result of a number of different causes.

Examine the example shown in Figure 17 of the multiple causes of poor sales performance from a team.

The first task in drawing such a diagram is to identify the output in which you are interested. Generally we take a single output or effect and examine the several causes leading to it. We could try to draw a multiple-cause diagram for two or more effects but the diagram would quickly become impossibly complex.

Having identified the effect we are exploring, we then add the first, or primary, causes of that effect. In this case, we have established two primary causes. These are lack of sales literature and poor effort. We then consider each of these and add their causes. Three causes of poor effort are shown in the diagram. We then move backwards through the different levels of causes until we are satisfied that we have a comprehensive diagram to explain the multiple causes of the poor sales performance.

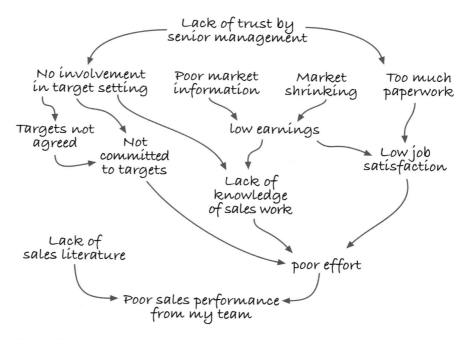

Figure 17 Causes of poor sales performance – a multiple-cause diagram

Box 5 Important points about multiple-cause diagrams

1   We are examining the multiple causes of a single output, so all arrows lead along a path to the output.

2   There needs to be a logical cause-and-effect relationship between each link. For example, the link between low earnings and lack of knowledge of sales work may not be clear, and another element such as high staff turnover could be included in the path.

3   A single cause can have a number of effects. An example in the diagram is low earnings that lead to lack of knowledge of sales work and to low job satisfaction. Often these points are the key ones to address: an improvement (on low earnings) will lead to multiple benefits.

4   Consider how the diagram can be developed to make it more effective. Important paths can be highlighted – perhaps the lines can be coloured or made thicker. Key elements can be underlined or bordered.

Drawing multiple-cause diagrams helps in exploring and in communicating complex issues. Practice improves drawing skills and deepens understanding – draw one today!

Task breakdown chart

A task breakdown chart is a useful planning technique that breaks down the task or project to be planned into its component parts. An example is given in Figure 18. It is more logical and structured than a mind map (see Mind mapping). You start with the whole job that has to be done and then ask the question: 'What are the two or three (or four or five) main elements that make up this piece of work?' Each one of those is then considered in turn and broken down in the same way to whatever level of detail is helpful to you. Thus you work in hierarchical fashion from the top down.

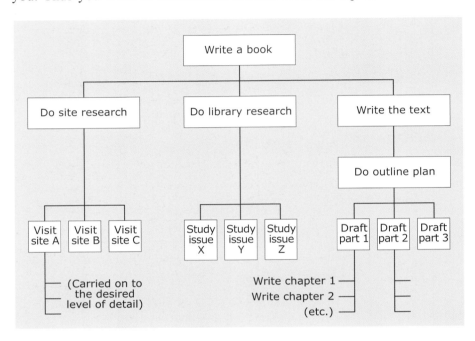

Figure 18 The first stages of a task breakdown chart for writing a book

The advantage of a task breakdown chart is that it follows a hierarchical approach. However, it may miss some ideas and concerns that occur to you, since they cannot be captured on the chart unless you annotate it.

Activity sequence flow diagram

One of the weaknesses of simple charts for planning and control, or for analysing activities or problem situations, is that they do not show how tasks are related to each other. Issues, functions, resources and so on may be recorded in 'balloons' or boxes that have some relationship to what is being investigated or considered, but the nature and direction of each relationship is not defined. Activity sequence diagrams define these relationships. They are useful in the early stages of analysis, particularly for collecting together preliminary thoughts and ideas prior to more detailed analysis. Consider the following scenario:

Anja has just been appointed Managing Clerk at a legal practice. Her role also includes that of office manager. The legal practice has eight qualified solicitors, two part-qualified staff, Anja, and eight support staff – a receptionist, secretarial staff and two accounts clerks. The procedure for accepting new business is as follows. Potential new business is identified by telephone call or letter to the senior solicitor, Patrick. He decides which solicitor will handle the business and, after brief consultation, informs Anja. In turn, she informs the accounts department and it is recorded in the business record book. The accounts department then liaises with the solicitor chosen to undertake the work and produces an estimate. Anja then sends the estimate to the potential client. If the client confirms the business, this is noted on the business record.

Anja feels that the process could be streamlined, particularly for relatively routine business. As a first task in her investigation, she draws up an activity sequence diagram to consider the current situation. Anja's diagram is shown in Figure 19.

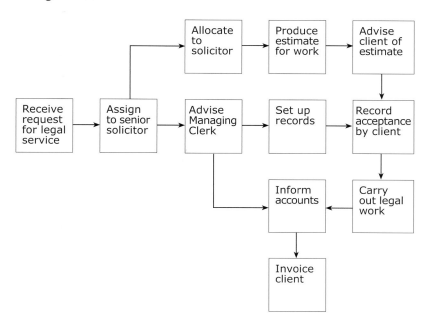

Figure 19 Activity sequence diagram – new business

The diagram shows how the component parts are connected and how they influence one another.

Network analysis

For large or complex tasks it is necessary to know which tasks are critical to achieving the deadline; some tasks will depend on the completion of others, for example. Network analysis (or critical path analysis) is used to identify those tasks which must be started before others, those that must be completed on time, and those which are not critical on the completion of other tasks and can be delayed if resources are needed to keep the critical tasks on schedule. The 'critical path' is found as a result of the analysis of the network of tasks. This critical path also identifies the minimum time required to complete the project. It is a useful tool for both planning and managing projects. It is often used in conjunction with Gantt charts (see Gantt charts).

There are many computer software packages which can help a manager to carry out a network analysis but the principles are straightforward.

Figure 20 shows part of a preparatory diagram for a critical path for converting surplus retail space into a warehouse. Each task is represented by an arrow; the length of an arrow does not relate to the duration of the task. The junctions (called nodes) where arrows meet would normally be numbered. You may come across other formats which use slightly different terms from those we have used.

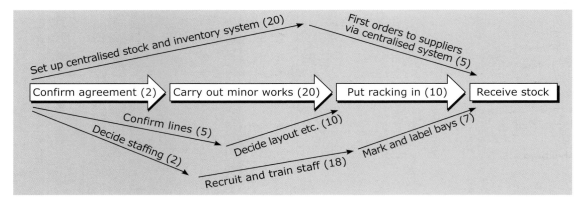

Figure 20 Activity sequence diagram – new business

Box 6 Network analysis: some key points to bear in mind

1   Some tasks depend on the completion of other tasks to enable them to start.

2   A string of such tasks makes a path through your plan, and that path has a very significant effect on the timescale for your project.

3   The path will tend to define the shortest feasible timescale for the accomplishment of the project, irrespective of the tasks elsewhere.

Gantt charts

Planning involves identifying the tasks that need to be done in the appropriate sequence. The most commonly used tool for setting out the tasks in this way is the Gantt chart, a form of bar chart (see Bar charts). A Gantt chart is simply a grid with the tasks listed down the left-hand side of the page, a timescale across the top of the page, and bars to indicate the timing of each task (i.e. the length of the bar shows its duration). A simplified chart for the warehouse project is shown in Figure 21.

Gantt charts are adaptable. Some people show a dotted line continuation of a bar to indicate how far a task could overrun its set timescale without causing difficulty. Another variation is to leave sufficient space under each bar to draw in a second line in a different colour to indicate progress to date.

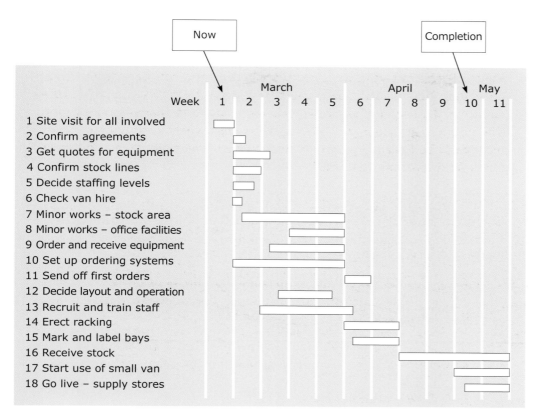

Figure 21 Gantt chart for the warehouse case study

One of the main strengths of the Gantt chart is that it gives an overall picture of the work to be done on a single page. It can be broken down into sub-projects in the case of large, complex projects.

One of the weaknesses of the Gantt chart, however, is that it does not display how tasks are dependent on each other. In the example, task 7, minor works in the stock area (which would typically involve electricians and heating/air conditioning engineers in overhead work), probably needs to be completed before task 14, erecting the racking (special metal shelving for stock), is started; and that in turn needs to be complete before the stock comes in (task 16 on the bar chart). More information on the interdependence of tasks can be provided through a technique called network analysis (see Network analysis).

Computer software is available for producing Gantt charts, often as a component part of project software which will carry out critical path analysis (see the Network analysis). Such software can automatically identify resourcing problems, such as when tasks involving one or more of the same people overlap. This is an important aspect which needs to be considered when drawing Gantt charts manually, especially when projects involve small teams.

Key events table

Simple tables can be a useful means of communicating the overview of a plan, perhaps for senior management. An example of one, a key events list, is shown in Table 9.

Table 9 A key events list for the warehouse case study

Date	Key event	Other events
9 March	Site agreed and confirmed	Other initial work in progress
8 April	Staff on site and trained	Goods handling equipment ordered
17 April	Racking installed	Bays marked and labelled
20 April	Receive stock	
15 May	Supply small stores	

The dates shown are broadly in line with the bar chart and case study to illustrate the technique; actual dates from the plan might vary a few days either way.

A key events list is not a primary planning tool. It should always be derived from a more detailed planning document, not least to ensure that the dates you show on the document are realistic.

The dates on a key events list are one way of recognising markers to indicate where you should be at a particular time or stage.

Problem-solving and decision-making
Ways of thinking about problems

Making decisions and solving problems are a key part of managerial activity. Decisions can be made without problem-solving: many times during a working day, managers are presented with known problems to which there are known or standard solutions. Similarly, in a crisis a decision needs to be made: why the crisis occurred may be investigated later. Then there are situations in which there are some obvious solutions but finding the 'right' solution requires investigation to ensure that it is the most effective one in the context. In yet other situations, solutions cannot be developed until the problem is investigated. This is because the problem could have more than one cause together with exacerbating factors. In such situations, we often see only the symptoms of the problem – its effects. Once a problem is investigated, effective action can be taken.

The term 'problem' often seems negative. Essentially a problem is simply a gap between a situation that exists now and what is desired, that is, between what is and what should be. So, the word problem can mean:

- something has gone wrong
- expectations have changed
- something needs improving, e.g. with suitable changes a system may be capable of delivering more, perhaps because it never worked properly in the first place

- something is needed that isn't in place, e.g. an online booking service.
- more than one of the above has happened, for example, performance has worsened just when expectations have increased.

Often we see that improvements can be made. We see this as an opportunity rather than a negative situation. However, when we attempt to make the improvement we must go through the same thinking process as when we are problem solving.

Boundedness

Not all problems - or opportunities – are straightforward and self-contained. There may be many causes of a problem and many of them may be outside a manager's control. A solution may have implications for other parts of the organisation and other people beyond a manager's influence. We need to look carefully to see what kind of situation we are dealing with.

One way of thinking about this is to consider the degree to which a situation is part of a related set of problems or situations – that is, how 'bounded' a problem is. Whilst it is probably best never to think of a problem or situation as being unconnected, routine day-to-day difficulties tend to be bounded and often have limited implications.

The characteristics of a bounded problem or difficulty are:

- you know what the problem is
- you know what needs to be known
- you know what would be a solution
- priorities are clear
- there are limited implications
- the problem can be treated in isolation from other issues
- few people are involved
- the timescale is limited.

In organisations where there are robust systems for routine work and established rules and procedures for dealing with situations, problems are more likely to be bounded with few risks and uncertainties surrounding them.

At the other end of the spectrum are unbounded problems.

Typical features of unbounded problems are the opposite of those of a bounded problem:

- you are not sure what the problem is
- you don't know what needs to be known
- you don't know what a solution might be
- priorities are called into question
- the problem cannot be isolated from its context
- the implication are uncertain, may be great, and are worrying
- a number of people are involved
- there is a longer and uncertain timescale.

Further, resources are ill-defined and may alter over time; it is not clear who the significant players are; urgency is unclear. The situation may well be highly political too, with reputation, career progression and the status of business units and staff groups at stake. Unbounded problems are more typical where work is less routine, for example in non-routine project work where there may be risk, uncertainty and, almost certainly, ambiguity. Assess the boundaries of a problem by asking:

Why has this problem arisen: is there an underlying problem that should be dealt with first?

Has it arisen before and in what circumstances?

How has the problem appeared: is it part of a network of related problems that need to be considered together?

What further information is needed to clarify the problem?

Are other people affected by the problem and should/how should I involve them?

Known or unknown?

A second way of viewing problems is to consider problems and solutions as a matrix of known and unknown problems and solutions.

	Known problem/situation	Unknown problem/situation
Known solution/s	Requires: decision-making (choosing between options); may also require problem-solving	Requires: Insight
Unknown solution/s	Requires: problem-solving	Requires: creative problem-solving

Figure 22 A problem-solution matrix

Figure 22 is a guide to what is required in particular circumstances, although circumstances are often not clear cut.

In the case of the *Known problem/Unknown solution*, the problem is likely to require some further or re-investigation so that a solution can be found which resolves it satisfactorily. Known problems are not necessarily fully understood problems which in turn makes solution-finding harder.

To understand the *Unknown problem/Unknown solution*, consider a situation in which a manager wants to make an improvement to a system. The ultimate goal is known – improvement – but any current problems within the system are not known, so the solution that will improve the system is not known.

Unbounded problems have features of both *Known problem/Unknown solution* and of *Unknown problem/Unknown solution.*

The *Known problem/Known solution* cell of the matrix is usually covers the bounded problem. If the situation is a recurring one for which several standard but flexible options are available, then decision–making in the sense of choosing between options may be all that is required.

In the case of the *Unknown problem/Known solution* the same 'solution' is tested on every 'problem' regardless of whether the solution is appropriate. A manager may favour one solution, say, pay incentives, as a way of improving performance. This may be effective in some cases but not if the person requires training or the person is not being provided with adequate resources to do the job. In these cases, if there is a need for a decision, then it must address the problem.

Same or different?

Problems are often complex and messy. Problem X may look like problem Y which you identified and resolved with Solution Z last week, but closer investigation reveals that the similarity was superficial. In each case the solution will be different. Conversely, two situations might appear very different at first, but be similar at a deeper level. For example, two similar marketing initiatives are not running to plan: the same design company is being used for each project and is failing to deliver on time. However, investigation reveals that in one project, the commissioning brief has been altered a number of times by the marketing team, leading to delays, while in the other project, a specialist supplier the design company uses has closed down unexpectedly.

Most situations require at least a little investigation to find if there really is a problem. Where a situation is well-understood, familiar and routine, where information is easy to obtain and the situation is clear cut, there are often procedures, routines or rules to deal with them. Then, a decision, or deciding between options, is all that is necessary. Other situations will require investigation – how and how much depends on many other factors, as does the solution you arrive at!

Bounded rationality

Problem-solving and decision-making are rarely easy. Herbert Simon, an eminent psychologist, was the first to identify what is known as bounded rationality. He noted that organisational contexts, politics and limitations on time and resources mean that managers are often not able to approach a problem or decision completely rationally. A simple example is the case where information is simply not available for some reason, and a 'best guess' is needed instead. Problems and decisions, then, may not be addressed in an optimal way: solutions and decisions may be simply 'the best in the circumstances.' This is known as satisficing.

It is important to separate bounded rationality from irrationality, however. Bounded rationality conforms to logic – the logic can be seen – whereas irrational thinking is simply poor thinking. A simple example is pursuing a solution that will not solve the problem encountered. A manager who is told that there is no budget for a new marketing initiative decides to develop one anyway. However, the initiative will not be funded and the sales team is fully occupied for the next year with the current and planned initiatives. While the manager might see some logic in his thinking, it is not clear. This is not the case with bounded rationality: rational, 'good enough' thinking can still be achieved even under difficult circumstances.

Decisional bias

The effectiveness of problems, solutions and decisions can be affected by decisional bias; that of the manager who is solving a problem or making a decision, or that of others. Decisional bias can result from the following:

- preferring some approaches to a solution (and problems) rather than considering equally possible alternatives
- previous experiences in similar situations
- a simple view of uncertainty
- misconceptions
- overconfidence.

One way for managers and organisations to overcome such bias is to ensure that different views can be freely discussed. This will depend on how problems are solved and decisions are made in an organisation, who is consulted and the extent to which the problem-solving and decision-making processes reflect the culture and values of the organisation. In some organisations it may be important that senior people have been involved or consulted even if they are not experts in the problem area.

Problem-solving – a framework

Problem-solving is what we do when it would be inappropriate to make a decision without investigating a situation. Deciding on a solution before investigating risks making a decision which doesn't actually solve the problem.

So, how do people normally go about problem-solving in a way that is most likely to be effective? If you were to take many examples of how people solve problems effectively, a core 'model' emerges. This model, of course, needs to be described step by step although, in practice, people frequently work through the steps in an iterative way. This may involve working backwards then forwards, or on several steps at once.

For example, as you encounter a problem a number of possible solutions may occur to you immediately. While investigating the problem – what caused it - you might also be evaluating these possible solutions to see which one might be most appropriate given the causes of the problem you are uncovering. Then, finally, when you decide on the solution that best addresses the problem, you find there are implications that you had not considered before. It is clear that that solution will not work or needs changing significantly.

Few people work through the model in the order set out. Rather, the stages are those which are important to have covered in effective problem-solving. This is the basic framework:

Analyse the problem

Draw conclusions from your analysis

Set the criteria for a solution

Identify an appropriate solution

Draw up an action plan.

Exploring the framework

Analysis

To decide if there is a problem and what kind of problem it is, you will need to analyse it. In doing this you will also define the problem. One way of doing this is to ask yourself three seemingly simple questions:

1   What is happening to make you think there is a problem that needs dealing with?

2   How and when is it happening and to whom?

3   Why is it happening?

By asking these questions you are likely to find that those involved in the situation have different perspectives and describe the problem differently. These can be useful in indentifying misunderstandings or current or potential conflict. They may also help to give a broader picture. This can show how the problem is related to others.

Normally a complex problem is the result of several related problems (or just one, deeper problem), so you may need to break it down into its component parts. Diagrams are useful tools to help you do this: they can help to reveal the relationship between different aspect of a problem and the different components of a complex one. You will find the following diagrams and how to use them in Section 2 of Tools and Techniques:

Systems thinking

Fishbone diagrams

Multiple cause diagrams

Network analysis

When analysing the problem it is useful to have in mind the desired situation. The desired situation may be far from clear, but you can ask yourself the following questions in order to clarify what kind of solution would be appropriate:

What are we trying to achieve?

What are we trying to keep or preserve?

What are we trying to avoid?

What are we trying to eliminate?

When you have done all this, you will have described, defined and analysed the problem: you will know what the key features of the problem are, its symptoms, what is affected (and who), how and why. You should also have identified and dealt with any assumptions you (or others) have made.

Dealing with assumptions

An assumption is something that we think is true, when it may or may not be true. When we are solving problems it is essential to know when we are making important assumptions. Many assumptions are possible to check but if we don't know we are making them, we don't investigate them (see Box 7). When we identify assumptions (and check them) we can develop better solutions and argue for them in a more convincing way. Other people are able to follow the logic of the case or argument.

When assumptions can be identified but cannot be tested, the appropriate action is to state the assumptions we are making. It shows that we are aware that our case is built on at least some assumptions that, if wrong, would alter the case, conclusions and recommendations. It alerts others to the possibility that our conclusions may be wrong.

Box 7 An example of assumptions

Air wrenches used in assembly plants are extremely noisy – a health and safety hazard for workers. The problem you want to resolve is how to reduce the noise level. You can see two possible solutions: sound proofing the room in which the wrenches are used, or putting silencers on the wrenches. In your thinking however, you have made the following assumptions:

> Air wrenches are noisy. (But are all air wrenches noisy?)

> We must use air wrenches. (Is there something else that can be used?)

> People must use air wrenches. (Could the wrenches be operated by robots?)

> The wrenches must be used in the assembly plant. (Could they be used in a separate building, or could the work be out-sourced to a specialist company?)

(Adapted from Harris, 2008)

Drawing conclusions

Conclusions are what you infer from your analysis, that is, they are judgements about the situation derived from your analysis.

For example, your analysis of customer complaints may show that a part of a system is failing because when clients telephone the organisation, only one person has sufficient information to identify the correct department for each client. So you conclude that there is insufficient resource in this part of the system.

Similarly your analysis of why no entrepreneurial activities are being carried out in your part of the organisation in the past month may reveal that 75% of your time is being spent handling disturbances and 25% on administrative matters. You conclude that this is leaving you with no time for entrepreneurial activities.

Thus, conclusions follow logically from analysis. Conclusions help you to clarify and state your goals for a solution in the next stage in the problem-solving process.

Set the criteria for a solution

A solution is an action or set of actions to produce the desired situation. It should solve the problem in appropriate ways. Before identifying an appropriate solution, however, you will need to have goals or criteria which your solution needs to achieve. When you identify these goals you will be setting objectives for a solution. In the case of too much time being spent on disturbance handling, the first aim may well be to find a way to reduce this, but the main aim is to provide more time for more entrepreneurial activities. Note that goals can often be achieved in a number of ways and themselves have the potential for creative approaches and thinking.

Identify an appropriate solution

Now you need try to develop solutions and choose the one that best matches the criteria you set. An evaluation matrix may help. A matrix is set out in Table 8 in this section. The solution must relate to the problem and match what you are trying to achieve, keep or preserve, avoid or eliminate. When clients are not being connected to the correct department the solution might be to train one or more extra people to route calls or for clients to select for themselves the department they need. In the second example, the solution might be to delegate more of the disturbance-handling work to others. If several courses of action are available, a decision tree may help. How to develop one is covered later in this section of Tools and Techniques.

A solution to a problem is likely to be presented as a set of recommendations. This will be usual when a decision needs to be made by a person other than yourself, or by your team, or when the participation and involvement of others is necessary as part of the decision-making process.

Recommendations are proposals for action; they set out what needs to be done to produce the desired situation. Your recommendations, of course, will depend on, or be constrained by a number of factors in your organisation. Such constraints might include other objectives, current systems, personnel, costs, culture, the cooperation of others, the availability of information and, importantly, the time available to resolve the problem. Your proposals will also be shaped by the nature of the desired outcome: do you want to resolve the problem 'once and for all' or do you need a simple solution that will serve for a short period until your department is reorganised in three months' time?

When making recommendations, always make sure that they are as SMART as possible. The letters in SMART are an acronym. They represent:

Specific – Proposals or objectives must state clearly what is to be achieved.

Measurable – They must state how success will be measured.

Agreed – They must be agreed with the person who will carry out the proposals and, ideally, with anyone affected by the process or result.

Realistic – They must be achievable within the constraints of the situation and in alignment with other objectives.

Timed – There must be a target time set for achieving the objectives.

Develop an action plan

When you have drawn up a set of SMART recommendations, you will need to turn them into an action plan. You will need to consider the steps in the implementation process, who will be involved, time and cost, and communication. You will also need to consider how progress will be monitored to ensure that the objectives are met. Some of these steps will merit discussion under the heading of 'Implications, advantages and disadvantages', along with implications, advantages and disadvantages that may not be so obvious. Remember, an action can result in unintended negative consequences. You may be able to avoid these if you consider them early and make suitable plans.

Implications, advantages and disadvantages

It is wise to consider the consequences of your proposals, for example, the time and cost implications of doing nothing and of implementing the plan or how the use of resources might change.

There are likely to be some positive outcomes – advantages – to your proposal which will help to 'sell' it to others. Examples of advantages are outcomes such as cost savings or new opportunities that might arise as a result of implementing your proposals.

Disadvantages are the negative consequences of your proposal, such as the disturbance associated with changing a process. Setting out the disadvantages of a solution should not weaken your argument. By recognising that a solution has some disadvantages you demonstrate that you have developed solutions carefully. Your argument will be further strengthened if you also set out ways to minimise these disadvantages. Of course, if the disadvantages of a solution outweigh the advantages, you may need to rethink your solution to the problem!

We can never be certain that every part of a solution will work, or that circumstances will remain the same. We cannot remove uncertainty. You should therefore identify the main uncertainties involved, and be aware of the level of risk that you are taking. It can be helpful to try to estimate the probability of events happening as predicted (such as the planned number of operations actually being performed, costs turning out as estimated, a project being completed on time). To do this, you can examine past experience. If a similar event has happened repeatedly in the past, you may be able to use information about it to predict the probable outcomes of future events. Alternatively, you can make subjective estimates based on past experience or simply make a guess. Where a lot of data are available, more sophisticated analyses can be made. However, many managerial problems are hard to quantify. It is helpful to apply some form of risk analysis in all situations. This is because it is rare for there to be certainty about a desired outcome.

Further steps in the problem-solving process

Markers and monitoring. It will necessary to identify markers that need to be achieved at each stage of implementation to enable progress to be monitored, and to have a clear idea of how you will assess whether the solution has been effective.

Communicating with and involving others. This framework for problem-solving has been presented as if you are primarily acting alone. This will often not be the case. The input of other people - those who carry out the work, who receive the services provided, whose work is connected to your own work - will usually help you at every stage in the problem-solving process. However, where others may be strongly opposed to your solution, involving them at an early stage may increase their opposition. In this case, you may decide to investigate the problem without their knowledge. More usually, talking to and consulting with others can help you to define and analyse a problem, and decide between possible solutions. Once a decision has been made, or the recommendations for resolving it, it is important to communicate the outcome to everyone who needs to know about it. This should include anyone who may be affected in any way by the proposed action. If you have involved others in each stage, the decision will include their ideas as well as yours and is more likely to be acceptable. To be effective, a decision needs to be of good quality and acceptable: if it is not acceptable, it cannot be effective. If the decision is damaging to others, we can expect them to resist.

The overall framework

The basic framework for problem-solving is set out in Figure 23. The curved arrows show the logical direction of the process while the straight lines show some of the iterative process that problem-solvers go through. Problem-solving in action is considerably messier than the framework suggests. Firstly, the process is iterative. Secondly, it is likely that a problem itself may be found to be less well-defined than it seemed at first. Thirdly, there may be an underlying problem. Other possibilities are that our information about a situation may be incomplete or that we may make wrong assumptions. In all cases there are demands and constraints – risks, cost, time – that limit our choices. Usually there are other people to be considered at every stage. Even an ideal solution may not work if people are unwilling to cooperate.

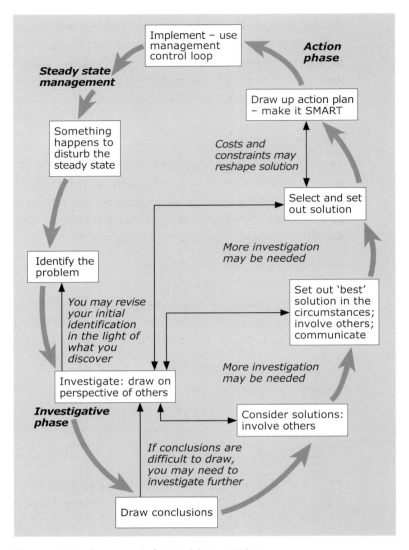

Figure 23 A framework for problem-solving

Making decisions: Comparing options and making choices

A decision is a commitment to do something. It may form part of a problem solving process covered earlier in this section of Tools and Techniques, but may not. Here, we assume it does not. Table 10 Comparing options and making choices shows the main steps in decision-making to help you choose the one best option from among those you have.

Table 10 Comparing options and making choices

Step 1 Set objectives	Specify what you need to achieve
Step 2 Set the decision criteria	Establish realistic criteria for a successful outcome. Make sure the criteria are SMART (Specific, Measurable, Agreed - with those who will be affected by the decision - Realistic and Timed).
Step 3 Compare the options	Assess each option against the criteria established in Step 2
Step 4 Select the preferred option	Make the decision, based on Step 3
Step 5 Plan the implementation	Prepare an action plan that is SMART, that is measurable, agreed, realistic and timed.

The steps seem simple but can be complex and demanding in practice. This is so when the decision to be made is not relatively well-structured, if information is not easy to find and if there too many non-routine elements and no policy guidelines. If the steps turn out to be too complex in practice, then it's best to treat the situation as a problem situation.

Set objectives

The most essential element in setting objectives is to be sure that, when you specify the desired outcomes that they actually address the situation. Ask the question: What are we trying to achieve here? Identify which outcomes are essential, which are desirable and what would be unacceptable. An example would be a solution does not involve upgrading computers.

Set the decision criteria

Specify the criteria or requirements for the desired situation or outcome as clearly as possible. Make sure the criteria are SMART. For example if the decision is to choose between different photocopiers,

Specific: 2000 copies a day; two sided copying facility

Measureable: evidence from suppliers and their customers

Agreed: acceptable to those who must use it

Realistic: can be bought within the budget

Timed: can be delivered within a week or ordering.

The criteria themselves can be in the form of a matrix such as that set out in Table 8 of Tools and Techniques (See Evaluation matrices).

Compare the options

Each option should be assessed against the objectives you set in Step 1 and the decision criteria you set in Step 2. Eliminate options that fail to match the objectives and the criteria. When selecting options, take account of financial implications. This often means evaluating the cost and resource implications of different options, for example, additional staff costs or savings, additional equipment. Also identify the main uncertainties involved, and be aware of the level of risk that you are taking. This should help you to estimate the probability of decision-making outcome happening as predicted. Past experience can help; otherwise a best guess may suffice.

Select the preferred option

Select the preferred option on the basis of Step 3. Communicate the decision to those who need to know about it, including anyone affected by it. If there is any likelihood that the decision will be rejected, it's best to know at this stage.

Plan and control the implementation of the decision

Depending on the nature of the options and the situation they were to address, implications may be as simple as ordering something or as complex as planning the implementation of a project. The more complex the decision, the more detailed the implementation plan will need to be. Make sure the plan is SMART. As the plan is being implemented, you will need to monitor progress to ensure that the overall objective is achieved.

Limitations of deciding between options

The limitations of any structured approach to decision-making are essentially the same as for problem-solving. The approach to decision-making is shown as being rational and clear. Complications, iteration and uncertainties are not indicated and the process of problem-solving appears to be linear. In practice managers tend to move forwards and backwards through the process. Whether you approach decision-making in a linear and rational way, or iteratively, some particular difficulties that might be encountered are:

- It can be hard or expensive to collect all the necessary information.
- It is not always easy to identify the objectives clearly in response to the needs you perceive. You may have to seek a compromise between competing or conflicting interests and objectives.
- Generating options can be time-consuming and expensive.
- You may not be able to find the time for creative thinking.
- Evaluation of alternatives can also be a time-consuming process.
- Predicting future outcomes will often carry a high degree of uncertainty.
- Even if you reach what you believe to be an ideal decision, it may be rejected!

Some alternative techniques, based on the ideas of de Bono (1982), are:

A less than ideal approach. Try to visualise the ideal solution and then choose an option that will be accepted and is as close as possible to the ideal.

An intuitive approach. Make your choice intuitively, as you often will, but be honest with yourself. State the real reasons why you opted for that choice. Could you justify them openly, or were they bad reasons based on, for example, laziness or fear? Should you perhaps think again?

A negative approach. Instead of looking for the best options, look for reasons to reject options. Eliminate the weaker options one by one until you are left with the least bad option.

A changing circumstances approach. You can eliminate options by considering how valid they would be if your forecast of the future turned out to be inaccurate. Change those circumstances to which the situation appears most sensitive. Choose the option which remains best in the changed circumstances.

Decision trees

A decision tree is useful when several, linked courses of action are available for solving a problem or making a choice between options in order to make a decision. It allows you to show the various options and the relationships between them, and it helps you to identify different levels of decision. The method is illustrated using a case.

Box 8 Tom's decision tree

At just 25 Tom had become manager of a busy health centre offering the services of doctors, nurses, midwives and other health professionals. Staff and visitors regularly complained that they could never get anything to eat or drink there. Tom realised that the number of people using the centre meant there was a potentially profitable opportunity to provide catering on the premises - and there was spare capacity to accommodate a refreshments area. But Tom became confused at the number of options he had to consider.

Should he investigate an automatic drinks dispenser? Should there be food as well? Or should he outsource the catering. As well as commercial organisations, there were one or two local not-for-profit organisations who might want to operate a small cafeteria. But then he needed to work out how to operate a tendering exercise, who to invite to tender – and how to decide between them. A not-for-profit organisation would be more consistent with the community ethos of the health centre, but a commercial organisation might be able to offer additional benefits. But any organisation tendering would have to adopt the health centre's healthy eating policy.

Tom struggled to sort out how best to proceed. Each time he started to think about any one option he would quickly switch to others. He was going round in circles. Then he produced a decision tree. This was no more than a diagram of his options, but it helped him to clarify them in his mind and he was able to think them through.

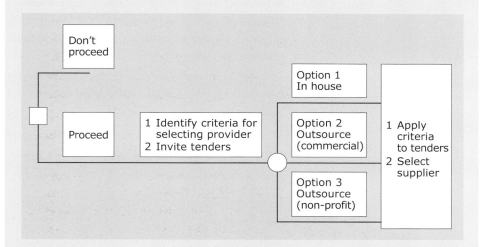

Figure 24 Tom's decision tree

You can see that, in this example, there were two separate decision points, and at each one there were two or more options to choose from.

Ways 'into' problems

There are two ends of the spectrum of difficulties we may face when trying to solve problems or make decisions. At one end is a blank sheet of paper and an accompanying blank mind; at the other is a tangled web of information, ideas, hunches, possible solutions and difficulties to avoid, which is seemingly impossible to tease apart.

Problems can often be difficult to analyse and resolve, especially when you are close to them. Here are some different methods you might try in order to enter a problem. Don't worry if using a method takes you only so far down the problem-solving route: if it has set you off on a productive line of thinking then it has been effective.

> *Start in the middle.* For example, you might begin by assuming that the work involved in developing a new system has been done. Then work forwards and backwards, working out how the system will operate, and how it might be developed.

> *Start with rival solutions.* Potentially, these could resolve the problem. Consider each and ask:

> Why would this solution work?

> Why would this solution not work?

By giving detailed consideration to each solution, you will work through at least a basic analysis of the problem, which you can then focus on with more insight. The eventual solution you develop may be different from both the original ones, or combine the best elements of them.

- *Use metaphors.* What is the problem most like – a machine, an underground transport network, an eco system? You can use these metaphors to visualise aspects of the problem and how they are related, and to consider some possible solutions.
- *Share it.* Tell one or more people and invite them to tell you their thoughts. You will not really be asking them to solve the problem for you; rather you will be seeking different perspectives on it.
- *Work backwards.* Start with the desired solution and work backwards. This may be a good method to apply to the issue of quality improvement as well as problem solving.

If you are having difficulties recognising the problem, then basic problem-finding techniques may help. Setting out to find a problem may seem odd – recall the old adage 'If it ain't broke don't fix it' – but if you want to improve something and can't quite see how, then you will need to identify ways in which things can be done better.

Creative problem-solving, devised by Sidney J. Parnes in the 1950s and developed by many people since then, suggests the following stepped problem-finding method described by VanGundy in 1988.

Box 9 Creative problem-solving

Step 1 Mess finding. Sensitise yourself (scan, search) for issues (concerns, challenges, opportunities, etc.) that need to be tackled.

Pose suggestions to yourself such as: 'Wouldn't it be nice if …' and 'Wouldn't it be awful if …'. Then brainstorm ideas to identify desirable outcomes and obstacles to be overcome. This is an 'opening up' or divergent technique. (See Classical brainstorming.) Conversely, narrow down or converge your thinking to highlight hotspots for improvement. For example, ask yourself a series of questions beginning with: 'In what ways might …?'

Step 2 Gather information. Ask the five 'wh' questions (who, why, what, when, where), and how. Then compose a list of 'wants' and who expressed them (sources). List all the 'wants' as a series of questions and compile a list of possible sources of answers. Follow up these for each source, and list what you find.

Alternatively use mind mapping to sort and classify the information gathered. Then restate the problem in the light of your richer understanding of it. (See Mind mapping.)

Step 3 Problem finding. Convert a fuzzy statement of the problem into a broad statement.

Step 4 Generate as many ideas as possible. Brainstorm ideas and identify promising ones.

Step 5 Select ideas. Shortlist the best ideas generated in Step 4.

Step 6 Gain acceptance for the ideas. Ask yourself how the idea or ideas you have just chosen can be presented persuasively and implemented. Action plans are better developed in small groups of two or three rather than in a large group (unless you particularly want the commitment of the whole group). For 'people' problems it is often worth developing several alternative action plans.

(Source: based on Van Gundy (1988), pp. 295–303)

Lateral thinking

Lateral thinking is a technique for trying to gain new perspectives – useful when you find that your thinking is in a rut such as when you 'go over the same ground' again and again and seem to make little progress.

Lateral thinking, a term coined by Edward de Bono, relies on a willingness to free your mind from its usual disciplined thought patterns and allow it to be stimulated into unpredictable and unaccustomed flights of imagination, which can sometimes be rich and innovative.

It advocates the suspension of all judgement until many ideas have been generated, on the grounds that one idea, although possibly 'wrong', can stimulate further ideas which might prove to be 'right'. De Bono argues that it is better to have enough ideas, even if some of them are wrong, than to be right by having no ideas at all (de Bono, 1982). Similarly, he suggests the deliberate use of 'discontinuity' as a way of triggering new lines of thought. Totally random words can be thrown into the melting pot in the hope that they will spark off new ideas.

The restructuring of problems is also a valuable device for compelling you to look at them in a new light in the hope of coming up with a new solution. 'What if the problem were not to achieve this but to avoid that?' 'What if this factor did not constrain us, what would we do then?' 'What if we did not have to make this assumption?' 'What if that rule did not apply?'

In these ways, it may be possible to redefine a problem or situation. For example, the problem of how to reduce graffiti in the lifts in high-rise residential housing can be redefined as potential problems of:

- how to reduce the time available for scribbling
- how to encourage creative graffiti
- how to make people think someone is watching
- how to use the lift for information collection
- how to occupy people's minds.

Such redefinitions can be achieved using brainstorming. Redefinitions of a situation open up the possibilities for dealing with it in ways that would not have been apparent, and may catch the imagination of those whom the solution is designed to target.

For some people, lateral thinking is a way of life and they are entirely happy to allow their ideas to roam around in apparently unconnected ways. Others, however, may find it very different from their normal ways of thinking and therefore hard to adopt.

Classical brainstorming

Brainstorming is a method of generating ideas and can be used for a wide variety of situations, from problem solving to making the most of a new opportunity that has arisen. Brainstorming can be carried out by one or many people. The key to successful brainstorming is to separate creative thinking from judgemental thinking. Ideas generated by creative thinking are only later assessed by judgemental thinking to identify the best or most appropriate.

These two principles – suspension of judgement and the generation of as many ideas as possible – lead to four practical rules:

1 *No criticism.* This is to ensure that judgement is deferred, and it is the most important of the four rules. It precludes not only explicit criticism, but also any spoken or unspoken gestures or actions that can create a critical atmosphere, or that any participant feels are critical.

2 *Freewheel.* Expression of ideas must be uninhibited. Whatever comes to mind is welcomed including random thoughts, images that are funny or apparently irrelevant.

3   *Go for quantity.* The more ideas recorded, the more chances there are of finding one that is likely to succeed.

4   *Hitch-hike.* As well as contributing your own ideas, it is important to build on those of others. This encourages the improvement and elaboration of ideas and enhances group interaction.

Only when you have an exhaustive list, that is, no one can think of any more, should you begin to sift through and gradually discard some. However, it is useful to take one or two offbeat or seemingly senseless ideas and try to turn them into useful ones. This 'wildest idea' technique, developed by Rawlinson (1981), can sometimes lead to valuable suggestions. Rawlinson reports that in a brainstorming session on how to attract customers into a shop, a wild idea was that the staff threw nails on the road outside the shop to stop buses. This led to a number of additional ideas such as asking the bus companies to place a bus stop outside the shop, arranging an upper-floor window display that could be seen by passengers on double-decker buses, and placing advertisements on buses.

Brainstorming sessions can be structured. The procedure for the classical form is set out in Box 10.

Box 10 Basic procedure for brainstorming

1   Well before the meeting, a suitable problem statement is developed, and a suitable group (of five to ten participants) is selected and invited. A person to record the ideas at the session is identified.

2   Two or three days before the meeting, participants receive a note giving the background to the problem, a problem statement, how the session will run and the four brainstorming rules.

3   The room is set up appropriately. The recorder prepares a good supply of pre-numbered blank sheets of flip-chart paper (or equivalent).

4   The session starts with a review of the brainstorming format, the four rules, and a warm-up session (unrelated to the problem).

5   The recorder prepares a new set of recording sheets. The problem statement is displayed prominently with a brief question time for clarification. The four rules are repeated.

6   Participants call out ideas as they occur to them, and the recorder writes them down. The facilitator checks that the four rules are followed. It is important the recorder is seen to record every idea (including quiet asides, jokes, etc.) in the contributor's words, or an agreed re-phrase. It helps if the contributors signal each idea clearly and adjust their pace so that there is time to record each idea. It is usually best that the recorder does not contribute, though in a very small group s/he might do so. Terminate the process when the idea flow begins to run dry – it should certainly not exceed 30 to 40 minutes.

7   As a separate activity, collate, sort and evaluate the ideas generated in any suitable way, providing the original participants with copies of the results.

A disadvantage to the method is that participants and facilitator need to be skilled and compatible, since adverse group processes can severely reduce its effectiveness.

Nominal group technique

The nominal group technique has the advantage that it allows everyone to participate actively in generating ideas and expressing their preferences, and may be appropriate where forceful individuals or status differences inhibit involvement. The steps are set out in Box 11. The procedure may seem rather elaborate but it has been carefully designed to separate idea generation from evaluation, to deal with disagreements safely (with the focus on ideas not individuals) and to provide a sense of closure to the process. It is particularly useful in temporary work groups which have to make complex decisions, such as inter-departmental or inter-agency groups, and it has been widely used in many settings, including community development.

Box 11 Nominal group technique (NGT)

NGT has the following stages:

1 Preparation: Select groups of six to ten members. Larger groups can be divided up. Give each group a flip-chart.

2 Brief group members: Outline the technique and explain the task or question under consideration. For example: 'Our task is to devise new ways of campaigning for a safer environment' or 'Our task is to identify the key problems which lead people discharged from prison to re-offend'.

3 Silent generation of ideas (5–10 minutes): The group members are asked to write down their ideas silently and independently.

4 Round robin to record ideas (15–20 minutes): Ask each group member in turn for one idea. The group leader briskly records all the ideas on a flip-chart, using brief statements in the original words of the person concerned whenever possible. Continue until everyone has offered all their ideas and a complete list has been made. At this stage the ideas are NOT discussed.

5 Brief discussion (20–40 minutes): Taking one item at a time, members have the opportunity to eliminate obvious duplications, clarify the meaning of ideas, and defend or argue against ideas. Lengthy debates are discouraged as the purpose is to clarify ideas, not to resolve differences of opinion.

6 Preliminary vote on importance (10 minutes): Each person is asked to rank, for example, the top five items in order of importance (the more items on the list the more 'priority items' participants can identify). This is usually done by giving each participant five slips of paper, on which they write their priority items, giving each an appropriate number of votes (5 for top priority, 4 for second top and so on). The slips of paper are collected and the votes for each item are recorded on the flip-chart. This should be done without discussion. The totals for each idea are calculated and clearly displayed.

7   Discussion of preliminary vote (20–30 minutes): The vote is then discussed to examine inconsistent voting patterns and to provide an opportunity to discuss items which are perceived as having too many or too few votes. This allows members to clarify their positions and assures that split votes reflect genuine differences of opinion rather than unequal information or misunderstandings.

8   Final vote (10 minutes): A final vote is taken as in step 6.

9   Selection of items: Based on the votes, the most important items are selected. The group will need to use its own judgement and set ground rules for which items are included and which are excluded.

10 Aggregation of several groups: If several groups are functioning, then their separate votes will need to be aggregated on one main list for final selection by the group as a whole.

Note: It is not always necessary to repeat the voting procedure – especially if a clear understanding of an agreement on the issues has emerged. The times given above are only indicative and will vary according to the size of the group and the nature of the issue being discussed.

This idea of different kinds of thinking is illustrated in Figure 25. You can see that you are using creative or 'divergent' thinking as you open up the possibilities, but you change to analytical or 'convergent' thinking when you start to narrow down the possibilities towards the final choice.

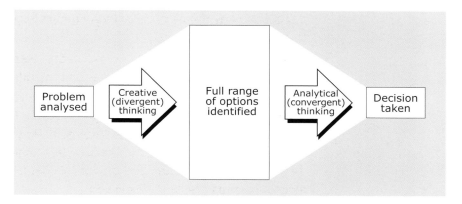

Figure 25 Creative and analytical thinking in the decision-making process

Brainstorming is not a complex technique. The concept is very simple, but it is not necessarily easy to apply. The main obstacle centres on attitudes. It can seem stylised and artificial, and careful handling may be necessary to break down any natural reluctance to engage in games of this kind. The technique cannot work without a leader who is committed to making it succeed, and who will guide the group through the various stages. The group members should preferably bring a variety of experience and expertise, but the technique is unlikely to succeed if the members of the group are from a wide range of levels of management – the presence of senior staff may constrain the juniors and vice versa. In these circumstances you need to provide safety by using a structured approach such as the nominal group technique. Similarly, the presence of non-participating observers is likely to act as a constraining factor. People need to feel free to sound silly and frivolous if they are to brainstorm without restraint. It is a technique that must be introduced with care and sensitivity.

PIPS: Phases of Integrated Problem Solving

PIPS, or Phases of Integrated Problem Solving, devised by Morris and Sashkin (1978), does more than define the various analytic steps required in problem solving: it also defines the interpersonal activities needed for each step, as shown in Table 11, showing the distinction between problem solving and interpersonal tasks.

Table 11 Outline of PIPS activities, showing the distinction between problem-solving and interpersonal tasks

Problem-solving phase	Problem-solving tasks	Interpersonal tasks
1 Problem definition	• Search for information about the problem • Detailed understanding of problem situation • Agreeing group goals	• Ensure that all members of the group are involved in the information search • Encourage open sharing of information about the problem • Consensus building
2 Solution generation	• Brainstorm ideas • Elaborate and refine ideas • Develop tentative list of solutions	• Encourage all to brainstorm • Encourage 'no criticism' • Encourage co-operation when listing solutions
3 Ideas into action	• Evaluate strengths/ weaknesses of each idea • Try combining good ideas • Select a tentative solution	• Avoid non-productive criticism • Resolve conflicts over combining/modifying ideas • Consensus building
4 Action planning	• List steps needed for implementation • Identify resources needed • Assign responsibilities for each step	• All participate in listing steps • Group adequately evaluates potential of available resources • Develop real commitments

5 Plan evaluation	• Success measures for each stop	• All contribute to developing success measures
	• Timetable to measure progress against	• All comfortable with timetable
	• Contingency planning in case steps need modifying	• Real commitments for contingency plans
6 Evaluate product and process	• How well do effects of solution match original goals?	1 How much group participation is there overall?
	• Identify any new problems created	2 Can members express themselves freely and offer support?
	• Are any future actions needed?	3 What has the group learned about itself?

PIPS is not a technique to be used alone, however. It is designed to be used with a problem-solving group and a facilitator, plus one observer to monitor the problem-solving tasks and another to monitor the interpersonal tasks. Ideally the observer roles should be rotated, for example, at the end of each phase the previous observers swap with others in the problem-solving group.

The authors of the PIPS technique also provide a questionnaire (considerably more detailed than Table 11) which all participants have for reference, but which the observers fill in. At the end of each step there is a general review of process issues, and members only continue to the next step when all tasks of the previous step have been adequately completed.

The full PIPS process may be good for training, but is probably too cumbersome for routine problem solving. However, the general principle of placing explicit interpersonal goals alongside the task goals of any problem-solving method is extremely useful.

Checklists

Checklists are useful to ensure that something – or nothing – has been overlooked. Checklists can be created for every activity and are useful both in recurring situations – in which it is worth making your own personalised checklist – and for unfamiliar situations in which it would be easy to omit something. For the latter situations, the best checklists have been compiled and tested by those who are very experienced. You can then annotate or add to them any special element of your task that you need to remember. Checklists are often in the form of questions – these help you to think. But remember, no checklist is infallible.

Problems: preliminary questions

When you are faced with what seems to be a problem or a situation that needs exploring it can be helpful to know the basic questions to ask. This list of questions is conveniently grouped under the 'wh' questions – who, when, why, what and where. The questions will help you to explore the situation and to gather and categorise basic information about it.

Who

- Who is affected by the problem?
- Who else has it?
- Who says it is a problem?
- Who would like a solution?
- Who would not like a solution?
- Who could prevent a solution?
- Who needs it to be solved more than you?

When

- When does it occur?
- When doesn't it occur?
- When did it appear?
- When will it disappear?
- When do other people see your problem as a problem?
- When don't other people see your problem as a problem?
- When is the solution needed?
- When might it occur again?
- When will it get worse?
- When will it get better?

Why

- Why is this situation a problem?
- Why do you want to solve it?
- Why don't you want to solve it?
- Why doesn't it go away?
- Why would someone else want to solve it?
- Why wouldn't someone else want to solve it?
- Is it easy to solve?
- Is it hard to solve?

What

- What might change about it?
- What are its main weaknesses?
- What do you like about it?
- What do you dislike about it?
- What can be changed about it?
- What can't be changed?

- What do you know about it?
- What don't you know about it?
- What will it be like if it is solved?
- What will it be like if it isn't solved?
- What have you done in the past with similar problems?
- What principles underlie it?
- What values underlie it?
- What problem elements are related to one another?
- What assumptions are you making about it?
- What seems to be most important about it?
- What seems to be least important about it?
- What are the sub-problems?
- What are your major objectives in solving it?
- What else do you need to know?

Where

- Where is it most noticeable?
- Where is it least noticeable?
- Where else does it exist?
- Where is the best place to begin looking for solutions?
- Where does it fit in the larger scheme of things?

Adapted from VanGundy (1983)

Implementation checklist

Where you are implementing a plan, it is useful to carry out a series of checks to ensure that you have not missed any essential features. VanGundy (1988) and Isaksen et al. (1994) have provided checklists, but they approach it from slightly different perspectives, so both lists are included here.

Implementation checklist 1 (Adapted from VanGundy, 1988)

Resources: Are resources (time, personnel, equipment, money, information) adequate for implementing this idea?

Motivation: Do others possess the motivation and commitment needed for successful implementation?

Resistance: Is the idea likely to encounter 'closed thinking' and/or resistance to change in general?

Procedures: Are there procedural obstacles to overcome?

Structures: What structural obstacles need to be overcome (e.g. communication channels that might block implementation)?

Policies: What official/unofficial policies need to be overcome?

Risk: How much risk taking is likely to be tolerated by those responsible for implementation?

Power: Are there any ongoing power struggles within the organisation – even if unrelated to the idea – which might block implementation?

Clashes: Are there any interpersonal conflicts that might prevent or hinder the idea from being put into action?

Climate: Is the organisational climate one of cooperation or distrust?

Implementation checklist 2 (Adapted from Isaksen et al., 1994)

Relative advantage

> Does your plan demonstrably improve on what's currently done?
>
> What advantages/benefits might there be to accepting it?
>
> Who may gain from it?
>
> How will adopting it reward others or me?
>
> How to emphasise its benefits to all?

Compatibility

> Does it show consistency with current practice/thinking?
>
> Can it be shown to meet a particular group's needs?
>
> Is it a better path to an already shared goal?
>
> What group(s) would endorse it, its goals and actions?
>
> Can it be named/packaged more favourably?

Complexity

> Is it easy to understand?
>
> Can it be explained clearly to different people?
>
> Does it take long to communicate to others?
>
> How might it be clarified, made simpler/easier to understand?
>
> Can I demonstrate the new idea/object's ease of use?

Trialability

> How to reduce uncertainty concerning its new elements?
>
> How can the adopter try out sections, before deciding to use it all?
>
> How to encourage adopters to try part of it?
>
> If it needs full adoption, but they insist on partial trials, what then?
>
> How to change it to make it more easily tried?

Observability

> How easy is it for an adopter to find/obtain it? Is it visible?
>
> Can it be made more visible? How?

How to make it easier to understand?

How to best communicate it?

Are there reasons for not making it visible now?

Other questions to help gain acceptance for your plan

What other resources could help? How best to use them?

What important obstacles are there? How to overcome them?

How to deal with challenges/opportunities it creates?

What might initiate action? And the next steps?

How to build feedback into it to allow future improvements?

References

Buzan, T. (1982) Use Your Head, London, Ariel Books.

de Bono, E. (1982) Lateral Thinking for Management, Harmondsworth, Penguin.

Harris, R. Case study – 'assumption articulation'. http://gloriahuston.org/ps/quotes.html. Accessed 28 May 2008.

Isaksen, S.G., Dorval, K.B. and Treffinger, D.J. (1994) Creative Approaches to Problem Solving, Dubuque, IA, Kendall/Hunt.

Morris W.C. and Sashkin, M. (1978) 'Phases of integrated problem solving (PIPS) in Pfeffer, J.W. and Jones, E. (eds) The 1978 Handbook for Group Facilitation, La Jolla, CA, University Associates Inc., pp. 105–116.

Peckham, M. (1996). 'Teams: Wrong box, wrong time' Management Development Review, Vol 9 (4). http://www.emeraldinsight.com/Insight/ViewContentServlet? Filename=Published/EmeraldFullTextArticle/Articles/0110090405.html. (Accessed 28 May 2008).

Rawlinson, J.G. (1981) Introduction to Creative Thinking and Brainstorming, London, British Institute of Management Foundation.

Rawlinson, J.G. (1986) Creative Thinking and Brainstorming, Aldershot, Wildwood House.

Van Gundy, A.B. (1983) 108 Ways To Get a Bright Idea, Englewood Cliffs, NJ, Prentice-Hall.

Van Gundy, A.B. (1988) Techniques of Structured Problem Solving (2nd edn), New York, Van Nostrand Reinhold.

Acknowledgements

Grateful acknowledgement is made to the following sources:

Cover image: © Fotosearch

Tables
Table 3.1: Lynn, J., Straube, B. M., Bell, K. M., Jencks, S. F. and Kambic, R. T. (2007) 'Using population segmentation to provide better health care for all: The "bridges to health" model', The Milbank Quarterly, Vol. 85, No. 2, 2007. Blackwell Publishing Ltd;

Table 4.1: Dresler-Hawke, E. and Veer, E. (2006) 'Making healthy eating messages more effective: combining integrated marketing communication with the behaviour ecological model', International Journal of Consumer Studies, Vol. 30, No. 4, July 2006. Blackwell Publishing Ltd;

Figures
Figure 5.3: Elischer, T. (2008) 'Rediscovering and climbing the donor pyramid', 2008 Expedition, July 2008.